Scala Microservices

Develop, deploy, and run microservices with Scala

Jatin Puri
Selvam Palanimalai

BIRMINGHAM - MUMBAI

Scala Microservices

First published: September 2017

Production reference: 1150917

Published by Packt Publishing Ltd.
Livery Place
35 Livery Street
Birmingham
B3 2PB, UK.

ISBN 978-1-78646-934-2

www.packtpub.com

Credits

Authors
Jatin Puri
Selvam Palanimalai

Reviewer
Mark Elston

Commissioning Editor
Kunal Parikh

Acquisition Editor
Chaitanya Nair

Content Development Editor
Siddhi Chavan

Technical Editor
Supriya Thabe

Copy Editor
Safis Editing

Project Coordinator
Prajakta Naik

Proofreader
Safis Editing

Indexer
Francy Puthiry

Graphics
Abhinash Sahu

Production Coordinator
Nilesh Mohite

About the Authors

Jatin Puri is a passionate engineer and programming language enthusiast. He holds a master's degree in mathematics. He is a Lightbend-certified Scala trainer and is involved with spreading goodness of Scala through Hyderabad Scala Meetup, Stack Overflow, training workshops, and open source contributions.
When he is not programming, he teaches meditation and stress elimination techniques under the aegis of The Art of Living foundation.

To my family who mean the world to me. And to my guru, His Holiness Sri Sri Ravi Shankar Ji, who made the world my family.

The authors are grateful to some lovely people who were instrumental with different aspects of the book: Sri Sunil Vyas Ji for making it happen; Rajmahendra Hegde for the original idea; Nabarun Mondal and Lekha Sachdev for the metaphors; Aayush Surana, Mohit Mandokhot, Niraj Patel, Danish Puri, Mannat Vij, Kshtregya Vij, Aarushi Vij, Shravya Vij, Agam Dhall, Samidha Dhall, Nityesh Sachdev, Prakhar Srivastav, and Deepak Agrawal for the proofreads.

Selvam Palanimalai is a Production Engineer currently working in data pipeline automation using Kubernetes and Spark in downtown Toronto. He is passionate about technology-driven problem solving, clean data, and merciless automation. He is active in the open source community on GitHub, contributing to the Statistical group (SOCR) at the University of Michigan, Ann Arbor.

I would like to thank my Dad for all the inspiration and motivation in life. And my co-author, Jatin, for his energy and guidance in writing this book. This book wouldn't have been possible without the valuable feedback of Nehil Jain, Keshav Raghu and Mark Elston

About the Reviewer

Mark Elston has been a software developer for 30+ years and has developed software in a wide number of fields, including Systems Simulation, Embedded Hardware Control Systems, Desktop Applications, and Tester Operating Systems for Semiconductor Test systems. He has been with Advantest America for 20+ years as a software engineer and a software architect.

Advantest, his current employer, produces a wide variety of test equipment for the semiconductor industry.

He has also reviewed the book *Mastering Android Wear Application Development* by Packt.

www.PacktPub.com

For support files and downloads related to your book, please visit www.PacktPub.com.

Did you know that Packt offers eBook versions of every book published, with PDF and ePub files available? You can upgrade to the eBook version at www.PacktPub.com and as a print book customer, you are entitled to a discount on the eBook copy. Get in touch with us at service@packtpub.com for more details.

At www.PacktPub.com, you can also read a collection of free technical articles, sign up for a range of free newsletters and receive exclusive discounts and offers on Packt books and eBooks.

https://www.packtpub.com/mapt

Get the most in-demand software skills with Mapt. Mapt gives you full access to all Packt books and video courses, as well as industry-leading tools to help you plan your personal development and advance your career.

Why subscribe?

- Fully searchable across every book published by Packt
- Copy and paste, print, and bookmark content
- On demand and accessible via a web browser

Customer Feedback

Thanks for purchasing this Packt book. At Packt, quality is at the heart of our editorial process. To help us improve, please leave us an honest review on this book's Amazon page at https://www.amazon.com/dp/1786469340.

If you'd like to join our team of regular reviewers, you can e-mail us at customerreviews@packtpub.com. We award our regular reviewers with free eBooks and videos in exchange for their valuable feedback. Help us be relentless in improving our products!

Table of Contents

Preface

Microservices is an architectural style and pattern that is becoming very popular and adopted by many organizations because of the advantages that it offers. In this book, you will learn what it takes to build great applications using microservices, the pitfalls associated with such a design, and the techniques to avoid them.

We will start by shedding light on traditional monoliths, and the problems faced in such architectures and how microservices are an obvious evolution to tackle such problems. We will then learn to build performant web-services using Play Framework. You will understand the importance of writing code that is asynchronous and non-blocking and how Play leverages this paradigm internally for a higher throughput.

Next, you will learn about the Reactive Manifesto and understand its practical benefits by leveraging it in your design. We will introduce the Lagom Framework, which serves two purposes: building reactive applications that are scalable and resilient to failures, and solving the problems associated with microservices architecture, such as service gateway, service discovery, inter-microservice communication and streaming, and so on. Message passing is used as a means to achieve resilience, and CQRS with Event Sourcing helps us model data for highly interactive applications.

We will proceed by learning about effective development processes for large teams. Using good version control workflow and continuous integration and deployments, we can achieve high confident shipment of code. Next, we will contrast it with an operating system level virtualization using Docker.

We will look at the theory of distributed systems first. This justifies the need for cluster orchestrator, such as Kubernetes, for efficient use of docker containers.
Finally, we will look at the actual end-to-end deployment of a set of Scala microservices completely in Kubernetes, with load balancing, service discovery, and rolling deployments.

What this book covers

Chapter 1, *Introduction to Microservices*, introduces the term microservices and what we mean by it. It sheds light on the problems faced with monoliths and how Microservices architecture helps us solve those problems gracefully.

Chapter 2, *Introduction to Play Framework*, provides a brief overview of the Play Framework. We will also look at Play-related elements such as Guice and Play-JSON.

Chapter 3, *Asynchronous and Non-Blocking*, thoroughly discusses the importance of being asynchronous and how the Play Framework leverages this paradigm for scalability and high performance. You will learn about the Scala Future API and Work Stealing in Play.

Chapter 4, *Dive Deeper*, demonstrates how to build a sample search engine to screen developers. This is built in a microservices-based architecture using the Play Framework. In the process, we also become aware of the problems faced in building microservices.

Chapter 5, *Reactive Manifesto*, introduces the Reactive Manifesto. You will learn about the different guidelines provided by the manifesto to build responsive applications that are resilient to failures.

Chapter 6, *Introduction to Lagom*, provides an overview of the Lagom Framework and how it handles problems usually faced in the Microservices-based architecture. We will explore Lagom Service API in this chapter.

Chapter 7, *CQRS and Event Sourcing*, explains Event Sourcing and CQRS and the advantages they provide in the scenarios they best fit in. We will adapt this paradigm in an example using the Lagom Persistence API.

Chapter 8, *Effective Communication*, explains the importance of asynchronous communication using message passing in building robust Microservices. It introduces Apache Kafka as a broker, and we will explore the Lagom Message API as a means for message passing.

Chapter 9, *Development Process*, talks about a scalable development model to build microservices using code versioning, continuous integration, and testing. It talks about the basics of docker containers and images.

Chapter 10, *Production Containers*, looks into server automation, deploying, and managing containers on production systems. It also delves deep into a popular container orchestrator called Kubernetes its internals, monitoring, and security.

Chapter 11, *Example Application in K8s*, helps dockerize all the services from our example application from Chapter 4, *Dive Deeper*. Using Kubernetes, it will deploy our application microservices with load-balancing and service discovery features.

What you need for this book

You will require Java 8 and SBT for this book.

Who this book is for

It is assumed that the reader knows Scala or is proficient in a competent programming language, such as Java, C#, or Ruby, with some exposure to Scala. Some experience with writing web services would also be ideal but is not mandatory.

This book is for software developers and architects who wish to have a comprehensive understanding of microservices and build them in Scala.
If any one of the following is true, this book is for you:

- You have a huge monolith that is making development painful for your team
- You wish to get started with Play Framework
- You wish to build scalable microservices using the Lagom Framework
- You want more axis to scale your application by effectively modeling data with CQRS and making it elastic and resilient using message passing
- You want to deploy already existing microservices
- You want to start using Docker

Conventions

In this book, you will find a number of text styles that distinguish between different kinds of information. Here are some examples of these styles and an explanation of their meaning.

Code words in text, database table names, folder names, filenames, file extensions, pathnames, dummy URLs, and user input are shown as follows: "If the computation fails, the `Future` object will contain the cause for the failure (throwable)."

A block of code is set as follows:

```
import scala.concurrent.Future
import scala.concurrent.ExecutionContext.Implicits.global

val future: Future[Double] = Future{math.sqrt(100000)}
```

When we wish to draw your attention to a particular part of a code block, the relevant lines or items are set in bold:

```
implicit val currentThreadExecutionContext =
  ExecutionContext.fromExecutor(new Executor {
    def execute(runnable: Runnable) {
      runnable.run()
    }
  })
```

Any command-line input or output is written as follows:

```
cd first-app
sbt
```

New terms and **important words** are shown in bold.

Warnings or important notes appear like this.

Tips and tricks appear like this.

Reader feedback

Feedback from our readers is always welcome. Let us know what you think about this book--what you liked or disliked. Reader feedback is important for us as it helps us develop titles that you will really get the most out of.

To send us general feedback, simply e-mail feedback@packtpub.com, and mention the book's title in the subject of your message.

If there is a topic that you have expertise in and you are interested in either writing or contributing to a book, see our author guide at www.packtpub.com/authors.

Customer support

Now that you are the proud owner of a Packt book, we have a number of things to help you to get the most from your purchase.

Downloading the example code

You can download the example code files for this book from your account at http://www.packtpub.com. If you purchased this book elsewhere, you can visit http://www.packtpub.com/support and register to have the files e-mailed directly to you.

You can download the code files by following these steps:

1. Log in or register to our website using your e-mail address and password.
2. Hover the mouse pointer on the **SUPPORT** tab at the top.
3. Click on **Code Downloads & Errata**.
4. Enter the name of the book in the **Search** box.
5. Select the book for which you're looking to download the code files.
6. Choose from the drop-down menu where you purchased this book from.
7. Click on **Code Download**.

Once the file is downloaded, please make sure that you unzip or extract the folder using the latest version of:

- WinRAR / 7-Zip for Windows
- Zipeg / iZip / UnRarX for Mac
- 7-Zip / PeaZip for Linux

The code bundle for the book is also hosted on GitHub at `https://github.com/scala-microservices-book/book-examples/`. We also have other code bundles from our rich catalog of books and videos available at `https://github.com/PacktPublishing/`. Check them out!

Downloading the color images of this book

We also provide you with a PDF file that has color images of the screenshots/diagrams used in this book. The color images will help you better understand the changes in the output. You can download this file from `https://www.packtpub.com/sites/default/files/downloads/ScalaMicroservices_ColorImages.pdf`.

Errata

Although we have taken every care to ensure the accuracy of our content, mistakes do happen. If you find a mistake in one of our books--maybe a mistake in the text or the code-- we would be grateful if you could report this to us. By doing so, you can save other readers from frustration and help us improve subsequent versions of this book. If you find any errata, please report them by visiting `http://www.packtpub.com/submit-errata`, selecting your book, clicking on the **Errata Submission Form** link, and entering the details of your errata. Once your errata are verified, your submission will be accepted and the errata will be uploaded to our website or added to any list of existing errata under the Errata section of that title.

To view the previously submitted errata, go to
`https://www.packtpub.com/books/content/support` and enter the name of the book in the
search field. The required information will appear under the **Errata** section.

Piracy

Piracy of copyrighted material on the Internet is an ongoing problem across all media. At
Packt, we take the protection of our copyright and licenses very seriously. If you come
across any illegal copies of our works in any form on the Internet, please provide us with
the location address or website name immediately so that we can pursue a remedy.

Please contact us at `copyright@packtpub.com` with a link to the suspected pirated material.

We appreciate your help in protecting our authors and our ability to bring you valuable
content.

Questions

If you have a problem with any aspect of this book, you can contact us at
`questions@packtpub.com`, and we will do our best to address the problem.

1
Introduction to Microservices

Generally, the probability of a great idea striking is higher when one is in a joyful state of mind. So, one day during your holiday, while interacting with your friends, a fantastic business idea comes to your mind. The idea is to build a search engine as a tool for **HR (Human Resources)** to find the best talent. The HR would be able to search for their ideal candidate for the respective profession.

However, because you believe that this is a very vast idea and each profession has its own complexities, it would be wise to start with a single profession. Being a programmer yourself, you decide to write a search engine that will help the HR find their ideal developer with a single click. The initial intended idea is to be able to search for people based on the respective technology tool and location. For example, Android developers in London.

In this chapter, we will design our search engine for HR using the conventional methods first. In doing so, we will cover the following topics:

- Designing all functionalities embedded as part of a single application
- Understanding the advantages and issues faced with such a design
- Introducing microservices as an alternative yet obvious approach

Business idea

To be able to implement a search engine, you need to decide the source of data. You decide to implement a search based on the data available at Stack Overflow, GitHub, and LinkedIn.

Data collection

The data has to be scraped from Stack Overflow, GitHub, and LinkedIn. We will need to write a web crawler that will crawl all the publicly available data on each source, and then parse the HTML files and try extracting data from each. Of course, we will need to write specific parsers for Stack Overflow, GitHub, and LinkedIn, as the data that you wish to extract will be differently structured for each respective site. For example, GitHub can provide the probable location of the users if the developer has mentioned them.

GitHub also provides an API (`https://developer.github.com/v3/`) to obtain the desired information and so do Stack Overflow (`https://api.stackexchange.com/docs`) and LinkedIn (`https://developer.linkedin.com/`). It makes a lot of sense to use these APIs because the information obtained is very structured and intact. They are much easier to maintain when compared to HTML parsers--as parsers can fail anytime as they are subject to a change in the page source.

Maybe you wish to have a combination of both, so as to not rely on just APIs, as the website owners could simply disable them temporarily without prior notification for numerous reasons, such as a higher load on their servers due to some event, disabling for public users to safeguard their own applications, high throttling from your IP address, or a temporary IP ban. Some of these services do provide a larger rate limit if purchased from them, but some don't. So, crawling is not dispensable.

The data collected individually from the aforementioned sites would be very rich. Stack Overflow can provide us with the following:

- The list of all users on their website along with individual reputation, location, display name, website, URL, and more.
- All the tags on the Stack Exchange platform. This information can be useful to generate our database of tags, such as Android, Java, iOS, JavaScript, and many more.
- A split of reputation gained by individual users on different tags. At the time of writing, Jon Skeet, who has the highest reputation on Stack Overflow, had `18,286` posts on C#, `10,178` posts on Java, and so on. Reputation on each tag can give us a sense of how knowledgeable the developer is about a particular technology.

The following piece of code is the JSON response on calling the URL
`https://api.stackexchange.com/docs/users`, which provides a list of all users in
descending order in respect to their reputation:

```
{
  "items": [
    {
      "badge_counts": {
      "bronze": 7518,
      "silver": 6603,
      "gold": 493
    },
      "account_id": 11683,
      "is_employee": false,
      "last_modified_date": 1480008647,
      "last_access_date": 1480156016,
      "age": 40,
      "reputation_change_year": 76064,
      "reputation_change_quarter": 12476,
      "reputation_change_month": 5673,
      "reputation_change_week": 1513,
      "reputation_change_day": 178,
      "reputation": 909588,
      "creation_date": 1222430705,
      "user_type": "registered",
      "user_id": 22656,
      "accept_rate": 86,
      "location": "Reading, United Kingdom",
      "website_url": "http://csharpindepth.com",
      "link": "http://stackoverflow.com/users/22656/jon-skeet",
      "profile_image":
      "https://www.gravatar.com/avatar
        /6d8ebb117e8d83d74ea95fbdd0f87e13?s=128&d=identicon&r=PG",
      "display_name": "Jon Skeet"
    },
    .....
  }
```

In a similar manner, GitHub can also provide statistics for each user based on the user's
contribution to different repositories via its API. A higher number of commits to a Scala-
based repository on GitHub might represent his/her prowess with Scala. If the contributed
repository has a higher number of stars and forks, then the contribution by a developer to
such a repository gives him a higher score, as the repository is of a higher reputation. For
example, there is strong probability that a person contributing to Spring's source code
might actually be strong with Spring when compared to a person with a pet project based
on Spring that is not starred by many. It is not a guarantee, but a matter of probability.

LinkedIn can give a very structured data of the current occupation, location, interests, blog posts, connections, and others.

Apart from the aforementioned sources, it might be a good idea to also build an infrastructure to manually insert and correct data. You could have a small operations team later, who will be able to `delete`/`update`/`add` entries to refine the data.

Once the data is collected, you will need to transform all the data collected to some desired format and have persistence storage for it. The data will also have to be processed and indexed to be made available in-memory, maybe by using Apache Lucene (`http://lucene.apache.org/core/`), and be able to execute faster queries on it. Querying data that is readily available on RAM are manifold times faster to access when compared to reading from disk.

Linking users across sites

Now that we have planned how to collect all the developer data based on the data available, we will also have to build our single global developer database across all websites comprising of such developer of information a Name, Contact Information, Location, LinkedIn handle, and Stack Overflow handle. This would, of course, be obtained by scraping from data generated by a web-crawler or API.

We need to have the ability to link people. For example, a developer with the handle *abcxyz* on LinkedIn might be the same person with the same/different handle on GitHub. So, now we can associate different profiles on different websites to a single user. This would provide much richer data that would leave is in a better position to rate that particular person.

Rank developers

We also need to have the ability to rate developers. This is a difficult problem to solve. We could calculate a rank for each user for each website and do a normalization over all the other websites. However, we need to be careful of data inconsistencies. For example, a user might have a higher score on GitHub but a poor score on Stack Overflow (maybe because he is not very active on Stack Overflow).

Ultimately, we would need a rank of each developer for each specific technology.

User interaction

Now that our backend is sorted out, we will of course need a fancy but minimal user interface for the HR manager to search. A query engine will be needed to be able to parse the search queries the users enter. For example, users might enter Full Stack Engineers in Singapore. So, we will need an engine to understand the implication of being Full Stack.

Maybe there is a need to also provide a **Domain Specific Language** (**DSL**) that users could query for complex searches, such as Location in (Singapore, Malaysia) AND Language in (Java, JavaScript) Knowledge of (Spring, Angular).

There will also be a need for the user interface to have a web interface for visualization of the responses, and store user preferences, such as default city or technology, and past searches.

Now that most of the functionality is sorted out on paper, coupled with confidence with the business idea and its ability to have an impact on how people search for talent online, confidence is sky high. The spontaneous belief is that it has all the potential to be the next market disruptor.

Implementation

Fundamentally, there are two parts to the application:

- We have a web-based user interface, which is the source for queries and visualizing the result set
- We have a lot of background batch work where we obtain data, extract content, run machine learning algorithms, and rank users

For the second part, we write background batch jobs that collect all the information from different sources, extract content, rank developers, and then persist them in some respective storage.

To expose the results that we have generated in the second part, we will write a set of standard service classes for each type of source (Stack Overflow, LinkedIn, and so on) that implement a common interface (just like any other traditional application):

```
interface SiteService{
  List<Developers> getTopDevelopers(Location location, Tech tech,
  int responseCount);
                  . . . . .
  }
```

```
class LinkedInSiteServiceImpl implements SiteService {...}
class StackoverflowSiteServiceImpl implements SiteService {...}
class GithubSiteServiceImpl implements SiteService {...}
```

Similarly, we have **Data Access Objects (DAO)** to query persistence storage and provide results.

For the first part, we plan to build the web interface, just like in any other traditional approach, to be **Model View Controller (MVC)** based. We need to have security as well as session management for the user so that they don't have to login each time. For the user interface, we could either use templates (play templates, velocity templates, and so on) or rather a **Single Page Application** (https://Wikipedia/wiki/Single-page_application) where the page is dynamically loaded and built using the network calls in the background using either Ajax or WebSockets.

As we can see, the application is growing in magnitude as we think deeper to solve our problem. The complexity has increased and so has the functionality. There is, therefore, the need for more people to be involved with the project.

Development issues

Now we have backend developers, database architects, frontend developers, and architects all working on the same project.

Configuration and maintenance hazards

Now, some of the developers in the team realize that there is a need for each type of service to use its own persistence mechanism. The data received by querying Stack Overflow is by itself very complete (suppose there is a developer who has 10 k points only under the Scala tag; now, this by itself provides a summary of the user). So, this information can be easily stored using any standard relational database.

However, the same might not apply for GitHub, where it could get complex, as a project can have multiple developers and each developer can contribute to multiple projects with varying contributions. Developers decide that Neo4J (https://neo4j.com/), a graph database, best fits the schema to persist data associated with GitHub.

The LinkedIn based implementation might settle with a relational database again, but might use MongoDB to store the preprocessed response so that it is faster to respond with JSON rather than building it again and again.

Worse, all three of them might use a different caching mechanism to store their results. So, the reliance of different technologies has increased in the application. This means the configuration setup, such as URL and port, the authentication mechanism with the database, the database connection pool size, the default time zone to be used by the database, and other configurations have significantly increased.

This is only the backend part of our application. In the frontend, we might use CoffeeScript or Scala.js, coupled with some JavaScript framework, such as Angular, to develop responsive user interfaces.

Because it is one large application that is doing everything, the developers working on one thing cannot turn their backs on other modules. If some configuration is set incorrectly, and throws an exception when a module is started or, worse, does not let the whole application start or causes a build failure, it results in a waste in productivity and can seriously impact the morale of the developers at large.

By the end, the number of configurations have increased.

Modularity is lost.

We have defined service objects that provide us top developers for respective locations and technologies for each of Stack Overflow, LinkedIn, and GitHub. These service objects rely on the following:

- Data Access Objects to obtain information from the persistence storage.
- Cache objects to cache content. Multiple services might refer to the same cache objects for caching. For example, the same in-memory cache may be used to cache data associated with LinkedIn and Stack Overflow.

These service objects may then be used by different parts of our application, such as controllers that receive HTTP requests from the users.

The user information is also stored in relational database. The SQL Database was used to store Stack Overflow data, so we decide to use the same SQL instance to persist user information, as well as reuse the same database drivers, database authentication, connection pooling, transaction managers, and so on. Worse, we could use a common *class*, as nothing stops us from not preventing it.

With increasing functionality, the intended boundary designed initially gets lost. The same *class* may be used by multiple modules to avoid code duplication. Everything in the application starts using everything else.

All this makes refactoring the code harder, as any changes in behavior of a class may knowingly or unknowingly impact on so many different modules. Also, as the code base grows bigger, the probability of code duplication increases as it is difficult to keep track of a replicated effort.

Difficult to get started

People leaving teams and new people joining happens all the time. Ideally, for a new person joining the team, it should be straightforward to get started with development. As the configuration and maintenance gets messier, and the modularity is lost, it becomes difficult to get started.

A lack of modularity makes it necessary for developers to become well accustomed with the complete code base, even if one intends to work on a single module in the project. Due to this, the time needed for a new recruit in the team to contribute to a project increases by months.

New functionality

Our current system ranks developers based only on Stack Overflow, LinkedIn, and GitHub. We now decide to also include Topcoder, Kaggle, and developer blogs in our ranking criteria. This means that we will increase our code base size by incorporating newer classes, with reliance on newer/existing databases, caching infrastructure, additions to the list of periodic background cron jobs, and data maintenance. The list is unending.

In an ideal setup, given a set of modules, *m1, m2, m3 .... mn*, we would want the net developmental complexity to be *Max(m1, m2, m3 ,,,,, mn)*. Or *m1 + m2 + m3 + ... mn*. However, in case of our application, it tends to be *m1 * m2 * m3 * mn*. That is, the complexity is dramatically increasing with the addition of new functionalities.

A single module can affect every other module; two developers working on different modules might knowingly or unknowingly affect each other in so many possible ways. A single incorrect commit by a developer (and a mistake missed by the reviewer), might not only impact his module but everything else (for example, an application startup failure due to a module affects every other module in the application).

All of this makes it very difficult to start working on a new functionality in code base as the complexity keeps increasing.

With time, if a decision gets taken to expand the application search engine to not only include developers but also creative artists and photographers, it will become a daunting task to quickly come up with newer functionalities. This will lead to increasing costs, and worse, losing business due to delays in development time.

Restart and update

A user reports a bug with the application and you realize that the bug is associated specifically with the Stack Overflow engine we have created. The developers in your team quickly find the fix in the Stack Overflow engine and are ready to deploy it in production. However, in disarray, we will need to restart the complete application. Restarting the application is overkill, as the change only affects one particular module.

These are very common scenarios in software development. The bigger the application, the greater the number of reasons for bugs and their fixes, and of course, the application restarts (unless the language provides hot swapping as a first class functionality).

 Hot swapping is the ability to alter the running code of a program without needing to interrupt its execution. Erlang is a well-known example that provides the ability to hot swap. In Erlang, one can simply recompile and load the new version at runtime. This feature makes Erlang very attractive for applications that need near 100% availability in telecom and banking. Common Lisp is another such example.

For JVM, Zeroturnaround's proprietary JRebel offers the functionality to hot swap Java code (method bodies, instance variables, and others) at runtime. Because JVM by itself does not provide an interface inbuilt to exhibit it, JRebel applies multiple levels of smartness by the dynamic class rewriting at runtime and JVM integration to version individual classes. In short, it uses very complex yet impressive strategies to exhibit hot swapping, which is not a first class feature in JVM. Although, as a side effect, JRebel is mostly used for faster development to avoid restarts and not normally in production.

Testing and deployment

We now have one giant application that does everything. It relies on a number of frontend modules, frameworks, databases, build scripts, and other infrastructure with ton of configurations.

All this not only makes integration testing difficult, but also makes the deployment process frustrating and error prone. The startup time would significantly increase as the number of operations increase. This, in most cases, would also apply for test cases where the application context loading time would impact the time it takes to start running test cases, thus leading to a loss of developer productivity.

Moreover, there can always be a range of hiccups. In between version upgrades, there might be a range of database operations that need to be performed. There might be single or multiple SQL files that contain the set of SQLs to be run for version upgrades. Multiple modules might have a different set of SQL files. Although, sometimes, due to eventual tight integration, a few of the modules might rely on common tables. Any schema/DML upgrades on the table by one module might unintentionally impact other modules. In such cases, the change has to be appropriately communicated to other teams. Worse, we might not know all the affected teams and this would lead to a production failure.

Scalability

The famous *Pokemon Go* mobile app had 15 million global downloads within a week of its launch. On August 3, in Japan, people watched an airing of *Castle in the Sky*. At one point, they took to Twitter so much that it hit a one-second peak of 143,199 tweets per second. The average then was 5,700 tweets per second; thus, there was a 25 times increase in traffic all of a sudden (`https://blog.twitter.com/2013/new-tweets-per-second-record-and-how`).

In technology businesses, such events are not rare. Although the surge might not be as dramatic as Twitter's, it can nonetheless be significantly higher than anticipated. Our application design is not designed to be scalable. As the load increases, we might vertically scale by adding more memory and CPU, but this cannot be done forever. What if the application goes down or a database starts misbehaving, taking eternally long to respond?

Apart from adding memory and CPU, we could scale it horizontally by having multiple instances of the same application running and a load balancer could route requests to different servers based on the load on individual servers (the application server with the lower load could be routed to more traffic). However, this leaves a lot of unanswered questions:

- What do we do with our databases? Will we have a single database that multiple application servers access? If we go with this setup, then a higher load on this database server would affect all the cloned servers, ultimately increasing the response time of all the servers as they all access the same database.

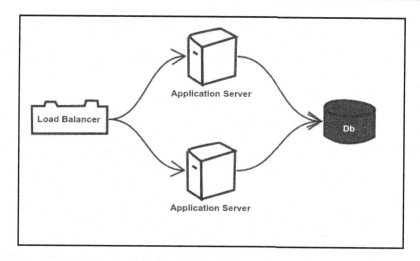

- Do we have a separate database for each application server? Then how do we deal with the consistency issues across databases? The data written on one database would have to be copied to the other database server for consistency. What happens if the data was not timely copied and the user requested the data?
- To solve this problem, a solution could be to ensure that the application servers interact timely with each other to sync up. What if there is a network partition and the application servers cannot access each other? What happens to the consistency issues in such scenarios?

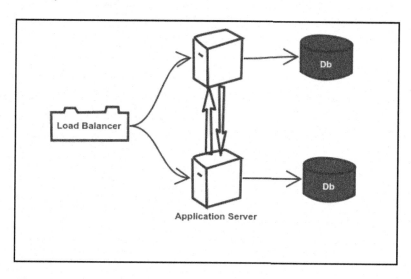

- How many servers do we have installed? If we install more, but the traffic load is low, then it results in wastage of resources and money (at the time of writing, a standard 8 core 32 GB RAM instance would cost 4,200 USD per annum on **Amazon Web Services (AWS)**).

In short, our current setup is ill-equipped to scale. It needs to be redesigned from the ground up to handle different ranges of issues, and not an ad hoc mechanism to fix it. What if you scale from 10 to 100,000 requests per minute without a complete revamp effort, but just a configuration change? This ability has to be incorporated as an abstraction and designed to scale from ground zero.

Sudden higher load are opportunities to excel as business. You would not want the application to fail when many users try accessing it for the first time. It would be an opportunity lost.

Isolation

What we currently have is this:

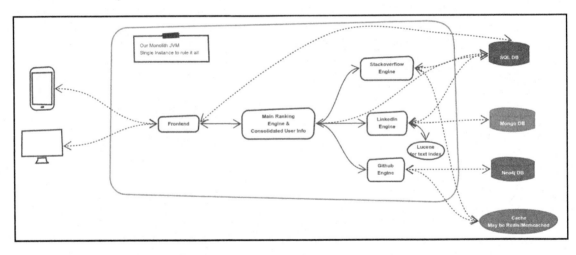

As humans, we are affected by our surroundings. At work, our peers affect us in positive or negative ways. Countries get affected by the peaceful/destructive atmospheres of neighboring countries. Even in the human body, long-standing hypertension can affect the kidneys. Deranged kidney function leads to accumulation of waste products that were normally excreted from the body. These metabolites or waste products then affect brain function. And worse, in the case of kidney dysfunction, water is not excreted effectively, which can lead to cardiac dysfunction. So, if the kidneys start dysfunctioning, they go on to affect everything else.

In the case of the human body, the organs' behavior to impact each other is not by design but rather by designoid. in software are inevitable and they cannot be avoided. Though it is good to write code that can prevent failures, failures can come in all unexpected forms: bug/mistakes in code, network failures, an unstable host due to high CPU/memory utilization, disk failures, JVM crash, thundering herd problem, and many others. How do we design to deal with failures? One strategy to handle failures is to have a backup mechanism. For example, Windows has layered device drivers (https://msdn.microsoft.com/en-us/library/windows/hardware/ff543100(v=vs.85).aspx). So, if one layer is not functional, the next higher layer can start working, thus potentially eliminating downtime. Another example is an octopus which has three hearts and nine brains.

If you are brainy and heartbroken, that should cheer you up.

They have those extra components in place because they want to be resilient and fault tolerant (at least they would like to believe so). Humans have two kidneys and can still survive on one kidney if the other fails. The whole of evolutionary biology teaches us how to be componentized.

But what happens if the backups also start failing? Backups fix the problem and certainly makes it more resilient when compared to the previous state, but they are not full proof. An alternative approach to handle failures is to accept failures and embrace them. Because we accept the fact that failures do happen, we try devising a strategy where other parts of the application remain unaffected by them. Though, of course, we will try everything in the world to prevent them, we accept that failures they are a reality.

A way to remain unaffected by failures in surroundings, is to provide the right isolation across modules. We quantify isolation as isolation in both space and time.

Isolation in space

With software, modules of an application do impact each other for good or bad. CPU utilization, memory consumption, and resources utilized by one part of our monolith significantly affects the application. In our application, an `OutOfMemoryError` caused by the Stack Overflow engine in our application would destabilize the complete application. Excessive locking in the database or higher CPU on the database server due to higher load (or abuse?) by the LinkedIn engine on the database would obstruct other modules from using the database server.

What we need is isolation in space. That is, for the modules to be completely separated in all forms so that they cannot impact each other. Perhaps splitting our application into different applications, with a separate:

- LinkedIn engine application
- GitHub engine application
- Stack Overflow engine application, and so on

Maybe we could deploy them on different hosts in a cloud service. Sometimes we have multiple instances of the same application running with a load balancer in front to handle higher load. In such cases, these multiple instances could be even in different continents so that a natural calamity at one location does not impact the other instances running on different locations.

Having them as different applications allows failures to be captured, signaled, and managed at a fine-grained level instead of letting them cascade to other components. But this does not fully solve the problem yet. Applications could interact with each other using REST via HTTP. In our case, the Stack Overflow engine might wish to push the consolidated ranks to our main developer-ranking application. If the developer-ranking application was down at that moment, our Stack Overflow engine would not be able to push the data.

If applications interact with each other, then it is required that:

- They are both alive at that moment
- The operation was a success

Failure of any one then leads to failure of the operation.

One way of dealing with such a failure is to retry the same operation at a future interval. This adds to extra boiler plate code and could get tedious if there were too many different API calls across applications.

To handle such failures, we need a further graceful solution to tackle this scenario and that is by being isolated in time.

Isolation in time

By isolation in time, we stress that it is not needed for both of the applications to be responsive at the same moment for communication to be possible. This quality has to be treated as first class. We do this by using message-passing as a mode of communication across applications.

When an application sends a message to another via a message broker, the message broker could persist all the incoming messages. By doing this, a few things are clear:

- If the sender sends a message and the receiver is dead, then the message is not lost but rather persisted by the message carrier (we could use Apache Kafka as the means to do this, for example). When the receiver becomes alive again, it will simply take the message from the queue and do the respective action.
- If the sender sends a message and immediately dies, we do not need to worry, as the receiver will receive the message and reply back. The original sender can then proceed from where it left off once it is alive.
- If both the sender and receiver are alive at that moment, then the receiver could quickly respond back. This experience would be very similar to the conventional mode of working with synchronous HTTP calls.

The aforementioned mode of communication is asynchronous by nature. It not occurring or existing at the same time. Another unseen advantage of this is that once the sender sends a message, it does not have to wait for the receiver to reply back. It could go on to do other stuff, thus utilizing the resources effectively. Once the message is received, it will then take the responsive action.

Isolation in time and space makes us very powerful by being location transparent.

Two separate modules, running as different processes on two different continents, can communicate with each other via messages. They can also communicate if they are running on the same process, as have to send the message to themselves. There is no difference in interaction provided the communication protocol remains the same. This makes us very powerful, as we could scale up our application by increasing the RAM and CPU of our process. Or split it to multiple applications running on different hosts. There is no dependency on the location of the sender and receiver. So, by design, the application becomes much more scalable by being independent or transparent of the location.

We will cover in depth the asynchronous mode of communication in Chapter 3, *Asynchronous and Non-Blocking*.

Overview of application design till now

In designing our search engine to search for the best talent, we have come to a stage where we realize that we are ill equipped to handle many real life issues and our giant application has serious shortcomings, such as:

- The inability to scale the application spontaneously
- Failure of one module significantly impacts on other modules
- Higher development time as the code base grows bigger with increased dependencies

Just like with programming, we need an appropriate design pattern that solves problems to meet our needs.

Microservices

Microservices are one such design pattern that aids in fixing problems we have faced until now. But what exactly are microservices?

Code example

Let's look at a simple program. We have an array of floating point numbers. We need to sort them in ascending order and finally print them rounded to the closest whole number. And, because we believe that the word Yo has power to inspire the young generation, we will also append Yo while printing the numbers. A simple code for this would be as follows:

```
double[] arr = ....// array to sort

//sort the array
for (int i = 0; i < arr.length; i++) {
    for (int j = i + 1; j < arr.length; j++) {
        double temp = 0;
        if (arr[i] > arr[j]) {
            temp = arr[i];
            arr[i] = arr[j];
            arr[j] = temp;
        }
    }
}
 //loop at every element of the array
for(double num : arr){
    //round it to nearest whole number and print
    long temp = (long) num;
    if(num - temp > 0.5)
        System.out.println("Yo - "+(temp+1));
    else System.out.println("Yo - "+temp);
}
```

The preceding code definitely doesn't look pretty, though it is a very simple piece of code. Here's a quick summary of the problems with the code:

- It looks complex and appears to do so many things.
- The sort implementation cannot be vouched for just by looking at it; it has to be tested.
- The same applies with the logic for rounding up.
- We are mixing the rounding up of numbers and printing them. Writing a test case for rounding would be difficult, as we would have to check the output of the program to test.
- If we have to sort at some other place in the code base, we will have to rewrite it.
- Any change in the sort or round-up logic would require testing of the complete code.

The code is difficult to read and difficult to test. The program does four primary things--sort, round to the closest whole number, append Yo to the number, and print.

We can, of course, simplify it by splitting each functionality as a different function, as shown here:

```
sort(arr);
for (double num : arr) {
    long round =round(num);
    System.out.println(getYoed(round));
}

private static String getYoed(long num){
    return "Yo - "+Long.toString(num);
}
```

The advantages of the preceding code include the following:

- The code is readable; we can clearly see that we are sorting, iterating, rounding up, and printing.
- We can reuse the sort and round methods.
- It is easier to test the sort and round methods.
- We could individually optimize the sort algorithm or even rewrite it completely without changing any part of the code. Just that the contract of argument type has to be maintained.
- We could cache results as part of the sort implementation if the input array is the same as previously invoked.
- Supervising strategy: let's suppose you implement your sort algorithm based on heuristics, which is faster than the default sort available as part of JDK, you can always call your sort implementation; however, if the implementation throws an exception or provides incorrect results (remember it is heuristics based), you can catch the exception and call the inbuilt JDK available to sort as backup. Thus, there is a supervisor to handle failures and not let the program crash.
- The code is more maintainable when compared to the previous code.

So, using the right abstraction is important. Years ago, writing an assembly was the only alternative, but, with evolution, came several paradigms. Languages such as C made programmability easier with a procedural and functional type of coding. Lisp showed the power of functional composition and recursion. Languages such as Erlang introduced the actor model as an abstraction to write highly concurrent code. And now we have all sorts of paradigms such as polymorphism with inheritance, parametric polymorphism, ad hoc polymorphism, F-based polymorphism, structural typing, pattern matching, immutability, and so on--the list is never ending. However, each abstraction gave us the ability to express in a better manner than before.

Microservices is not a new concept but an abstraction. It is trying to do exactly what we attempted doing before by extracting our modules from a single giant application (often called a **monolith**) to different standalone applications (often called **microservices**). Each microservice will have necessary isolation with other modules of the application. The communication protocol of each microservice would be well-defined. Our application will now be a collaboration of different microservices. The advantages expected by doing this would be as follows:

- We would have clear semantics of different part of applications
- It would be easier to scale as we can target each microservice individually
- It would be easier to test each module
- Development must be easier as developers, who clearly know their constraints, can focus on one module at a time
- Failures are easier and more effective to handle

Restructuring

In our talent-search engine application, we can split the application to a set of individual microservices:

- A separate application/process for each Stack Overflow engine, GitHub engine, and LinkedIn engine, which will collect and process data for each kind of site and expose the final results comprising of the rank and score of each user of a respective site using a communication protocol, normally HTTP.
- A separate microservice to consolidate all the developer meta information. This will act as a single source of information related to all the developers on the platform. It will also link handles on different sites to a single developer (the same user can have accounts on each of GitHub, Stack Overflow, and LinkedIn, and it helps if they can be linked to a single user).

- A frontend server that will receive the searches. This will also store user preferences.
- A rank server that consolidates results from different microservices and generates a global rank of developers on the platform.

We have discussed isolation and the need to split up into a system of microservices, but how do we identify the basis to form a microservice and the boundary?

What exactly are microservices

Linux tools such as Unix Pipelines, Diff, ls, sort, grep, and others are interesting metaphors. Doug Mcilroy has documented the Unix philosophy and summarizes it at `https://en.wikipedia.org/wiki/Unix_philosophy`.

 This is the Unix philosophy--Write programs that do one thing and do it well. Write programs to work together.

A Linux command to search an exception message in a log file is:

```
tail output.log | grep Exception
```

This works great because we distinctively know what `tail` and `grep` do individually. They do one thing and they do it great. And then we integrate both of them to work together via a clean interface.

In the paper, *Program design in Unix Environment* by Unix authors Rob Pike and Brian W. Kernighan, they summarize it at

`http://harmful.cat-v.org/cat-v/unix_prog_design.pdf`.

Much of the power of the UNIX operating system comes from a style of program design that makes programs easy to use and, more important, easy to combine with other programs. This style has been called the use of software tools, and depends more on how the programs fit into the programming environment and how they can be used with other programs than on how they are designed internally. But, as the system has become commercially successful and has spread widely, this style has often been compromised, to the detriment of all users. Old programs have become encrusted with dubious features. Newer programs are not always written with attention to proper separation of function and design for interconnection.

The Unix philosophy tends to favor composability over monolithic designs.

There is no global definition for a microservice. But here we intend to define it as:

Do one thing and do it well!

This clarity makes the composition extremely powerful, as we understand the consequences of using a microservice very well. The semantics are clear, just like the Unix toolset. Everything that has to be done with respect to functionality will be done at one place. So, this means the developers working on a microservice will only be concerned with the code base of a single functionality, the database architects know the precise optimizations to be done, as there is precise clarity on usage (as before many modules using the same database complicates matters), and scalability is easier, as you would have to worry about a small portion of a problem rather than the complete application.

Sharing of a database

A microservice needs to do one thing and must do it well. There also needs to be clear a boundary in between microservices on what distinguishes them.

In software development, every application will have some state to be maintained and persisted. Can this state or database be shared across microservices? If it can, would it mean that the boundary is being crossed when microservices share the state amongst each other?

In order to answer this, we need to better understand what we mean by boundaries for each microservice so that isolation remains intact. In general, we want our microservices to be autonomous. Webster's Dictionary defines *Autonomous* as:

- Having the right or power of self-government
- Undertaken or carried on without outside control

So, an autonomous system must have the sovereign right over everything it does and no outside system must be able to influence or control it. This means an autonomous system must have the capability of existing independently in all situations and thus responding, reacting, or developing independently of the whole.

By this definition and understanding, it is important for a microservice to be immune to outside changes and have total control of what it does. So, it is very crucial for a microservice to own and command over its state. This means the persistence or a database cannot be shared across microservices. If they do, there is no clear boundary between microservices, and the systems cannot be truly autonomous. For example, if two microservices share a same set of tables across each other, then:

- Any update in the schema by one microservice will unknowingly affect the other.

- A write lock by one microservice will affect the reads of others.
- A microservice might decide to cache the data. If another microservice updates the entries in a table, this would mean that the cache of the first microservice now stores incorrect data and the cache will have to be invalidated. So microservices will have to communicate with each other to invalidate respective caches. This also means they will need to understand the internals of each other for an application to survive, adding to development and maintenance complexity.
- A table can either be optimized for faster reads or for faster writes with appropriate indexes. But rarely for both. One microservice might want the table to exhibit faster writes and the other microservice might wish for faster reads. In such a scenario, they are at crossheads.

This situation would be very similar to a monolith. It's like breaking different interfaces of a monolith into different applications, just that now they interact with each other over the network. Of course, this means more things can go wrong.

Services must be loosely coupled, so that they can be developed, deployed, and scaled independently and changes to one microservice state should not impact other microservices. For a microservice to be autonomous in the truest sense, it cannot share the same state or even the same database server. One could argue that there is no harm in sharing the same instance of a database server given they don't share the same set of tables in a database. But this adds to the unnecessary complexity where in time no one remains sure about what each microservice owns and the other doesn't. Maybe a solution could be to name tables with a prefix of the application that owns it.

But it doesn't solve the problem that if the database server is affected due to heavy load by one microservice, it inadvertently affects the other microservice. Moreover, each application might want to configure the database best for its usage patterns. In Microsoft SQL Server, we usually set the number of data files (data files contain data and objects such as tables, indexes, stored procedures, and views); for example, we could either set a 160 GB database as 1 * 160 GB file or 2 * 80 GB or 4 * 40 GB, and so. Each setup will provide the best performance for different scenarios.

In short, microservices do not share their persistence storage with each other. If they do, then the isolation is affected

However, sometimes things are not very straightforward. It might be that common tables need to be shared across microservices and we need to learn mechanisms to handle such scenarios.

Different things are inferred differently by different people. For example, if you are decorating a children's bedroom, as a parent you focus on the wall paint color, decor, a study table, height of the bed, and so on. But to the construction agency, they are only concerned about the dimensions of the room and not the decor. So, even though the domain is the same, the context of each is different. Hence, the modeling of the same domain by both of them would be different, which may means different schema even though both of them deal with a single object that is a room.

So, it might appear that it make sense to share the same state (a room here), but what they represent can be very different. We will jump into details of modeling such applications when we introduce domain driven design and its implication of architecting microservices in Chapter 8, *Effective Communication*, with strategies to set boundaries in complex domain designs. Then we will introduce design patterns on how to model them effectively in practice using event sourcing and CQRS.

Defining microservice

To summarize what we mean by a microservice:

- Microservices do one thing and they do it well.
- A microservice owns its own state. It does not share it with others microservices.

Micro in microservice

The word *micro* in microservice can be very misleading.

Micro in microservice does not mean that the microservice should be tiny in terms of the number of lines of code or shouldn't do many operations. There is no constraint on the size of a microservice. For example, in our search engine application, we could have a separate microservice for the Stack Overflow engine. Now the code base for this microservice has no limits. It could be a 1,000 lines of code or may be a hundred thousand lines of code long. It could use different types of databases to store content, different technologies to cache, and a plethora of libraries to function. All of this is irrelevant until the time it is in its own boundary, and does not interfere with others and everything related to Stack Overflow is done at this single place.

The size of the microservice is irrelevant until the time the right boundary across domains is maintained.

Polyglot

In our application, if one realizes that once the communication semantics are set, we could implement any of the Stack Overflow or LinkedIn engines in any programming language. A team might wish to do it in Haskell and someone else in Groovy and they will all have the independence and flexibility in which to implement it. Designing with microservices gives this as a first class mechanism.

The dark side of microservices architecture

Not everything is rosy. Just breaking different parts of the systems into different applications is not making things easy if we do not do it the right way. Worse, it becomes like a giant distributed system where the method calls are over the network. And the network always has numerous reasons to mess up. It becomes unpredictable and the application becomes difficult to debug.

With distributed systems, there could be other problems, such as:

- Deployment of many applications becomes painful as we now have numerous applications to deploy.
- As if tracking and monitoring the monolith was easy! We now have several microservices to monitor, adding to the workload.
- Collecting and viewing logs and restarting applications.
- Distributed transactions. With a monolith, transactions are easier, as it is a single application and one could lock across several tables (and modules) for a transaction. With distributed systems, transactions can get extremely complicated (or impossible) as they are different applications altogether and having a lock spread across all of them is a nightmare. We need to learn the skill to model data in distributed systems.
- An application will need the address of other applications to access them. If the communication is via HTTP then it will need to store the URL of all the applications it wishes to access. If another application changes its URL, this will have to be communicated to all the dependents to update their URL list. Worse, if the input format changes, such as the method signature of a service that takes HTTP requests, this change in signature has to be conveyed to all other teams. Not doing so will lead to errors.

- Logs are scattered across microservices. If something goes wrong, trailback gets difficult. This also makes finding the root cause of the problem difficult.
- Version management.
- One of the tactics mentioned in this chapter is to do asynchronous communication by message passing. But asynchronous communication can get very complicated as the response of the operation would be notified sometime in the future. This can add to code complexity and makes debugging difficult unless the right abstractions are used.

We need to be well equipped to handle all the scenarios better to see the true benefits of the microservices architecture. This book will be a journey on how to write great microservices at the beginning and then focus on tackling pain points effectively towards the end.

Why Scala

For the functionalities we desire, we need the right toolset to express them better.

Scala provides abstractions (such as a powerful type system, pattern matching, implicits, immutable collections, and many others) and syntactic sugar (such as case classes, for comprehensions, extractors, and many others) to express better. This results in code that is not only less verbose (and less code means less bugs) but also write scalable code that the language name is synonym with.

Coupled with the fact that Scala runs on a fantastic VM--Java Virtual Machine, which is one of the best platforms out there for high performance, this also gives the ability to access all the Java libraries. It makes Scala be the best of both worlds--great runtime execution thanks to JVM and an expressive Typesafe programming language.

If you would like to learn more about Scala, we suggest that you read the book, *Programming in Scala* by Martin Odersky, Lex Spoon, and Bill Venners, *Artima Inc.* Also the online free course, *Functional Programming Principles in Scala*, on Coursera (https://www.coursera.org/learn/progfun1), by Martin Odersky is a good introduction.

Summary

In this chapter, we tried architecting our search engine application as a monolithic application. During the process, we came across the pain points associated with large monolithic applications. We then tried defining microservices and how they help as a design pattern to build scalable applications with lesser nuisance during development. We briefly tried understanding the advantages associated with this approach, and we also acknowledged the pain points associated with a microservices-based architecture if it is not designed and executed well.

In the next chapter, we will try learning simple microservices using Play Framework in Scala.

2

Introduction to Play Framework

In the previous chapter, we briefly covered the essence behind microservices. In this chapter, we will introduce Play Framework, and build simple web services using Play Framework.

We will get started with Play Framework, and you will learn the following:

- How to write web services using Play
- Play internals such as router and controller
- REST and stateless
- Parsing JSON using Play-JSON

You can find the full source of the examples that we try in this chapter at `https://github.com/scala-microservices-book/book-examples/tree/master/first-app`. However, it is recommended to program the examples mentioned in this chapter by yourself, and use the source only as a reference.

Quick introduction to Play 2.66

Play is a refreshing modern web framework for Scala and Java, following the **Model-View-Controller (MVC)** architectural pattern. It is inspired by **Ruby on Rails (RoR)**, and prefers the convention over the configuration approach in building web apps. Play is designed from the ground up to be highly performant with minimal resource consumption (CPU, memory, threads) with asynchronous and non-blocking being its core nature (we will see later what this means). Built on top of Akka, it is lightweight and stateless (it does not hold any server-side state). Thus, it is easier to scale Play applications both horizontally (by adding parallel application instances because it is stateless) and vertically (by adding more CPU and memory), providing a robust toolset to scale predictably.

Play differs from other Java-based web frameworks in the sense that it does not comply to the servlet standard, and has its own mechanism to handle HTTP and WebSocket protocols. It internally uses the Akka-HTTP engine as the default HTTP server backend. Until the previous version of Play (specifically 2.5), Play used Netty (`http://netty.io/`) as the HTTP server backend. Being containerless (not running on servers such as Tomcat, GlassFish, and so on) makes it easy to compile, run, and deploy Play applications, as everything is prepacked by default. This also makes it simple to run Play applications on platforms such as Heroku (`https://www.heroku.com/`).

Play is also designed to be developer friendly with automatic reloading of code changes on browser refresh, and it also has great IDE support.

To see all the features that Play provides, you are recommended to go through the documentation at `https://playframework.com/documentation/2.66.x/Home`.

Getting started

To set up a `hello world play` project, you could either create the project straight out of your IDE by going to **File** | **New Project** | **Select `Play`** in the Scale IDE (eclipse), or in Intellij Idea. You can also create a new project out of the command line using SBT. SBT is a build tool that is *de facto* for most of the Scala projects. You will need to install SBT before proceeding; installation details can be found at `http://www.scala-sbt.org/0.13/docs/Setup.html`.

We will be following the command-line approach, as it helps to understand the specifics. Do not worry, there is not much to configure at this stage.

In your empty project folder named `first-app`, create three files as shown next:

```
first-app/
├── build.sbt
└── project/
    ├── build.properties
    └── plugins.sbt
```

The contents of these files will be as follows:

build.sbt
```
name := "first-app"
version := "1.0.0-SNAPSHOT"
lazy val root = (project in file(".")).enablePlugins(PlayScala)
scalaVersion := "2.12.2"2
libraryDependencies += guice
```

You will need to keep a redundant empty line in between the preceding lines, as it is required by SBT.

```
project/build.properties
  sbt.version=0.13.13
project/plugins.sbt
  resolvers += "Typesafe repository" at
  "https://repo.typesafe.com/typesafe/maven-releases/"

// Use the Play sbt plugin for Play projects
addSbtPlugin("com.typesafe.play" % "sbt-plugin" % "2.6.33")

addSbtPlugin("com.typesafe.sbteclipse" % "sbteclipse-plugin" %
"4.0.0")
```

Once the preceding three files are created, from your command line, use the following:

```
cd first-app
sbt
```

At first, it will take some time as it downloads a few dependencies over the network in the background, and will, ultimately, show the Play console as seen in this screenshot:

The Play console is a development console based on SBT, which allows you to manage a Play application's complete development cycle. You can input several commands, such as the following:

- `compile`: To compile your source files
- `test`: To run test cases
- `run`: To run your application
- `console`: To enter the interactive Scala console, which allows you to test your code interactively
- `exit`: To exit the Play console
- `reload`: To reload any configuration changes made in `build.sbt` file and the properties file (it is useful in the sense that you do not have to restart SBT to load any new changes)

If you enter `run`, it will start your application. Try visiting `localhost:9000` from your favorite browser, and you will see a red screen citing **Configuration error** as follows:

Note—To run on some other port number and not the default port `9000`, use the command `run -Dhttp.port=80`.

The error screen is displayed because we have not coded anything that tells the server what the response must be when we send a `GET` HTTP call to `/`. Thus, the server throws a `java.io.IOException: resource not found on classpath...`. In this case, it suggests that it anticipated some file that could tell it what to do when an `HTTP request` is made. This exception thrown by the server is then shown on the browser.

This feature that *any exception thrown by a server handling request is automatically shown on the browser* works with all kinds of exceptions—including the ones thrown by our application logic. This is a great development productivity booster, as you do not have to scroll over logs to find the cause. The stack trace and information is directly available on the browser, saving you precious time.

You can now import this project in your favorite IDE as follows:

- On Intellij—you simply have to go to **File | New | Project from existing sources | select SBT | next**, and so on
- On eclipse (Scala IDE)—you will need to follow these steps:

    1. Run the command `eclipse with-source=true` on the Play console.

    2. Compile using the `compile` command.

    3. Import the project in the IDE from **File | Import | General | Existing project... menu**.

For troubleshooting with the Scala IDE and Intellij, or to import a project in ENSIME or NetBeans, refer to the documentation at `https://www.playframework.com/documentation/2.5.x/IDE`.

Hello world

We will now create a `hello world` example, and this is what our project structure will look like:

```
|- first-app/
        |- app/
            |- controllers/
                    |- HomeController.scala
        |- conf/
            |- routes
            |- application.conf
        |- project/
            |- build.properties
            |- plugins.sbt
        |- build.sbt
```

You will first have to create a `conf/application.conf` file, which can be an empty file for now.

Create the file `conf/routes` with the following contents:

```
GET / controllers.HomeController.index
```

`routes` contains the mapping of the *request-path* with the Scala function that needs to be called when the `HTTP request` is received. In the preceding code, a GET call at / would correspondingly request an action from the `index` function in the `controllers.HomeController.scala` file. You will need to create `app/controllers/HomeController.scala` as follows:

```
package controllers
  import javax.inject.Inject
  import javax.inject.Singleton
  import play.api.mvc._
    @Singleton
    class HomeController @Inject()(cc: ControllerComponents)
    extends AbstractController(cc) {
      def index() = Action{
        Ok("Hello World!")
      }
    }
```

- `app/` is the root directory for the source files
- `controllers` is a Scala package containing a single Scala file

By default, Play Framework supports Google Guice (`https://github.com/google/guice`)for **dependency injection (DI)**

While working with a large-scale application, we usually use a dependency injection framework. We are not going to delve much into DI as it is a well-documented concept. This article by Martin Fowler is a good read to understand dependency injection—`https://martinfowler.com/articles/injection.html`. However, in a nutshell, we can explain it as follows:

When building services, your code will have dependencies on other services. Often, the specific implementations will vary between development, test and production environments, so it's important not to couple your code tightly to a concrete implementation class. Explaining it further:

- We do not instantiate our dependencies ourselves. That is, we do not use the `new` keyword or any other factory pattern to instantiate our dependent objects. Rather, we request `someone else` to initiate it, and ultimately, provide/inject it for us.

- For example—in our `HomeController` example, Play Framework would instantiate the `HomeController` class. The advantage is that if some other Scala object wanted to access the `HomeController` object, then they would request Play Framework to obtain the already instantiated object. Similarly, if an object wanted to access a database or a service, then the database or services objects can be injected to the one that needs it.
- The advantages include ease of coupling across dependent classes, and testing, as we could inject mock classes instead of the original ones.

Play Framework provides dependency injection support via the following two modes:

- **Runtime dependency injection**: It is called runtime because the dependency graph (configuring the dependencies of all objects) is created, wired (injecting the dependencies), and validated (whether the right dependency injection was configured; for example, if an object depended on a database access object, but was provided with an object to access an external web service, then it would throw an error at runtime citing invalid dependency injected). Please refer to the following points:
    - Any framework that is compliant with *JSR 330* (`https://jcp.org/en/jsr/detail?id=330`) is supported; Google Guice support is out of the box
    - We will be using Google Guice for all our examples in this book
    - There isn't a need to dive deeper into Guice at this stage, and we will cover most of the concepts as and when needed in this book
- **Compile-time dependency injection**: The dependent objects are wired at compile time. Please refer the following points:
    - Think of this as using *setters* of the object
    - The boilerplate associated with the manual calling of the setters can be avoided by using compile time DI frameworks such as Macwire (`https://github.com/adamw/macwire`)
    - Compile time DI has an advantage over runtime DI in that the dependencies are validated at compile time.

Coming back to our `HomeController` example:

```
@Singleton
class HomeController @Inject()(cc: ControllerComponents) extends
AbstractController(cc) {
```

Please refer to the following points:

- @Singleton: Implies that we only want a single object of the class HomeController to be created. If multiple other objects need an instance of HomeController, then they would all be provided with the same instance of HomeController.
- @Inject()(cc: ControllerComponents): Inject implies that the HomeController class is dependent on the object of type ControllerComponents. ControllerComponents contains some components needed by the controller. We will look at this in more detail later.
- Our class finally extends AbstractController: This provides HomeController with the ability to define *Actions* for an HTTP call. We will discuss this further in the next section.

Execute run in the Play console, and try accessing http://localhost:9000 from your browser; you will see Hello World! as the response.

Now try adding the following line in your routes file:

```
GET /:name controllers.HomeController.hello(name: String)
```

And add the following method in your controllers/HomeController.scala:

```
def hello(name:String) = Action{
  Ok("Hello "+name)
}
```

Try making a call to http://localhost:9000/Liverpool from your browser, and you will see the response as Hello Liverpool!.

Play automatically associates name in /:name with the string Liverpool in the request. We will discuss this further in the section on routing.

Note that you didn't have to stop the server, compile, and restart again, but you simply had to make a call from the browser. SBT automatically determines the source files impacted, recompiles only the changed files, and refreshes. This makes the development experience seamless, as you do not have to worry about redundant and expensive restarts to reload your code changes. To learn more about the Play console, it is recommended you refer to https://www.playframework.com/documentation/2.5.x/PlayConsole.

Structure of the Play project

Here is a brief overview of a simple Play project:

```
|- first-app/
        |- app/ → Application Source Files
            |- com.company → Application Source packages
            |- assets → Web-Assets like Play-Templates code. CSS,
                        Javascript for UI
        |- conf/ → Configuration Files (available on classpath)
            |- routes → Routes definition
            |- application.conf → Main configuration file
        |- project/ → Sbt configuration files
            |- build.properties → Marker for sbt project
            |- plugins.sbt → Sbt plugins including declaringing
                             Play plugin
        |- public/ → Public Assets
            |- stylesheets → CSS files
            |- javascripts → Javascript files
                |- images → images
        |- logs/ → Logs folder
            |- application.log → Default log file
        |- target/ → Compiled code, other generated code
        |- build.sbt → Main Application build script
```

Primarily, all the preceding folders can be segregated into three types—SBT-specific files such as `build.sbt` and `project/folder`, application-specific files such as `app/`, `conf/`, and `public/folders`, and finally, other meta files such as `target/` and `logs/`.

The `app/` directory contains all the executable Scala source code, templates, and compiled asset sources. Usually, the package structure is left as this:

- `app/controllers`
- `app/models`
- `app/views`

This is, of course, inspired by the MVC architectural pattern with a package folder for each. The package structure can be explained as follows:

- **models**: This is the behavior of an application; that is, all the logic, data, and rules
- **views**: This is the output that is shown to the user; it can be the HTML template files for a website/mobile
- **controllers**: This is the interface for input; it sends commands to the models, or even views, to update something

Usually, while building web apps, `models` represent the core logic of the application. We expose them via a service using `controllers`. `Controllers`, internally, then communicate with models. `Views` then provide the output.

Routing

Let us try to understand the code that we have just seen. Our `routes` file currently looks like this:

```
GET  /       controllers.HomeController.index
GET  /:name  controllers.HomeController.hello(name: String)
```

The following figure explains the flow of a HTTP call. Routes are a means to trigger the respective action for a HTTP call:

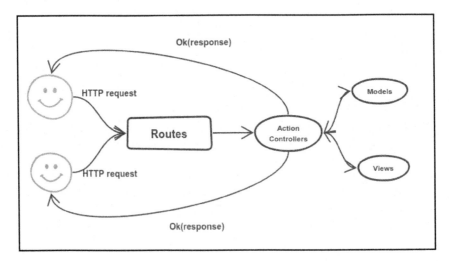

Routes

Router helps in the translation of each incoming message to its respective action. Each line contains these three aspects:

- HTTP method
- URI pattern
- Both are associated with a call to an action

The HTTP method can be any of the valid methods supported by HTTP (GET, PATCH, POST, PUT, DELETE, and HEAD).

The URI pattern defines the route's request path. The pattern can either be static or dynamic. Another example of a static path (we have created a new file, Users.scala, in the controllers package) is as follows:

```
GET /user/getAllUsers controllers.Users.getAllUsers
```

The path can also be dynamic like we saw earlier.

```
GET /:name controllers.HomeController.hello(name: String)
```

In the preceding line, :name is a dynamic part where it gets associated dynamically to exactly one URI path segment for a request. So, if http://localhost:9000/gerrard gets called, then the string gerrard would get attached to the field name. The default matching strategy for a dynamic part is defined by the regular expression [^/]+ (all characters excluding the forward slash / with at least a single character).
A path segment is automatically decoded before passing it to a route. Suppose http://localhost:9000/Love moves the world gets called, then the browser would encode it as http://localhost:9000/Love%20moves%20the%20world, and the route would decode and associate name with Love moves the world.

You can also have multiple path segments, as follows:

```
GET /user/:name/:age
controllers.Users.getUser(name:String, age:Int)
```

An action can be defined as this:

```
def helloDetail(name:String, age:Int) = Action{
  Ok(s"Hello $name of age: $age")
}
```

Upon calling http://localhost:9000/user/federer/36, Play will attach name with federer, age with 36, and the response from the server would be—Hello federer of age 36.

You could also implement this using the traditional GET parameters like this:

```
GET /user controllers.Users.getUser(name:String, age:Int)
```

You would now need to call http://localhost:9000/user?name=federer&age=36, and Play would automatically attach name with federer, and age with 36.

Another important aspect of the `routes` file is that it is compiled, please refer to the following points:

- Any mismatch in the action name in the `routes` file results in a compilation failure. For example, if there was a typo in `controllers.Users.getUser(...)`, then it would result in a compile-time failure.
- Further, many `routes` can match the same request. If there is a conflict, the first route is used as per the declaration order.

HTTP POST

To make an HTTP `POST` call, just like any other HTTP method, use this:

```
POST        /user/addUser          controllers.Users.addUser
```

In `controllers/Users`, implement the action as follows:

```
def addUser() = Action { implicit request =>
 val body = request.body

 body.asFormUrlEncoded match{
   case Some(map) =>
     //persist user information
   Ok(s"The user of name `${map("name").head}` and age
   `${map("age").head}` has been created\n")
   case None => BadRequest("Unknow body format")
 }
}
```

You can then make a call from the command line by using `curl` on Linux-based systems, like this:

```
jatin@puri:~$ curl \
--header "Content-type: application/x-www-form-urlencoded"  \
--request POST \
--data 'name=Nadal&age=31' \
http://localhost:9000/user/addUser
```

Instead of using `curl`, you can also download the Google Chrome extension to make `GET` or `POST` calls from the browser. One such tool is Postman (`https://www.getpostman.com/`). Using Postman, you can easily call different web services, and Postman will preserve the history and signature for you.

When a call is made either from `curl` or Postman, you can access the request body by using `request.body`, as shown in the preceding code. In this case, we expected the request to be of the content type `application/x-www-form-urlencoded`, and therefore, we added `body.asFormUrlEncoded` in the code. The following table gives you a list of content types and the corresponding methods for your reference:

Content-type	Method Name
`application/x-www-form-urlencoded`	`request.body.asFormUrlEncoded`
`text/plain`	`request.body.asText`
`application/xml`	`request.body.asXML`
`application/json`	`request.body.asJson`

Actions

We have seen that each row in the `routes` file contains three parts—the HTTP method, URI pattern, and the associated name of an action. A sample implementation of `Action` that we have seen is like this:

```
def index() = Action { Ok("Hello World!") }
```

We could also rewrite the preceding implementation as follows:

```
defindex() = Action { implicit request =>Ok("Hello World!") }
```

They both mean the same thing; it's just that, in the former, we have access to the request body and other `HTTP request` meta information.

We know that, in Scala, the preceding code is a syntactic sugar for this:

```
def index() = Action.apply{implicit request => Ok("Hello World!") }
```

In the preceding command, we, essentially, provide a `Request => Result` function that handles a request, and generates a result to be sent to the client. We mark the `request` as implicit so that it could implicitly be used by Play APIs that need access to the `request` object. The implicit is, of course, limited to the scope of the action.

The type of the result is `play.api.mvc.Result`. In the preceding code, `Ok("..")` is an implementation for `play.api.mvc.Result`, which returns a response to the client with the following:

- An HTTP 200 response
- `text/plain` as the content type

Apart from `Ok`, there are also other `play.api.mvc.Result` implementations. For example, there is a call that returns the square root of a number for the following entry in `routes`:

```
GET     /sqrt/:num      controllers.HomeController.sqrt(num:String)
```

The sqrt function is implemented in `HomeController.scala` as:

```
def sqrt(num:String) = Action{ implicit request =>
Try(num.toInt) match {
  case Success(ans) if ans >= 0 => Ok(s"The answer is:
    ${math.sqrt(ans)}")
  case Success(ans) => BadRequest(s"The input ($num) must be
    greater than zero")
  case Failure(ex) => InternalServerError(s"Could not extract the
    contents from $num")
  }
}
```

The following are the responses that we get for different inputs in the preceding code:

- Where the input is a valid number and greater than zero, we return `Ok`, which is an HTTP 200 response
- Where the input is a valid number and less than zero, we return `BadRequest`, which is an HTTP 400 response
- For all other failures, we return `InternalServerError`, which is an HTTP 500 response

There are multiple other sample `Response` objects that can be found at the `play.api.mvc.Results` trait, to name a few—`NotFound` (for HTTP 404), `Unauthorized` (for HTTP 401), `BadGateway` (for HTTP 502), `Redirect` (for HTTP 303), and so on.

As discussed, `Ok("")` is an implementation of `play.api.mvc.Result`. `Result` is a case `class`, and contains other `helper` functions to add cookies, HTTP headers, HTTP sessions, and so on.

```
def index() = Action{implicit request =>
Ok("Hello World!")
```

```
.withHeaders("Server" -> "Play")
.withCookies(Cookie("id", scala.util.Random.nextInt().toString))
}
```

The response sent back to the client on running the preceding code will contain the HTTP header "Server" with the value as "Play", and a cookie with the key as "id" and its value as a random number.

Auth

With the help of sessions, we can implement a simple HTTP authentication mechanism based on username and password. A session is just a cookie. You can find more information about HTTP cookies here—https://en.wikipedia.org/wiki/HTTP_cookie.

You can find the full source of the following implementation at https://github.com/scala-microservices-book/book-examples/tree/master/first-app.

There are primarily three calls in the controllers/LoginController file:

- /auth/index:
  - If the user is already logged in, we welcome him
  - If not, we ask him to log in by making a call to http://localhost:9000/auth/login?name=admin&password=1234
- /auth/login: We verify the username and password, and respond as follows:
  - If the password is validated, we log him in (by storing the session), and redirect the user to /auth/index
  - If the password fails, we reply saying wrong password
- /auth/logout:
  - If the user is already logged in, we log him out
  - Otherwise, we ask him to log in

```
def check(name: String, password: String) = {
  name == "admin" && password == "1234"
}

def isValidUser(name:String) ={
  name == "admin"
}
```

```
def login(name: String, password: String) = Action {
  if (check(name, password))
  Redirect("auth/index").withSession(("user", name))
  else BadRequest("Invalid username or password")
}
```

In the preceding code, if the username and password matches, we redirect the user to the /auth/index page after setting the session object, as follows:

```
def index = Action{ implicit request =>
  request.session.get("user") match {
    case Some(user) if isValidUser(user)=> Ok(s"Welcome $user")
    case Some(user) => BadRequest("Not a valid user")
    case None => BadRequest("You are currently not logged in. \n
    Please login by calling: \n" +
    "http://localhost:9000/auth/login?name=admin&password=1234")
  }
}
```

If the user has already logged in (that is, if the session was already set), then we welcome him. Otherwise, we ask him to log in first. You could try this locally by running the application, and making a call to http://localhost:9000/auth/index.

Templates

To build visual user interfaces, there are two approaches that are normally adapted. One is to use a template engine to auto-generate HTML files for us. The HTML files are auto-generated at runtime during a request. Play comes with Twirl (https://github.com/playframework/twirl), a Typesafe template engine based on Scala. A very simple template file would appear as follows:

```
@(customer: String)
<html><body>
<h1>Welcome @customer</h1>
</body></html>
```

If a file is created with the preceding body and named as index.scala.html under the app/views folder, you can then call it in the following manner just like any other Scala code:

```
def index() = Action{
val c: Html = views.html.index("Gerrard")
Ok(c)
}
```

An HTML will automatically be generated where the variable `customer` is initialized with the string `Gerrard`. By calling *Ok(c)*, we then return this HTML to the caller.

Twirl is quite powerful. The expressions we use in templates are not a new language, but Scala itself is. You can embed Scala code and use Scala expressions inside your templates. For example, `@customer` is a valid Scala object, and you could use all the methods of the `String` class (along with implicits) inside your template file. This not only makes it powerful and expressive but also `Typesafe`, as you would get compile-time errors if it was not a valid Scala expression.

Another alternative way to build user interfaces is to use pure JavaScript-based frameworks such as Angular.js, Ember.js, and so on. In such scenarios, all the UI-related logic and appearance is then coded in JavaScript, and it requests for information in the background using Ajax or WebSockets. The application simply provides the data in some format (usually, **JavaScript Object Notation (JSON)**). The JavaScript code then receives the extracted data from JSON, and renders it on the user interface.

So, the application server would only be worried about responding back to the JSON for a service. This JSON could either be used by our web pages, or by the mobile application. Better, other applications or servers could access our application using HTTP calls, and we could respond with JSON. This way, applications would be able to communicate with each other using JSON as the form of communication. In practice, we will be doing this a lot.

REST

REST expands to **Representational State Transfer**. In a RESTful web service, a request made to a resource URI will elicit a response that is in some format, for example, JSON, XML, HTML, or it may provide a hypertext link to another resource or a set of resources. Using HTTP, as is most common, the kind of operations available include those predefined by the HTTP verbs `GET`, `POST`, `PUT`, `DELETE`, and so on.

To briefly explain REST, it can be thought of as a simple mechanism to `get`, `create`, or `update` the state on the server as follows:

1. The client could make an HTTP `GET` call, and `/users`, and the server would return the list of all the users.
2. The client could then send an HTTP `POST` call, `/user:username`, and it would create a new user with a username.
3. An HTTP `PUT` call to `/user:username` with other attributes would be able to `edit/modify` the user information associated with that username.

4   An HTTP `DELETE` call to `/user:username` would delete the user from the
    application records.

Fundamentally, over the network, one is able to access and modify the application state.
Very similar to `getters`/`setters` that we write in our classes, but only over the network.

This is only a tiny explanation of REST. You could use HTTP `GET` for all—to get all users,
create, and delete users as well instead of using `POST`, `PUT`, and `DELETE`. But then you
would use a different URI for each. For example, you may have `GET /deleteUser` to delete
a user, and `GET /updateUser` to update the user details.

REST was originally architected and defined by Roy Thomas Fielding. The original
explanation can be found at `http://www.ics.uci.edu/~fielding/pubs/dissertation/`
`top.htm`. There are quite a few concepts and paradigms that REST introduces, but the one
relevant for us here is being **stateless**.

Stateless
Stateless means that the application does not carry a state. The original description from
Roy Fielding's paper is cited here:

> *...communication must be stateless in nature, ... such that each request from client to*
> *server must contain all of the information necessary to understand the request, and cannot*
> *take advantage of any stored context on the server. Session state is therefore kept entirely*
> *on the client.*
> *This constraint induces the properties of visibility, reliability, and scalability.*

Fundamentally, the application server does not maintain any state. If there is no state
maintained, then, of course, no state gets shared across multiple requests. If multiple calls
are made to the server, then they can be thought of as independent of each other. To explain
it further, if a request is made, then the response must not be affiliated to the previous
request made. A counterexample to being stateless would be to maintain the session
information of the user. For example, in an airline ticketing system, the user could search
for flights between Dubai and New York on a particular date. The server would preserve
the filter applied by the user. In a subsequent call, if the user wanted to change the
destination to London, the client would only request with the destination change in the
second search assuming that the server already remembers the previous filters applied,
such as the date and origin of the start. So, the subsequent calls are not independent.

A stateless solution would be one where the client would provide all the information, such
as origin, destination, and date for all subsequent calls without assuming that the server
stores the previous state applied.

This idea can be quite powerful. It is similar to the ideology of pure functions in functional programming languages. Just like the mathematical notion of a function which, when called with the same arguments, always returns the same results. A call to the square root of number four would always return the same value, two, independent of how many times we call it. This provides **reliability** and also **performance,** as the function could cache results for subsequent calls.

Similarly, a GET call, called as many times, should always return the same value from a stateless server. And just because a GET call is made, it should have no impact on other calls.

Another advantage of being stateless is that it is easier to scale. Just like in programming, a mutable state is an enemy for multithreaded code. If a variable, let's say var counter:Int, is shared across multiple threads, then each thread would be able to change the value. So, we would need an appropriate locking mechanism to change it, making it complex. It would also be difficult to backtrack in history to obtain information on a set of steps done to arrive at the current counter value.
With no changing state maintained by the application server, there is no need for explicit locking.

Scalability is improved by being stateless, because we do not have to store a state between requests, allowing the server component to quickly free resources. This further simplifies the implementation, because the server doesn't have to manage resource usage across requests. Further, instead of one application server, we could have multiple stateless application servers, and we could route the user requests to different servers. Because no state is maintained by any instance, it is not required that subsequent requests are routed to the original instance that catered to the first request of that user. Subsequent requests could be routed to any other instance which is relatively free, thus promoting scalability. This also promotes reliability--any server could be killed or started at any time, as all are stateless. If there was a state maintained, then information would have been lost if the application instance was killed.

In reality, however, it is impossible for an application to be completely stateless; that is, be void of all the data. There will always be some data, as without data there is no application. So some data/state will be maintained by the application, and it is usually delegated to someone else, which is, in most cases, a database. The database would then be the carrier for preserving and storing the state. For example, in an airline ticketing system, once a ticket is purchased, the database would contain the information of the ticket purchased, the remaining empty seats on the flight, other flight information, and so on.

Delegating state management to an external storage has advantages where the state is completely isolated and maintained by a specialized service, thus providing modularization.

To summarize, we can list the following points:

- When we say something is RESTful, it implies that the server can be accessed, and the state transferred externally using an interface which is HTTP.
- Being RESTful also means being stateless. **No state would be stored by the application server**. The server would access the state from external places, such as other web services and databases. Statelessness has the following advantages:
    - **Reliability**: The same call made multiple times would result in the same response. Restarting the instance would make no difference, as no information would be lost.
    - **Scalability**: No information would be preserved across multiple requests. We can create multiple instances of the application to handle higher load, and route requests to different instances.
    - **Visibility**: This is improved, because a monitoring system does not have to look beyond a single request datum in order to determine the full nature of the request.

JSON marshalling/Unmarshalling

Microservices can themselves expose their services in multiple ways. REST is one of them. Usually, JSON is the format used during communication. In Scala, there are multiple libraries to parse JSON. In this section, we will look at Play-JSON to parse JSON, but there are other good alternatives as well—Spray-JSON, rapture, and pure functional-approach-based ones, like argonaut and circe.

When dealing with JSON, we are, primarily, involved with the following two scenarios:

- Reading JSON--and sometimes, converting it to Scala objects
- Writing JSON--and sometimes, generating JSON from Scala objects.

You can find the full source of the following examples in the package /app/json/ under the first-app folder in the GitHub repository of the book.

Reading JSON

To read the contents of JSON, we use the following code:

```
import play.api.libs.json._
val jsonString = """{
    | "teamName" : "Real Madrid FC",
    | "players" : [ {
    | "name" : "Ronaldo",
    | "age" : 36
    | }, {
    | "name" : "Modric",
    | "age" : 30
    | }, {
    | "name" : "Bale",
    | "age" : 27
    | } ],
    | "location" : {
    | "lat" : 40.4168,
    | "long" : 3.7038
    | }
    |}
    |""". stripMargin
val jValue: JsValue = Json.parse(jsonString)
```

The simplest way to parse JSON is via `Json.parse`. It returns `JsValue`. `JsValue` is a sealed trait that signifies a JSON value. Its subclasses are as follows:

- `JsNull`: This represents a null value
- `JsBoolean`: This represents true or false
- `JsNumber`: This represents an int or floating point arithmetic
- `JsString`: This represents a JSON string
- `JsArray`: This represents a JSON array
- `JsObject`: This represents a JSON object

So, you can pattern match on `JsValue`.

This code is used to search for the value of a key in a `JsValue`:

```
(jValue \ "teamName").as[String] //returns Real Madrid FC
(jValue \ "location" \ "lat").as[Double] //returns 40.4168
((jValue \ "players")(0) \ "name").as[String] //returns Ronaldo
```

\ returns the property corresponding to the field name for a JsObject. You could even search nested as we did in the preceding code with (jValue \ **"location"** \ **"lat"**). If the value is an array, then we use the index position as we did in the preceding code using ((jValue \ **"players"**)(0) \ **"name"**).

In the preceding code, we directly tried reading the value from the result using as[String]. Now the actual value might not exist, or may be an integer, Boolean, or some JSON object, but not necessarily string. So, it may result in an exception if the value is not found. In such scenarios, validate helps us to be safe, as shown in the following code:

```
val validate: JsResult[String] = (jValue \
"teaName").validate[String]
validate match {
  case x:JsSuccess[String] => println(x.get)
  case e: JsError => println(e.errors)
}
```

validate[String] does two things—it verifies if the value exists, and if the value is a String.

You can search for all the values through JSON, as follows:

```
val names: Seq[JsValue] = jValue \\ "name"
names.map(x => x.as[String])
//would return List(Ronaldo, Modric, Bale)
```

\\ searches for the values in JsValue with the key as name in the JsValue, and all its descendants. In the preceding code, it will iterate over the complete JSON to get all values for the key, name. The key, name, could be anywhere in the JSON, and it will record all of them.

Note that \\ will return a sequence of JsValue, and each JsValue could either be a JsObject, JsArray, or integer, and so on. We inferred it as a string. But you must use validate for each value.

Now that we know how to parse JSON, we need to extract all the contents, and generate Scala objects for the same, as follows:

```
case class Team(teamName:String, players:List[Player],
  location:Location)
case class Player(name:String, age:Int)
case class Location(lat:Double, long: Double)
```

So, it is required to parse JSON, and fill the preceding objects. Doing so manually would be cumbersome. Play provides an alternative to automatically convert JSON to Scala objects using `Reads`.

The idea is that we declare the path, and associate each path with a Scala object. The path is represented using `JsPath`. For example, in our JSON, latitude and longitude in the location will have a path as follows:

```
val lat = (JsPath \ "location" \"lat")
val long = (JsPath \ "location" \"long")
```

Here, `JsPath` represents the root of JSON. Once we obtain the path, we use this information to get the value using `Reads`, as shown here:

```
val temp: Reads[Double] = (JsPath \ "location"\"lat").read[Double]
//now using Reads, obtain the value from the JSON
println(jValue.as[Double](temp))
```

We first defined a path, and then we generated a `Reads` object out of it. `Reads` **helps us to convert a** `JsValue` **to some specific type. It achieves this by using a path to obtain the value.**

We can merge multiple `Reads` for more complex `Reads`, as shown here:

```
import play.api.libs.functional.syntax._

implicit val locationReads: Reads[Location] = (
  (JsPath \ "lat").read[Double] and
  (JsPath \ "long").read[Double]
).apply((x,y) => Location.apply(x,y))
```

We define the path for `lat` and `long`, and then we club them both. Using both the values, we then generate the `Location` object by calling its constructor with the value `x` and `y`, as follows:

```
import play.api.libs.functional.syntax._
implicit val locationReads: Reads[Location] = (
  (JsPath \ "lat").read[Double] and
  (JsPath \ "long").read[Double]
)(Location.apply _)
implicit val playerReads: Reads[Player] = (
  (JsPath \ "name").read[String] and
  (JsPath \ "age").read[Int]
)(Player.apply _)
implicit val teamReads: Reads[Team] = (
  (JsPath \ "teamName").read[String] and
```

```
            (JsPath \ "players").read[List[Player]] and
            (JsPath \ "location").read[Location]
        )(Team.apply _)
        val teams = Json.parse(jsonString).as[Team]
```

`teams` will contain the value filled with all the information. We can summarize this preceding code as follows:

- We define a path for each value. The path is relative.
- Using each path, we generate a `Reads` object out of it. `Reads` helps in using the path to extract the value from `JsValue`.
- Using multiple `Reads`, we generate further `Reads` for complex objects.

Macro to generate Reads

To generate `Reads[Team]`, one could also automatically generate them (and save the hassle of manually writing all the preceding code). Play provides a macro for the same where we do not have to manually specify `Reads` for each class by ourselves, as shown here:

```
implicit val playerReads:Reads[Player] = Json.reads[Player]
implicit val locationReads = Json.reads[Location]
implicit val teamReads = Json.reads[Team]
val teams = Json.fromJson[Team](jValue).get
```

`Json.reads[Player]` automatically generates the `Reads[Player]` that we defined in the previous section. The macro will automatically create `Reads[Player]` by resolving the `case class` fields, thus generating the path by itself, based on the constructor information. So, ultimately, it is quite simple to build Scala objects from JSON directly.

In reality, most of the time, we use this handy macro to generate `Reads` for our Scala classes. In cases where a JSON string does not directly match with our `case class` structure, then there is a need to write custom `Reads`.

Generating JSON

Now that we know how to parse JSON to Scala objects, in this section, we will look at how to generate JSON.

We could generate JSON by directly building it ourselves, as follows:

```scala
val json: JsValue = JsObject(Seq(
  "teamName" -> JsString("Real Madrid FC"),
  "players" -> JsArray(Seq(
    JsObject(Seq(
      "name" -> JsString("Ronaldo"),
      "age" -> JsNumber(32))),
    JsObject(Seq(
      "name" -> JsString("Modric"),
      "age" -> JsNumber(29))),
    JsObject(Seq(
      "name" -> JsString("Bale"),
      "age" -> JsNumber(28)))
  )),
    "location" -> JsObject(Seq(
    "lat" -> JsNumber(40.4168),
    "long" -> JsNumber(3.7038)))
))
println(json.toString())
```

We simply provide the JSON structure using key-value pairs. Wherever the value is a string, wrap it with `JsString`. For numbers, we wrap them with `JsNumber`. For JSON objects which are just multiple key-value pairs, we wrap them with `JsObject` which contains a sequence of multiple key-value pairs. And so with `JsArray`.

We could simplify it using implicits. Most values do not need explicit `JsValue` classes, and they could be obtained using implicits, as follows:

```scala
val json: JsValue = Json.obj(
  "teamName" -> "Real Madrid FC",
  "players" -> Json.arr(
  Json.obj(
    "name" -> JsString("Ronaldo"),
    "age" -> JsNumber(32)),
  Json.obj(
    "name" -> "Modric",
    "age" -> 29),
  Json.obj(
    "name" -> "Bale",
    "age" -> 28)
  ),
    "location" -> Json.obj(
    "lat" -> 40.4168,
    "long" -> 3.7038)
  )
println(json.toString())
```

Suppose we had a simple Scala object, like this:

```
val team: Team = Team("Real Madrid FC", List(
  Player("Ronaldo", 31),
  Player("Modric", 30),
  Player("Bale", 27)
), Location(40.4168, 3.7038))
```

To generate JSON from the team Scala object, we would do the following:

```
Json.obj(
  "teamName" -> team.teamName,
  "players" -> Json.arr(
    team.players.map(x => Json.obj(
      "name" -> x.name,
      "age" -> x.age
    ))),
      "location" -> Json.obj(
      "lat" -> team.location.lat,
      "lat" -> team.location.long
    )
  )
```

But this is verbose, and can be automated using Writes. Writes is opposite to Reads. Writes **is a converter to convert a specific type to** JsValue. **In the preceding case, it will help in converting the** team **object to** JsValue.

Like Reads, we define Writes by the path. This path would then be used to automatically generate JsValue from the object based on the path:

```
implicit val locationWrites: Writes[Location] = (
  (JsPath \ "lat").write[Double] and
  (JsPath \ "long").write[Double]
)(unlift(Location.unapply))
implicit val playerWrites: Writes[Player] = (
  (JsPath \ "name").write[String] and
  (JsPath \ "age").write[Int]
)(unlift(Player.unapply))
implicit val teamWrites: Writes[Team] = (
  (JsPath \ "teamName").write[String] and
  (JsPath \ "players").write[List[Player]] and
  (JsPath \ "location").write[Location]
)(unlift(Team.unapply))
println(Json.toJson(team).toString())
```

In the case of `locationWrites`:

- We define the path for `lat` and `long`. We also specify that they are `Double`.
- We provide a `Location.unapply` extractor. It helps in getting the actual latitude and longitude values from the location object, as shown here:

```
valxx: Option[(Double, Double)] =
Location.unapply(team.location)
```

- Using multiple `Writes`, we generate further `Writes` for complex objects.

Macro to generate Write

To generate `Writes[Team]`, one could also automatically generate them. Play provides a macro where we do not have to manually specify `Reads`, as shown in this code:

```
implicit val residentWrites = Json.writes[Player]
implicit val locationWrites = Json.writes[Location]
implicit val positionWrites = Json.writes[Team]
println(Json.prettyPrint(Json.toJson(team)))
```

`Json.writes[Player]` automatically generates the `Writes[Player]` that we defined in the previous section based on the `case class` fields. The path is automatically generated using constructor arguments.

Play production mode

Play has the following two modes while running an application:

- Development mode
- Production mode

Until now, to run our Play application, we have been using the command `run` on the Play console. When the application server starts, it runs under the development mode. In the development mode, the server would be launched with the auto-reload feature enabled. This means that for each request, Play will automatically detect any change in the source files, recompile them, and restart the server for faster development. This mode is not recommended in production, as it can significantly impact the performance of the application.

To run the application in production mode, we first package our complete application along with its other JAR dependencies in a single ZIP file. To do this, run the `dist` command on the Play console. The `dist` task builds a binary version of your application, which you can deploy to a server without any dependency on SBT.

On doing this, it would generate a ZIP file in the `target/universal` folder. This ZIP file can be extracted and run on any server. The `bin` folder in the ZIP contains executables to start the server, as follows:

```
jatin@puri:~/first-app-1.0.0-SNAPSHOT/bin> ./first-app -
Dplay.http.secret.key='abcdefghijk' -Dhttp.port=80
[info] play.api.Play - Application started (Prod)
[info] p.c.s.AkkaHttpServer - Listening for HTTP on /0.0.0.0:80
```

Note that, in the preceding code, we used the command `./first-app -Dplay.http.secret.key='abcdefghijk -Dhttp.port=8080`. We provided these two JVM arguments:

- `-Dplay.http.secret.key='abcdefghijk'`: This is mandatory, as without this, Play would throw an error. The secret key is mandatory, as it is needed by Play to sign session cookies and for several other encryptions of its internal utilities.
- `-Dhttp.port=80`: This tells Play to start the server on 80 port.

It is, usually, preferred to provide the secret key via a JVM argument. The secret key can also be provided in `conf/application.conf` by adding the following line:

```
play.http.secret.key="abcdefgh"
```

This is not recommended, however, as the secret would be available to everyone who has access to the source files.

Play also provides functionality to auto-generate a secret key using the command `playGenerateSecret` on the Play console.

To know more about other techniques of deploying Play applications, please refer to—`https://www.playframework.com/documentation/2.6.x/Deploying`.

Summary

In this chapter, you learned the basics of Play Framework. You learned about the `routes` file, actions, responses, and the Play console. We also looked at what is meant by a stateless server, and the advantages associated with being stateless. Towards the end, you learned how to automatically convert JSON with Scala objects and vice versa.

In the next chapter, we will dive deeper into how Play helps us with writing great microservices by being asynchronous and non-blocking from its core. We shall explain the essence of asynchronous and the non-blocking paradigm, the advantages associated with them, and ultimately, how to apply the concepts in reality using Play.

3
Asynchronous and Non-Blocking

In `Chapter 1`, *Introduction to Microservices*, you learned that microservices are a single unit of autonomy. They exist in systems to form one large, usable application. Though it is important to have the appropriate communication protocols and coordination among them, it is equally important for each one to be solidly built internally. Therefore, we need to focus both on the inside world of microservices, that is, its internal implementation, and the outside world, that is, collaboration with other microservices.

We will introduce an important paradigm that can be applied to both the inside and outside world of a microservice. Although, in this chapter, the focus will only be on the inner implementation, and we will cover the following topics:

- The essence of being asynchronous and non-blocking
- Asynchronous code using Scala futures and promises
- Work Stealing in Play--what makes Play fast

Being asynchronous

One cannot spend all day coding. There are quite a few things that humans have to do for survival. Buying groceries is definitely one such mundane task. To make effective use of my time, I usually prepare a list of items I need for my usage over the next couple of weeks. Planning helps so that I can buy everything I need at once, and do not have to revisit the grocery store for repeated buying. Among the list of items, I also wanted a new mechanical keyboard for myself as my dog withered away the USB port from my current keyboard.

Scenario 1 - synchronous

Once I have the list ready, I'll get in my car and go to the closest megastore that usually contains groceries, stationery, electronic items, and so on. I will start collecting all the groceries I need in my trolley. Because I already prepared the list of my needs, it was quick to collect all my needed items. I ultimately check out by paying the bill at the counter and head back home.

Doing all this costs me a couple of hours (gosh, the traffic!), but now, I have all my necessities for the next couple of weeks.

Scenario 2 - synchronous

An alternative to going to the store and buying stuff by yourself is to request someone to get it for you. I asked my brother if he would go and get the groceries for me. Being in a good mood that day, he agreed to go to the store and get it for me. He borrows my car and heads down to the store.

In the meantime, I wait for a couple of hours for my brother to arrive. I am hungry for food and can't wait to look at my new keyboard. This makes me wait for him, desperately. I am too excited to do anything else in the meantime--all I can do is wait.

Just waiting for my brother to get stuff sounds like a stupid thing to do. But hey, most of our coding design pattern falls into this category.

Scenario 3 - asynchronous

Over time, I realized that this process of going by myself to get groceries regularly is turning out to be quite frustrating, as it wastes so much productive time. I would rather use that time playing some tennis, taking a swim, or maybe going through all my liked tweets or bookmarks over the last week, which one rarely revisits.

I could make productive use of my time even when my brother has agreed to get stuff for me and do my own hobby until the time arrives. However, unfortunately, there is too much melodrama involved in convincing him to get stuff for me repeatedly.

A better idea is to save time by ordering the groceries online. Luckily, the store I visit has an e-commerce site to order stuff online with some nominal home delivery charge. The groceries would be delivered in a few hours, and could be delivered faster for some extra charge.

By ordering online, I do not have to wait for stuff to arrive. In the meantime, I could proceed to go and do other stuff.

The preceding first two scenarios are examples of being **synchronous**. That is, either we go and buy stuff ourselves or ask someone to do it for us. However, in both the preceding scenarios, *we ultimately wait for the requested task to be completed*. To finish the task of buying groceries, we spend a couple of hours buying stuff ourselves, or I wait for my brother to get it for me and do nothing else in the meantime. Ultimately, for those two hours, doing/waiting for the task to be completed is the only course of action.

The third scenario is an example of being **asynchronous (non-synchronous)**, where we want a job to be completed but do not wish to physically wait for completion. Until the time the groceries are delivered, we have all the independence in the world to perform other tasks. Once the delivery person delivers the items, we can then perform corresponding actions, such as placing the respective items in the refrigerator and so on. We do not have to physically or mentally wait for the task to be completed. By the end of that day, I would have effectively utilized my time. Ultimately, for those two hours, I am doing other jobs rather than waiting for the deliveries to be delivered.

Scenario 4 - waiting

Consider a change to scenario 1: I decide to go out and buy stuff myself. At the grocery store, I realize that this store only has membrane-based keyboards and does not have mechanical keyboards. Being an avid fan of mechanical keyboards, I decide not to compromise. I have the following two options:

- Request the current store to order a mechanical keyboard. If my action was always synchronous, I would now have to wait physically at the store for my ordered item to be given to me. If there is a spare keyboard available in the store, in one of their inventories, I am alright with waiting for 10-15 minutes. However, if it is not available, and they have to order from the manufacturer, then this action could take days, or even months. Of course, it would be impractical and stupid to be synchronous and wait at the store for days to obtain my keyboard. So, I need to behave in an asynchronous fashion. I could head back home and the store could contact me some time in the future, once the product is available. This way, my valuable time could be spent doing other actions.

- An alternative way would be to head to other electronic shops nearby, and try purchasing the desired mechanical keyboard. I may ultimately find my keyboard after searching various shops, but at the expense of a few hours. I had informed my family that I would be back in an hour and we would go to dinner together. But now, I have already spent a good few hours buying all my stuff. The situation on arrival at home is best left to your imagination.

Failures during a task are inevitable. With the synchronous mode of communication, I would have to wait forever for the task to be completed. Or I could even set a limit for waiting time, that is, we will only wait for a stipulated time for the task to be completed. If it completes within this time frame, we are good. Otherwise, we mark the task as a failure. Like in the preceding example, we would probably spend a few extra minutes obtaining the keyboard from the grocery inventory. But how long should we wait?

Determining this waiting time does not have a simple answer. If we set a shorter time, we may preemptively stop waiting too early. And we might repeatedly fail with no conclusion to the problem, as we fail most of the time. If we set the wait time too long, then we are wasting our resources and capacity. We could complete so many other tasks in the meantime.

Consider the case of being asynchronous, that is, ordering online. I would request that the store order my mechanical keyboard. If they do not have one, I would request that they notify me once it is available. So, the expectation and semantics are very clear--I would be sent items when they are readily available. When they are not, I would be notified in the future on the product's availability.
So, there is no waiting involved or I am not being *blocked* on anything whatsoever. The resource utilization (in this case, my time utilization) is far superior.

However, there is a risk--what if I am never notified by my store regarding the keyboard? This might happen due to a software glitch where they have the product available but the software didn't notify me. It could also happen due to other reasons where the manufacturer of that keyboard stopped producing similar models and the store failed to notify me because the respective person failed to update the system.

In such a case, my desire for a new keyboard would never be satisfied. So, I will have to take a precautionary step and set a calendar notification that in case I do not receive any notification within a couple of days, I would order the keyboard online from some other store. In case it is not available, even from the newer store, I would have to try someone else and the cycle will keep repeating. If I am rich, I could hire a person whose job is to coordinate with as many stores possible to obtain my keyboard. And I would only asynchronously wait for a response from this person. But yes, being asynchronous does not come for free and we need to learn effective tactics to handle asynchronous scenarios better.

For all the advantages it brings to the table, we will be using the asynchronous mode of computing in most of the things we do. To rephrase:

- A synchronous operation **waits** until the operation completes.
- An asynchronous operation **does not wait** but only *initiates* the operation, and it will be notified in the *future* once the operation is completed. Although, with asynchronous operations, the operation could either be completed by someone else or by the process/person himself.

In asynchronous mode, the actual operation could be done by itself as well. You will learn more about this later in this chapter.

Another example that would help you understand the synchronous versus asynchronous analogy would be the following case:

Your boss calls you on the telephone and insists that you obtain and return the answer to a question on the spot; we all know that these moments are very tricky to get right. He expects the answer to the query on the spot and he waits for a response on the phone. This is the **synchronous** mode of computation, where the boss is **blocked** due to us.

What we rather prefer is to respond back within some time, once we have the solution. In the meantime, the boss could go on and do some other job instead of waiting on us. In this example, the boss is functioning in an **asynchronous** mode of computation. The boss is **not-blocked** by us.

Note that we have introduced two new words here--blocked and non-blocked. Although they may appear as synonyms to synchronous and asynchronous, they slightly differ in their meaning. We will dive deeper into the differences over the course of this chapter.

Sending and operating email is another asynchronous action we perform in our life. When we send an email to another person, we do not wait for him to reply. If we wait for the reply and do nothing else during the meantime, it would be a synchronous action. And this, of course, sounds incorrect--there is no need to wait for the reply where I could go on and do other things.

In reality, after sending the email, we proceed to do our other jobs. Only on receiving the response, do we take the necessary action to be taken for that email. This behavior results in higher throughput of our day, as we have spent time doing stuff rather than waiting on stuff.

Being asynchronous in Scala

The `scala.concurrent` package in Scala SDK provides quite a few utilities to do asynchronous and reactive programming in Scala (we will cover more about being reactive in Chapter 5, *Reactive Manifesto*). Among the classes in the package, `scala.concurrent.Future` is of relevant importance now.

When we initiate an asynchronous computation, the result of that computation will be stored in a `Future` object. Although, at any given moment, `Future` may or may not contain the final result:

- If the computation is successfully completed, the `Future` object will contain the final value
- If the computation is *not* yet completed, the `Future` object will *not* contain the result
- If the computation fails, the `Future` object will contain the cause for the failure (throwable)

The result whether success/failure becomes available in the `Future` object, once the asynchronous computation is completed. For example, consider the following code snippet:

```
import scala.concurrent.Future
import scala.concurrent.ExecutionContext.Implicits.global

val future: Future[Double] = Future{math.sqrt(100000)}
```

We create an asynchronous computation that computes the square root of the number `100000`. When we call the preceding `Future{math.sqrt(100000)}`, the thread itself does not compute the task but rather delegates it to someone else (`scala.concurrent.ExecutionContext.Implicits.global`, in this case). The thread on calling `Future{math.sqrt(100000)}` immediately returns with `Future[Double]`, without waiting for the job to be completed.

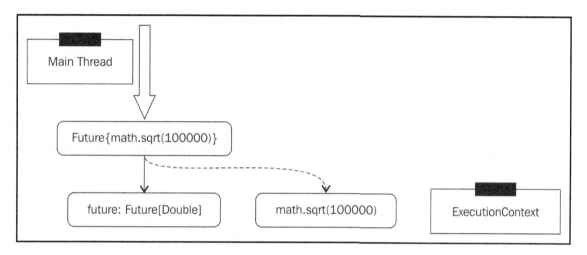

The actual body of the `Future` object will be computed by someone else. The `Main` thread would then have the `Future` object and it can proceed with the next line of code. This is the reason why I have called it an asynchronous operation, because it does not wait for the task to be completed. To verify this behavior. Please refer to the following code:

```
println("Before Future")

val future: Future[Double] = Future{
  Thread.sleep(5000)
  println("Inside Future")
  math.sqrt(100000)
}

println("Outside Future")
```

Executing the above program, prints the following statements:

- `Before Future`
- `Outside Future`
- `Inside Future`

`Outside Future` will be printed before `Inside Future` and the `main` thread will not wait
for the body of `Future` to be completed. To obtain the response of the body, we could block
ourselves and wait for the following result:

```
import scala.concurrent.Await
import scala.concurrent.duration._

val ans:Double = Await.result(future, 10 seconds)
```

We wait for the result for a maximum of 10 seconds. In case the `Future` object completes,
`Await.result` will return the value immediately as soon as it is available. If the waiting
time exceeds 10 seconds, then `Await.result` would throw a `TimeoutException`. By
using `Await`, our behavior no longer remains asynchronous, but is rather synchronous as
we wait for the task to be completed.

To remain asynchronous, you could do the following:

```
import scala.util.{Failure, Success}

future onComplete {
  case Success(x) => println("Success: "+x)
  case Failure(e) => e.printStackTrace()
}
```

In this case, we provide a *callback* that would be called once the *future object is completed*. This
could happen at, anytime, eventually. Whenever the `Future` objects get completed in time,
then our `onComplete` block will get called. If the `Future` object ends with success, then
the `Success(x)` case gets called. If it results in failure, the `Failure(e)` case gets called.
The
`onComplete` block is defined as follows:

```
def onComplete[U](f: Try[T] => U)
(implicit executor: ExecutionContext): Unit
```

It expects a function that takes `Try[T]` as its argument. It also needs an implicit argument of the `executor: ExecutionContext` type. This implicit argument is needed because the callback that we provide (`f: Try[T] => U`) would be executed by this `ExecutionContext` (a pool of threads). Hence, `onComplete` is also asynchronous because the calling thread does not wait for `onComplete` to be completed but rather `ExecutionContext` takes care of evaluation of the argument function `f`.

To summarize--implicit `ExecutionContext` will be used to execute the callback.

`Try[T]` holds a value. The `Try[T]` class has two subclasses--`Success[T]` and `Failure[T]`. `Try[T]` is a `Success[T]` when it holds a value and a `Failure[T]`, which holds an exception.

ExecutionContext

We have seen that we ask `ExecutionContext` to execute program logic asynchronously.

`ExecutionContext` is like a task executor; the tasks could be executed on a new thread or a thread from some thread-pool.

 Thread-pools are a pool of threads that wait for tasks. It is more efficient to use thread-pools rather than creating a thread specially for each task and destroying the thread once the task is executed. In a thread-pool, one can reuse existing threads rather than destroying them. Plus, maintenance is easier as only the pool must be maintained and not each individual thread. More information is available at `https://en.wikipedia.org/wiki/Thread_pool`.

For ease of usage, Scala SDK comes with the following in-built `ExecutionContext`:

```
val exec: ExecutionContext =
    scala.concurrent.ExecutionContext.Implicits.global
```

This `ExecutionContext` is backed by Java's ForkJoinPool (`http://docs.oracle.com/javase/tutorial/essential/concurrency/forkjoin.html`). The default size of the pool is the value returned by `Runtime.getRuntime.availableProcessors()`. If the processor is a four-core processor, then the default pool size would be `4`.

You could also create your own `ExecutionContext` by running the following lines of code:

```
import java.util.concurrent.Executors

implicit val exec =
  ExecutionContext.fromExecutor(Executors.newCachedThreadPool())
```

We provide `newCachedThreadPool()`, which is a thread-pool of infinite size. If a task is given to that pool, and if a thread in the pool is idle, then the thread is used for computation. Otherwise, a new thread is created by the pool.

Synchronous ExecutionContext

In `ExecutionContext`, the tasks could even be executed in the current thread instead of delegating to another thread. Although this is discouraged as then, the operation becomes synchronous because the task given to `ExecutionContext` would be executed by itself.

However, for the sake of fun, this is how you can implement `ExecutionContext`, which is synchronous:

```
implicit val currentThreadExecutionContext =
  ExecutionContext.fromExecutor(new Executor {
    def execute(runnable: Runnable) {
      runnable.run()
    }
  })
```

If you now use the preceding implicit and rerun the following program:

```
val future: Future[Double] = Future {
  Thread.sleep(5000)
  println("Inside Future")
  math.sqrt(100000)
}
println("Outside Future")
```

The output would be as follows:

```
Inside Future

Outside Future
```

The body of the `Future` object would be executed by the `main` thread; hence, the behavior of the output.

In Scala.js, `import` `scala.concurrent.ExecutionContext.Implicits.global` would work. This `ExecutionContext` would enqueue the job in a standard JavaScript event loop. The tasks would be executed asynchronously, but not in parallel since JavaScript has no notion of parallelism. Thanks to `ExecutionContext`, `scala.concurrent.Future` could even be used in Scala code to be compiled to the JavaScript platform. The experience is just the same for JVM or JS.

Future

The `scala.concurrent.Future` is quite powerful. It comes with many inbuilt utilities for effective asynchronous computation.

Suppose we wish to implement a simple `grep` search in Scala--`grep` is quite elaborative. In our case, we will implement a simple search to obtain a list of all files containing a desired word.

`grep` is a command-line utility for Unix-like systems to search plain text datasets for lines matching a regular expression. Check out `https://en.wikipedia.org/wiki/Grep` for more details.

The following program asynchronously searches for the occurrence of keyword `word` in the argument file:

```
import java.io.File

def search(word:String, file:File)
(implicit exec:ExecutionContext): Future[Boolean] = Future {
   val content = scala.io.Source.fromFile(file)
    content.getLines().exists(_ contains word)
}

val ans = search("hello", newFile("/home/user/someFile.txt"))

ans onComplete {
  case Success(x) => println(s"Found: $x")
  case Failure(e) => println(s"Failure ${e.getMessage}")
}
```

```
ans onSuccess {
  case true => println("Yay. Found")
  case false => println("Oops")
}

ans onFailure {
  case ex:Exception => ex.printStackTrace()
}
```

The onSuccess and onFailure callbacks are similar to onComplete in terms of signature. Both take an implicit ExecutionContext as an argument. The onSuccess callback will only be called if the Future object completes successfully and onFailure will only be called if the Future object completes as failure. The onComplete callback will always be called.

If the Future object completes successfully, then, in the preceding example, both onComplete and onSuccess would be called. Please note the following:

- The order of execution of the onComplete or onSuccess callback cannot be predetermined. In fact, the callbacks may be executed concurrently with one another. However, a particular ExecutionContext implementation may result in a well-defined order.
- If one of the callbacks throw an exception, the other callbacks are executed regardless.
- If some of the callbacks never complete (for example, the callback contains an infinite loop or gets blocked on a lock), the other callbacks may not be executed at all. The precise answer to this relies on the nature of ExecutionContext. If the pool size is 1, then that thread would be busy completing the task forever (as part of the task body) and the other callbacks would never be executed.
- Once executed, the callback is now available for garbage collection.

Note that we have defined our function as follows:

```
def search(word:String, file:File)
(implicit exec:ExecutionContext): Future[Boolean]
```

This is different from the following:

```
def search(word:String, file:File): Future[Boolean]
```

It is good practice to include `implicit exec:ExecutionContext` in your method argument, if your method would be dealing with `Future` and its callbacks in the method body:

- By explicitly mentioning this argument, we are requesting that the caller provide an `ExecutionContext`. This `ExecutionContext` would be used to execute any `Future` specific operations that our `search` function does.
- If we do not include an implicit argument (similar to the one in the preceding declaration), then our `search` function would need some other `ExecutionContext` in scope. It would either have to create a new one or use the default `ExecutionContext.Implicits.global`, both of which are not recommended in our example case as creating a new pool is expensive. Using `Implicits.global` is not recommended at all in production because that pool could be used by someone else as well.

 `ExecutionContext.Implicits.global` is recommended only for quick tests and not for production usage. This pool is global and shared with the complete application. A misuse of the pool by one part of the operation would have unexpected consequences on some other part using the same pool (for example, if one function uses all the threads of the pool, then no free thread would be available for other functions, or, worse, the other function tasks would never get executed).

Functional composition with Futures

Callbacks can quickly get messy, especially if we need the response of the `Future` object. In the preceding examples, we were simply printing the result in case of success. But in real life, we might wish to use that value for a larger purpose and not everything can be a part of callback. Functional composition can be quite handy in such scenarios.

Consider the following example where we wish to determine the list of all numbers less than `1000`, whose square root is an integer. An example answer would be—4, 9, 16, 25, and so on.

```
def isPerfectSquare(n:Int) =
  if(n < 0) throw new IllegalArgumentException("Invalid")
  else math.sqrt(n) % 1 == 0

val future: Future[Seq[Int]] = Future {
  (1 to 1000).filter(x => isPerfectSquare(x))
}
val str: Future[String] = future.map(x => x.mkString(","))
```

```
str onComplete{
  case Success(x) => println(x)
  case Failure(e) => e.printStackTrace()
}
//1,4,9,16,25,36,49,64,81,100,121,144,169
```

We are doing a map operation over a Future object. str would eventually be completed with string—1,4,9,16....

- A map operation is also an asynchronous operation and expects an implicit ExecutionContext in scope. The lambda provided to map would be executed by ExecutionContext.
- In case the Future object failed with exception, then str: Future[String] would also fail with the same exception.
  You can try this by doing (-10 to -1).filter(..) instead of (1 to 1000).

There are quite a few other methods such as map:

- **filter**: Checks if the Future object satisfies the predicate or not. If it does not, the resulting Future would fail with NoSuchElementException:

  ```
  val cont: Future[Seq[Int]] = future.filter(x => x contains
  100)//checks if the value in future contains number 100
  ```

- **fallbackTo**: A Future can fall back to another Future in case it fails:

  ```
  val f = Future { throw new RuntimeException("error") }
  val g = Future { 7 }
  val h = f fallbackTo g
  Await.result(h, Duration.Zero) // evaluates to 7
  ```

- **zip:** Zips the value of two Futures and returns a Future that contains the tuple of the result of both:

  ```
  val f = Future { 6 }
  val g = Future { 7 }

  val a: Future[(Int, Int)] = f zip g
  ```

There are many other functional compositions—flatMap, collect, withFilter and so on. Thanks to map, flatMap, and withFilter, one can also use Future with for-comprehensions:

```
val future: Future[Seq[Int]] = Future {
   (1 to 1000).filter(x => isPerfectSquare(x))
}

val str = for {
   x <- future
} yield x.mkString(",")
//this is syntactic sugar for: future.map(x => x.mkString(","))
```

To know more about for-comprehensions, you may refer: http://docs.scala-lang.org/tutorials/FAQ/yield.html.

The following is another simple example:

```
val sum: Future[Int] = for {
   i <- Future {1}
   j <- Future {2}
   k <- Future {3}
} yield i + j + k
```

sum Future would eventually be completed with value 6.

Future.sequence:

In the companion object of scala.concurrent.Future, there is an interesting function defined as sequence:

```
val ls : List[Future[Int]] = List(Future{1}, Future{2}, Future{3})
val a: Future[List[Int]] = Future.sequence(ls)
//a would complete with `List(1,2,3)`
```

The preceding Future.sequence converts List[Future[Int]] to Future[List[Int]].

A real-life example would be buying a new laptop, HDMI cable, and some stickers for the laptop. The laptop, cable, and stickers are to be ordered online from three different respective stores. Future.sequence would be to hire a person who would obtain the response from all the three stores for us, and package them together as a single shipment. So, we would receive one shipment that would contain the laptop, cable, and stickers. This is sometimes preferable to dealing with each shipment individually.

`Future.sequence` are as follows:

- Consolidates the success values of all the `Future` objects in a list to one common list as the final answer.
- If any of the `Future` objects fail, then the final `Future` object also fails.
- In the preceding code example, it will access `Future` objects from the list `ls` and append all the successful values in the same order as the original placement in the list. That is, the order of the values of computed `Future` objects in the final list will be the same as the corresponding `Future` in the original list.

 If we have a list of multiple tasks that would be completed in `Future`, `Future.sequence` merges the response of those results to form a single list that would contain the response of all the `Future` objects.

Now, let's implement our `grep` search to find all files containing your desired word:

```
def searchInAll(word: String, root: File)
(implicit exec: ExecutionContext): Future[Seq[File]] = {
  if (!root.isDirectory) {
    search(word, root).map(found => if (found) Seq(root) else
    Seq())
  } else {
    val all = root.listFiles().toList.map(x => searchInAll(word,
    x))
    Future.sequence(all).map(x => x.flatten)
    }
}

def search(word:String, file:File)
(implicit exec:ExecutionContext): Future[Boolean] = Future{
  val content = scala.io.Source.fromFile(file)
  content.getLines().exists(_ contains word)
}
```

The function takes two arguments—the word to search and the `root` folder which has to be searched.

- `root.listFiles()` returns all the files and folders in `root` folder.
- We iterate through all the files and folders in `root` folder. If we come across a directory, we recursively call ourselves to obtain an answer for that directory. If we come across a file, then we validate if the file contains our desired word. If it does, we preserve this file.

- The variable `all` is of type `Seq[Future[Seq[File]]]`. It is a sequence of answers for individual folders and files that we searched inside the `main` folder, folders inside those folders, and so on. We merge the response using `Future.sequence` to append all the answers we have found to one common list.

Blocking

Futures let us be asynchronous. In reality, we might call an external web-service via an HTTP call or call a database to obtain some results. In either case, by using `Future` objects, we delegate the task of waiting to obtain results to someone else. We might use `Future` objects and be asynchronous ourselves in a way, but the other thread executing the database call would have to wait for the SQL query to be executed. So, the other thread is blocked to obtain its results.

In software, there are several examples of a thread getting blocked:

- While calling a method that is synchronized (waiting for a lock to be released)
- Reading from an I/O stream in case of `InputStream.read` where the thread remains blocked till the input data is available
- Making a call to a SQL database using standard JDBC driver and so on
- Using `Await.result` to wait for the result

In all these cases, the thread executing the desired function remains blocked till the operation is completed. It is also a waste of computing resources, because the thread's stack would still be in memory. It may cause a memory leak if the thread created many objects and gets blocked, then those objects will not be collected by a Garbage Collector as they are still in scope. The more blocked threads you have, the more memory you will need.

But all the preceding are practical cases and we need to learn to better handle them.

scala.concurrent.blocking

See the following example:

```
val f = Future{
  getUserNameFromDatabase()
}
```

If the `getUserNameFromDatabase()` method takes ten minutes to be completed, then a thread of the `ExecutionContext` would be unavailable for any other task for those ten minutes. If the `ExecutionContext` had only four threads in its pool, then the other three would be available to execute more tasks. If many such preceding database operations must be performed, then all the threads of the `ExecutionContext` will be waiting and the task queue would keep piling up with tasks but no thread to execute them, because all the threads of the pool are waiting for their database operations to be completed. To handle such cases, implementing the following code:

```
import scala.concurrent.blocking
val f = Future {
  blocking {
    getUserNameFromDatabase()
  }
}
```

By wrapping the code under `blocking`, it signals the underlying `ExecutionContext` of this blocking operation. The `ExecutionContext` *may* decide to increase its thread count by one. If all the waiting tasks inside a `Future` are surrounded by `blocking`, then the thread pool count would keep increasing by one and the `ExecutionContext` would have the necessary thread's available to execute more tasks.

This preceding behavior of `ExecutionContext`, increasing its thread count by one in case of a blocking call, would not work with all kinds of `ExecutionContext`. An example where the execution context would *not* increase its thread count by using the `scala.concurrent.blocking` method is:

```
ExecutionContext.fromExecutor(Executors.newFixedThreadPool(4))
```

Though it would work with the default context:

```
scala.concurrent.ExecutionContext.Implicits.global
```

`scala.concurrent.blocking` is a preventive mechanism where it signals the underlying `ExecutionContext` of a blocking operation. The `ExecutionContext` may decide to act or not. The reason it works for `Implicits.global` is because it relies on Java's ForkJoinPool. ForkJoinPool has a property that if the task is an implementation of `java.util.concurrent.ForkJoinPool.ManagedBlocker`, then the pool would treat it as a `blocking` operation. By using `scala.concurrent.blocking`, the library wraps our code block with `java.util.concurrent.ForkJoinPool.ManagedBlocker` and hence the magic.

The reason it does not work with `newFixedThreadPool` is because that pool is not based on ForkJoinPool and hence it does not understand this mechanism.

Non-blocking I/O

We have seen that blocking is expensive and yet inevitable. I/O is one such operation where, usually, a lot of blocking is involved. Fortunately, operating systems provide a provision to do I/O operation in an asynchronous manner, where the process that issued an I/O request is not blocked till the data is available. Instead, after an I/O request is submitted, the process continues to execute its code and can later check the status of the submitted request.

Java provides provision for non-blocking I/O using the `java.nio` package and `Nio.2` upgrades in the same package with Java 7. It takes care of all the lower level implementations and provides an adequate high-level library.

There are some asynchronous I/O libraries available which go on to do some impressive things such as Akka IO (`http://doc.akka.io/docs/akka/current/scala/io.html`) and Netty (`http://netty.io`).

 The great part about async I/O is that a single thread can manage multiple I/O connections. The Play Framework has option to use Akka IO or Netty for its server.

Using `.nio`, a single thread can manage multiple I/O connections as the thread is not blocked on any connection. This phenomenon is implemented by Netty and Play leverages it for its internals. If you had to make `100` HTTP calls in parallel, in a synchronous world, you would need `100` threads. With non-blocking I/O, a single thread can manage all `100` HTTP connections by itself. We will learn more about it along with the procedure to make asynchronous HTTP calls to other services later in this chapter.

We have learnt that being asynchronous is great with Futures, but there are moments when the worker thread might get blocked due to a blocking operation. If the operation is based on non-blocking I/O, then no thread remains blocked and the overall throughput (work done) of the system remains high, as no one is waiting on anyone else. An application designed to be asynchronous with non-blocking I/O is a killer combination.

Blocking and synchronous, non-blocking and asynchronous

We have used the words blocking and synchronously in a synonymous manner and for non-blocking and done the same asynchronous as well. The differences between them is debatable and subtle, as terminology is not applied consistently across the whole software industry. Most of the time, they are used interchangeably and may be correct. Here is one such interpretation in the application development world:

 Synchronous is about an API. Blocking is about the implementation.

Interpretations of calling a method that is:

- Synchronous and blocking:
    - If we call a method and wait for method execution to be completed, then we are synchronous. For example, the thread executing the following statement will only move to the next line of code after the statement execution is completed:
    ```
    val a = getUserNameFromDatabase ()
    ```

      It can also be thought of as a blocking call, as the thread cannot move to the next line till the statement is executed. The thread may physically not be blocked on a lock or I/O but is waiting for the result of the task.

- Synchronous and non-blocking:
    - Generally, not possible.

- Asynchronous and blocking:
    - Async API can be implemented via blocking calls, as we have seen previously:

    ```
    val f = Future{
      getUserNameFromDatabase()
    }
    ```

      The main thread executing the preceding function is asynchronous, but the worker thread executing the future body is blocked for SQL queries being executed on a SQL database. This makes the worker action be a blocking action.

- Asynchronous and non-blocking:
    - When we call a method and it returns us a `Future` instance, and the worker thread running the actual method body does not get blocked. In the following example, no thread gets blocked:

```
def square(n:Int) = Future{
  math.sqrt(100)
}
val f = square(100)
```

- Another example in Play would be the following (we will go deeper on `WS` towards end of this chapter):

```
import play.api.libs.ws.{WS, WSResponse}
val f: Future[WSResponse] =
WS.url("http://google.com").execute()
```

- The main thread calling the preceding line is asynchronous and the worker thread will make an HTTP call to `google.com`. It will internally use non-blocking I/O to make the HTTP call, hence the operation is non-blocking as well.

In a purely technical sense, with I/O, there is a difference between asynchronous I/O and non-blocking I/O at a very low level. With non-blocking I/O, the thread may request for data on the stream, if no data is available, the thread will ask to check sometime later. Asynchronous I/O means that the thread would request for complete data from the stream, and it would be notified/provided eventually sometime later.
From our application development perspective, the library will internally take care of all the semantics. Hence in all my usage in this book, a non-blocking I/O will implicitly also mean that it is asynchronous.

We have learned in this chapter, what it means to be asynchronous. In the subsequent section, we shall evaluate the implementation of this paradigm in building a world-class web framework.

Work Stealing - what makes Play fast!

Programming is interesting and fun. But what if, as well as programming, you also love food? (I always wanted to be a food critic when I was a kid). And because life is too short to have leftover desires, you decide to share your love of food with others by opening a food takeaway restaurant serving your favorite dishes.

The idea is simple—to open a takeaway restaurant in the most crowded place in the city, where people would come for lunch. There is no seating at the restaurant (as you do not wish to spend a lot of your money), so people would need to stand in queue, pay at the counter, collect food, and head out.

At the initial stages, you decide to hire a cook. The cook would not only cook, but also take care of the money counter. We decide not to hire a special person for the counter management as we would like to save as much money as we can. Please refer to the following points:

1. At the takeaway restaurant, the cook is ready behind the payment machine.
2. A customer would arrive at the counter, browse the menu, order the food by paying the money.
3. The cook would collect the money and head to the kitchen behind to prepare the ordered item.
4. Once the food is ready, the cook would come back to the counter, package the food and provide it to the customer.
5. The customer would take his food and head out.
6. When the cook is preparing the food, in the meantime, if more people arrive at the store, they would all queue up.

It turns out the quality of food being served in the restaurant is great. The restaurant starts getting fame and more and more people start coming over to get their lunch. Realizing the demand, we decide to hire two others cooks who will also operate in the same fashion—We will now have three food counters and each backed by a cook. People would come to the counter and order, the cook will collect money, and go back to the kitchen to start preparing food.

The people coming would still stand in the single queue. As and when the counter gets free, they would head in that direction for the order:

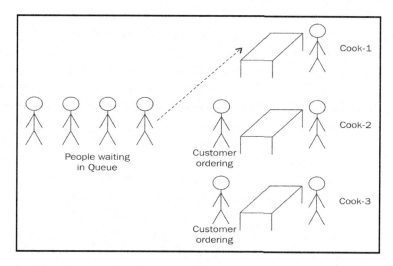

The restaurant starts to do well and we add more food items to the menu. The people's favorite turns out to be rice with tikka masala. When the customer orders rice with tikka masala, the cook notes the order and goes back to the kitchen to prepare the food. Because the restaurant believes in preparing the food fresh and not serving pre-processed food, preparing the ordered item takes quite a long time. So, in this case, the cook would:

- First prepare the rice by putting rice in the pressure cooker. This process would take about 20 minutes. In the meantime, the cook would do nothing else but wait for the rice to be ready.
- Then, prepare the curry. This would take 20 more minutes.
- Once the curry is ready, the cook will head back to the client.

In this case, preparing fresh food took around 40 minutes.

It is a standard queueing theory problem that if it takes long for food to be prepared, the queue length would keep increasing.

Once, for an order of rice with tikka masala, the cook realizes that the rice in the kitchen is out of stock, and he/she would have to go buy rice from the market. The cook rushes to the nearby grocery store, purchases rice, and gets back to kitchen. This consumes additional 15 minutes. He puts the rice in a pressure cooker for rice to be cooked. It would take about 20 odd minutes for rice to be completely cooked. In these 20 minutes, the cook happily sits down and takes a short power nap for the rice to be ready. He thinks it is alright for him to nap, because he thinks he has nothing else to be done.

In the meantime, the customer gets upset and restless for the food to become available. Not only the customer waiting at the counter for the food, but also other customers standing in the queue start getting annoyed. 20 minutes later, the cook collects the rice, prepares the gravy, and heads back to the counter to give the food to the customer. The total time taken to deliver the order was now close to 55 minutes.

In this duration, the length of the queue has significantly increased as technically, only two cooks were delivering food, as one cook was busy purchasing rice from a nearby store.

Turns out that freshly preparing food is starting to become expensive, but we believe in providing quality and are committed to providing freshly prepared food. The increasing queues are giving the restaurant a bad name, so we decide to hire seven more cooks for the restaurant. We now have 10 cooks in the kitchen serving orders. Even with 10 cooks, in a span of 120 minutes, our restaurant can only deliver 30 rice with tikka masala orders. 30 orders in 120 minutes is impacting the profitability.

Scheduling improvements - 1

Our current bottleneck is:

- While preparing the rice, the cook waits for rice to finish. In those 20 minutes, he does nothing productive.
- In some cases, like preparing the curry, there is a genuine case for the cook to be occupied for those 20 minutes.
- In calamities, like no availability of rice in the kitchen where the cook will have to go to the grocery to buy rice, the customer is not notified of the delay.

So, we make some changes to improve our response rate—**Let cooks multi-task.** This means if there is something to wait for, then the cook will pick up another task. In our scenario:

- The cook will not synchronously wait for rice to be cooked, but will start preparing curry. That is, the cook will first put rice in the cooker to be cooked, then he will start preparing the curry. Once the curry is ready, the cook will check for rice and serve them both together.

By doing so, serving one order of rice with tikka masala now takes just 20 minutes to serve rather than 40 previously. The reason it takes 20 is because the cook does not wait for rice to be ready but rather starts preparing curry. This small behavioral change results in our restaurant delivering 60 orders of rice with tikka masala in 120 minutes. That is 100% improvement over the previous case. This gain is without employing more cooks. So, we haven't invested any further money for this significant gain.

Multi-tasking further provides flexibility:

- While preparing the curry, after adding the masala and vegetables, it would take 10 minutes to simmer. There is no need for the cook to wait for simmering to end, but can rather head back to the counter to take another order.

By doing this, the cook saves 10 other minutes and can execute one order in 10 minutes instead. In 120 minutes, a single cook would have delivered 11 full orders of rice with tikka masala. Our overall restaurant capacity is now at 110 orders which is a 366% increase when compared to 30 orders previously thanks to **Work Stealing**.

Scheduling improvements - 2

We wish to cut down our costs to improve the profit margin. We cannot keep increasing the number of counters to manage more customers. Each counter contains a computer for billing, credit card payment machine, the furniture, and not to mention the space occupied.

One way to cut down costs is to reduce the number of counters. We decide to maintain only two counters but hire people to take orders from customers; instead of cooks taking orders directly, the cashier will now take the orders. Two new cashiers would be hired for this purpose. Please refer to the following points:

1. A customer would head to a counter and order food.

2. The cashier will collect the money and notify the cook about this new order.

3. The cashier in return will provide a ticket number to the customer. This ticket number is for reference purposes. Let's say the ticket number is 7.

4. The cashier would request the customer to stand by the side and let the other person in the queue come and give the order.

5. The next person waiting in the queue will then come forward to give his order.

6. Once the food is ready for ticket number 7, the cashier would announce it on the mic and the customer holding ticket 7 would come forward to collect his item:

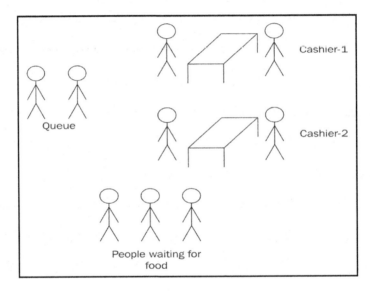

The responsibilities are segregated and clear in this manner. The cashier knows his job well and the cook must only worry about preparing his food.

Just by having two counters, we can do the same amount of work as previously when we had 10 counters. To scale further, to manage more customers, there is no need to build further counters to manage higher load. These two counters would be able to take many orders. If the need arises, we could maybe have a few more counters, but the count would be lower when compared to our previous setup.

Maybe there is even no need to hire cashiers, as people could swipe their cards directly at the counter, or select their order on an iPad or computer. But for the sake of discussion, let's use the cashier analogy.

The advantages of this setup are as follows:

- A few cashiers can handle many customers.
- Cooks could get smarter. If they realize that they have two orders for the same item, they could prepare the item in a large quantity and provide two orders in the timespan it takes to do one.
- Cooks could interact with other cooks and reuse or share the material they have prepared with others.

These optimizations are only possible if there is clear segregation of responsibilities. The Play Framework internally uses this strategy to be high performant.

Work Stealing in Play

The first scenario which we observed, where the cook collects the order from the customer, waits for rice to be cooked completely before heading for curry preparation, and 40 minutes later delivers the order to the customer, is the case of web-servers that work on the **request-per-thread** model.

In this model, when a web-server receives an HTTP request, the thread executes the code logic written in the controller, calls the database, or does some computation as coded. Once the response has been formed, the thread would output the data in the output stream of the request and the client would now receive the data. The thread would not handle any other requests till the time this request processing has been finished.

Servlet-based specification works on the request-per-thread model.

Play framework works on the **Work Stealing** model. When an HTTP request is received, the thread from the pool would receive the request using asynchronous I/O. Thanks to asynchronous I/O, this thread in practice can actively handle over 1000 parallel concurrent connections. For each HTTP call, the thread will then proceed to execute the `Action` body:

```
def index = Action {
 Ok("Howdy!")
}
```

Just like the case of our restaurant cook in later cases, the thread from Play's default pool is busy doing several tasks:

- It is handling HTTP requests and doing i/o by reading and writing to requests
- Executing the body of `Action`, like returning a response with the content `Howdy!` in the preceding case

The net throughput of the system is high as the thread is always busy doing something. Like in the preceding case, it is busy either executing the Action body, or writing the response to the output stream, or reading HTTP calls for other requests. This feature is the crux of what makes play so scalable.

Play thread pools

Play Framework is an asynchronous Play Framework from the ground-up. There are two primary thread pools/ExecutionContext:

- Netty Thread Pool—this is used internally by Netty for handling Netty I/O. Application should never access this pool.
- Play default ExecutionContext—this can be accessed by:

```
import play.api.libs.concurrent.Execution.Implicits._
```

This is the ExecutionContext in which all the application code is executed. The Action body is executed by this thread pool.

The default thread pool can be configured using application.conf under akka namespace:

```
akka {
  actor {
    default-dispatcher {
      fork-join-executor {
        parallelism-factor = 1.0
        parallelism-max = 24
      }
    }
  }
}
```

The parallelism factor is one. Which means the default pool size would be—(Available cores * parallel-factor). If the processor is a four-core processor, then the pool size would be four. The max-cap has been set as 24 above, which means the max count of pools would not exceed 24 even if it is a 50 core processor that is, min (available cores * 1, 24) is the size of the pool.

On a 4-core machine, this thread pool of size four would handle all the requests requested on the server. Because these threads use asynchronous I/O, each thread can handle many requests. In my own personal experience, I have seen Play respond with 4000 requests per second per thread. This is a phenomenon. This is only possible because asynchronous and non-blocking are distilled deep down in its philosophy. Thread pools in Play are tuned to use fewer threads than in traditional web frameworks, since I/O in the Play-core never blocks.

As said, this pool would also execute the `Action` body. **This behavior is like our cashier metaphor we previously used**. Each cashier is a thread of this pool, in this case:

- A thread takes requests from multiple requests—A cashier taking orders from multiple customers
- Then they process the request body themselves or delegate it to someone else to execute— A cashier fulfilling the order himself (if the order was a quick order such as Cola) or requesting the cook to prepare the item
- The thread replys by pushing the result to the respective output stream to the caller —Once the food for the ticket is ready, provide the food to the respective ticket holder

Just like a few cashiers could take orders from so many customers, in our case, a tiny pool can process orders of multiple requests.

As said, these threads execute the `Action` body as well. If the `Action` body makes a blocking call, then it would significantly impact the performance of the application:

```
def index = Action {
  Ok(getUserNameFromDatabase())
}
```

On a four-core machine, if four such calls are made to the server, then it would clog all the other requests as well. Because all the HTTP accepting threads are busy waiting on a database call and are not available to handle other HTTP calls. Hence, we need to be extra precautionary of the Action body.

To fix our problem in the preceding case, let's try delegating the database call to another `ExecutionContext`. You could either create your own `ExecutionContext` by:

```
implicit val exec =
ExecutionContext.fromExecutor(Executors.newFixedThreadPool(10))
```

Or better, you could ask play to create it for you by setting the `pool` properties in `application.conf`. This method is preferable as all the configurations are in one place:

```
contexts {
  db-lookups{
    throughput = 1
    thread-pool-executor {
      fixed-pool-size = 10
    }
  }
}
```

We configure the pool property in the configuration file and obtain the reference to that pool by doing `dispatchers.lookup`. Let's now use the preceding `ExecutionContext` to make a database call:

```
import javax.inject.{Inject, Singleton}

import akka.actor.ActorSystem
import play.api.mvc._
import scala.concurrent.Future
@Singleton
class Application @Inject() (cc: ControllerComponents, akkaSystem:
ActorSystem) extends AbstractController(cc) {
  implicit val exec = akkaSystem.dispatchers.lookup("contexts.db-
  lookups")

def getUserName = Action.async {
  Future{
    Ok(getUserNameFromDatabase())
  }
 }
}
```

There are couple of interesting things happening here. We use `Action.async`, instead of just using `Action`. Secondly, we return a `Future[Result]` inside the action body instead of plain `Result`.

With `Action.async`, we return a `Future` object. Once the `Future` object is completed, the response of the `Future` is automatically returned to the client. The operation is asynchronous in nature. This way, the thread from the default thread pool would not be blocked on anything. As soon as the future is completed, the thread from the default thread pool would push the response to the caller.

To sum-up:

- Play is an asynchronous web framework
- All the I/O operations performed by Play are asynchronous by nature
- A tiny thread pool manages all the HTTP requests
- The `Action` body is executed by this pool, so the action body must be asynchronous and non-blocking

Mixing synchronous and asynchronous code

As much as I love being asynchronous, the reality is that synchronous sometimes cannot be avoided. Mostly, this happens when making database calls to a SQL database. JDBC is a gold standard for Java-based database drivers and most of the database drivers comply to this standard. JDBC API is synchronous in nature. Not just from a driver perspective, but also a database perspective, most of the major databases provide asynchronous database drivers for JVM. Hence, blocking I/O is inevitable.

Apart from this, there can be multiple other places where threads can get blocked. So, in such cases, to adhere to being asynchronous at the expense of blocking, we would wrap these blocking calls with a `Future`. These `Future` objects would need an `ExecutionContext` to be available. We have learned in the previous section, that it is a bad idea to use Play's default thread pool for our blocking purposes.

 An alternative is to create a new `ExecutionContext` and use it for all only our blocking calls.

This looks like a reasonable statement to make, but it is a bad idea. During the life of our application, we will be making several kinds of blocking calls—database calls, synchronous calls to external web services, reading from a file, and CPU intensive tasks. If we use one common `ExecutionContext` for all of them, then one type of usage might impact the others:

- Suppose the size of this thread pool is 20. This pool would be used for all blocking calls.
- If the number of database calls increase to 20, and each query would take longer to execute, then no thread would be available to compute other kinds of `Future` tasks, like computing some CPU task.

- This reduces predictability of the response time and behavior of the application, leading to unexpected delays in response time. Because, if the pool is busy doing only certain kinds of tasks (such as doing only database calls because database calls take a long time to execute), then others won't get their due.
  In such setups, you will find that the response time would vary drastically, maybe a few minutes if it should have taken a few seconds.
- Spikes in CPU and memory usage (if suddenly all 20 threads get busy in CPU computation or heavy-memory centric operations). Worse, deadlocks.

Each type of blocking has a nature of its own. It is alright for a pool to be of size 20 to manage database connections, but it might not be alright to have a pool of high thread count if that pool is going to do expensive CPU computation such as image processing. In such cases, maybe the ideal pool size would be four, so as not to burden the CPU entirely. Similarly, there would be CPU computations which would be quick to execute and a reasonable pool size is desired.

There cannot be one pool size that would fix all our blocking use cases. Worse, various kinds of scenarios might require different types of thread pools. The database ExecutionContext would need the underlying thread pool to be a fixed-size-pool with count set to the number of parallel database connections desired. If 20 database connections can be handled in parallel, then the count of the pool must be 20. But a ForkJoinPool might be preferable for CPU prone tasks.

It is a good idea to implement a good idea. The good idea here is to use different ExecutionContext for different scenarios.

You could configure them in application.conf as:

```
contexts {
  db-lookups{
    throughput = 1
    thread-pool-executor {
      fixed-pool-size = 10
    }
  }
  expensive-db-lookups {
    executor = "thread-pool-executor"
    throughput = 1
    thread-pool-executor {
      fixed-pool-size = 20
    }
  }
  cpu-operations {
    fork-join-executor {
```

```
            parallelism-max = 2
        }
    }
}
//Contexts.scala
@Singleton
class Contexts @Inject() (akkaSystem: ActorSystem) {
    val dbLookup = akkaSystem.dispatchers.lookup("contexts.db-
    lookups")
    val expensiveDBLookup =
    akkaSystem.dispatchers.lookup("contexts.expensive-db-lookups")
    val cpuLookup = akkaSystem.dispatchers.lookup("contexts.cpu-
    operations")
}
```

Another advantage of segregating pools based on the type of tasks, is that it becomes easier to fine tune each.

Asynchronous WebService calls

Play manages all the dirty asynchronous I/O code internally and provides a higher level API to execute HTTP calls to other servers using non-blocking I/O. Of-course, if the call is made using non-blocking I/O internally, the API would provide us a Future which would be eventually completed with the response:

```
import javax.inject.{Inject, Singleton}
import play.api.libs.ws.WSClient
import play.api.mvc._
@Singleton
class SearchController @Inject() (cc: ControllerComponents,
ws: WSClient) (implicit ec: ExecutionContext)
extends AbstractController(cc) {
    def get(name:String) = Action.async { implicit request =>
        //below will make a call to
        //http://httpbin.org/get?username=ronaldo
        ws.url("http://httpbin.org/get")
        .withHeaders("Content-Type" -> "application/json")
        .withQueryString("userame" -> name)
        .get().map { response =>
        Ok(response.body)
      }
    }
}
```

We inject `WSClient` to the class. `ws.url("").get()` returns a `Future` and we `map` over this `Future`. We, of course, need an `ExecutionContext` in scope and we use Play's default thread pool for this purpose. This is injected to us by Play, thanks to the following constructor argument:

```
(implicit ec: ExecutionContext)
```

Play default `ExecutionContext` would be injected by this line of code.

It is alright to use the default pool in this scenario as the body of `map` is minimal.

`ws.url` internally uses `.nio` to make a call. This makes the operation both asynchronous and non-blocking.

There is flexibility to make HTTP `GET`, `POST`, `DELETE`, and so on, calls with custom header information and much more. The full details of usage and configuration can be found at `https://www.playframework.com/documentation/2.6.x/ScalaWS`.

Summary

In this chapter, we have learned the importance of being asynchronous and non-blocking. We have seen that adhering to this paradigm provides us with the ability to achieve higher throughput (do more work in limited resources) and scalability to handle a large number of loads. We had a brief overview of Future objects in Scala and operations defined in it.

We have seen how Play has applied the concept of being asynchronous and non-blocking in its core ideology, and we have seen how Play applies this internally by having a default tiny pool to handle all the user requests. The `Action` body must then be asynchronous and non-blocking in nature.

We have also seen the technique for methods to gracefully handle blocking calls by using a separate `ExecutionContext` for different kinds of blocking calls.

We are now equipped with the understanding and tools to build a robust microservice. In the next chapter, we will be building a sample application using the techniques we have learnt, using the asynchronous mode of communication across microservices.

4

Dive Deeper

In Chapter 2, *Introduction to Play Framework*, we covered the basics of the Play Framework. In Chapter 3, *Asynchronous and Non-Blocking*, we understood the advantages of being asynchronous and how the Play Framework leverages this aspect to be highly scalable.

In this chapter, we will build a sample application with a host of microservices. In doing so, we will also learn more about the Play Framework functionalities, setting up multi-build Play projects in SBT and later, toward the end, understand the practical problems faced in building microservices.

The source code for the application discussed in this chapter can be found on http://github.com/scala-microservices-book/book-examples/chapter-4.

We will cover the following topics in this chapter:

- Talent search engine
- Play framework functionalities and building Play projects in SBT
- Introduction to Slick
- Pitfalls in building microservices

Talent search engine

In chapter 1, *Introduction to Microservices,* we introduced a business idea to build an application that will help individuals and companies find the best developers in a city. Here are the details:

- Intention is to build a search-engine where people can search for awesome developers:
    - In a city.
    - A programming language.
    - The data would initially be based on the data available at http:// stackoverflow.com and http://github.com. We also need to have a provision so that it is easier to incorporate other data sources as well.
    - Application must only be accessible to authorized users.
    - Authentication for inter-microservice communication.

Building it based on microservice architecture makes a lot of sense here as different teams can collaborate with each other. We will be using the Play Framework to build our microservices. (maybe using Play Framework might be overkill for a few of the microservices that are not very complex). Please refer to the following points:

- The data would initially be based on the data available at http:// stackoverflow.com and http://github.com. We also need to have a provision so that it is easier to incorporate other sources as well. Please refer to the following points:
    - Application must only be accessible to authorized users
    - Authentication for inter-microservice communication

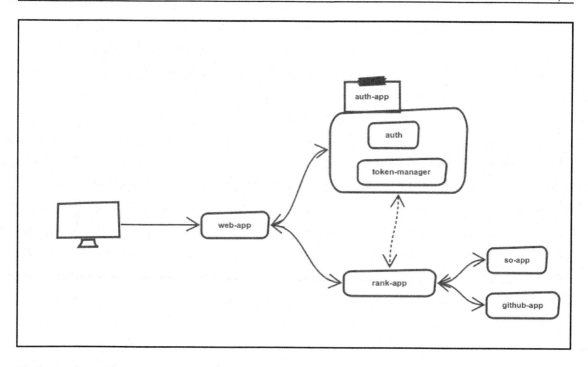

We have five microservices:

- **web-app**: This is our main web server for the application.
- **auth-app**: This takes care of the user authentication. It also manages tokens that are used to authenticate inter microservice communication.
- **rank-app**: This is the main application that is responsible for collaborating results of ranking developers available across Stack Overflow, GitHub, and different platforms.
- **so-app**: This contains all the Stack Overflow related information and ranking of developers available on the Stack Overflow site.
- **github-app**: This contains all the GitHub related information and ranking of developers available on the GitHub site.

Note that we have cooked up the data and developer profiles rather than originally extracting from Stack Overflow and GitHub. Although, you can very well extract them. In case of Stack Overflow, Stack Exchange publicly publishes their monthly data, which can be accessed from `https://archive.org/details/stackexchange`.

Project structure

One can have an individual microservice as a standalone project with a distinct deployment/development process for each. This usually works in larger teams, but seldom in smaller teams. For this application, I have organized the code base as a collection of subprojects under one umbrella. Each subproject in a build has its own source directories, generates its own JAR file when you run packages, and, in general, works like any other project.

This setup is convenient in the sense that each project still has its own independence and is not impacted by the setup and dependencies of other projects in the build so it provides a good degree of independence and yet one could share common build-related files and common projects across projects if needed. For example, for maintenance purposes, we wish to use the same Play version across all our projects. In which case, we could organize our SBT files to use the same version across all our projects. One could, of course, use different, if intended.

The build.sbt file

We will define the `root` project as a collection of Projects in our `build.sbt` file:

```
import sbt.Keys._

name := "chapter-4"

version := "1.0"

lazy val `chapter-4` = (project in file(".")).aggregate(
  `web-app`,
  `auth-app`,
  `so-app`,
  `github-app`,
  `rank-app`
  , commons)

lazy val commonSettings = Seq(
```

```
organization := "com.scalamicroservices",
scalacOptions := Seq("-unchecked", "-deprecation", "-encoding",
"utf8"),
scalaVersion := "2."12.2",
resolvers ++= Seq("Typesafe Releases" at
  "http://repo.typesafe.com/typesafe/releases/",

"JBoss" at "https://repository.jboss.org/")
)
```

This chapter defines seven subprojects—six microservices and one common-utilities project based out of SBT. The `commons` project contains common code that could be reused across microservices.

Here, we define settings that are reused by our microservice projects:

```
def BaseProject(name: String): Project = (
  Project(name, file(name))
  settings (commonSettings: _*)
)

def PlayProject(name: String): Project = (
  BaseProject(name)
  enablePlugins PlayScala
)
```

We defined the base project with `commonSettings`. Any subproject that uses the preceding `BaseProject` will include `commonSettings`. So, changing `scalaVersion` at `commonSettings` would reflect the same in all the dependent subprojects.

`PlayProject` uses `BaseProject` with a single change where it includes the `PlayScala` plugin. Please refer to the following code:

```
lazy val commons = BaseProject("commons")
.settings(libraryDependencies ++= Seq(specs2 % Test, playJson))


lazy val `web-app` = PlayProject("web-app")
.settings(libraryDependencies ++= Seq(parserCombinator, ws, specs2
% Test, guice, scalaTest))
.dependsOn(commons)

lazy val `so-app` = PlayProject("so-app")
.settings(libraryDependencies ++= Seq(h2, jbcrypt, slick,
playSlick, specs2 % Test, playSlickEvolutions, guice))
.dependsOn(commons)
```

```
lazy val `auth-app` = PlayProject("auth-app")
.settings(libraryDependencies ++= Seq(h2, jbcrypt, slick, playSlick,
 specs2 % Test, playSlickEvolutions, guice))
.dependsOn(commons)

//and others
```

We have defined an SBT project by the name commons. This contains common case classes that would be reused by other microservices. We then define Play projects that are our microservices with their own respective dependencies. These microservices depend on the commons project, which is reflected by the .dependsOn(commons) statement.

lazy is used instead of eager evaluation to prevent initialization order problems. The libraryDependencies used in the preceding projects are defined further in the following file:

```
val slickV = "3.2.1""
val h2V = "1.4.193"
val playSlickV = "3.0.1"
//...

val slick = "com.typesafe.slick" %% "slick" % slickV
val slickHikariCP = "com.typesafe.slick" %% "slick-hikaricp" %
slickV
val h2 = "com.h2database" % "h2" % h2V
val playSlick = "com.typesafe.play" %% "play-slick" % playSlickV
//...
```

To run a microservice, we will start the sbt console at the root project, chapter-4, and trigger the subproject. For example, to run the web-app microservice, we would execute the following piece of code:

```
jatin@puri:~/book-examples/chapter-4$ sbt
[info] Loading global plugins from /home/jatin/.sbt/0.13/plugins
[info] Loading project definition from /home/jatin/book-
examples/chapter-4/project
[info] Set current project to chapter-4 (in build
file:/home/jatin/book-examples/chapter-4/)
> ; project web-app; run 5678
```

Running ; `project web-app;` `run 5678` does two things—it sets the current project as `web-app` first and then starts the `web-app` application at port `5678`. The behavior is similar to the following piece of code, where we provide the project selection and run command's separately:

```
jatin@puri:~/IdeaProjects/book-examples/chapter-4$ sbt
[info] Loading global plugins from /home/jatin/.sbt/0.13/plugins
[info] Loading project definition from
/home/jatin/IdeaProjects/book-examples/chapter-4/project
[info] Set current project to chapter-4 (in build
file:/home/jatin/IdeaProjects/book-examples/chapter-4/)
> project web-app
[info] Set current project to web-app (in build
file:/home/jatin/IdeaProjects/book-examples/chapter-4/)
[web-app] $ run 5678
--- (Running the application, auto-reloading is enabled) ---
```

In general, just entering `web-app` project opens up the console with the current project as `web-app`. The `run 5678` command starts the Play app at port `5678`.

Note that we also provide a semicolon '`;`' while performing ; `project web-app;` `run 5678`. Using a semicolon is a way of telling SBT that the statement we wish to provide is a collection of multiple commands. There is no need to provide a semicolon at the start of the statement if you do not intend to provide multiple commands.

For the sake of development, and in general, we have also defined a way we can run all our microservices using a single command on the `sbt console:` `runAll`.

We define its behavior in `build.sbt` as follows:

```
val runAll = inputKey[Unit]("Runs all subprojects")

runAll := {
 (run in Compile in `web-app`).partialInput(" 3000").evaluated
 (run in Compile in `so-app`).partialInput(" 5000").evaluated
 //and others
}
```

runAll will start the microservices declared with their port number. So, the web-app project will be started on 3000 port and the so-app microservice on 5000 port. The logic behind this is that by using partialInput(" 3000"), it appends the " 3000" string to the run command. So, technically, this is analogous to the run 3000 sbt command. The reason we provide space before port 3000 is that, if we do not, then the statement will correspond to run3000. By providing a space, it will get converted to run 3000. You could very well put other flags associated with the run command.

Similarly, we provide the run statements of all microservices in the runAll block defined earlier. Note that this has been built for development purposes only and, in production, it is recommended that each microservice is initiated individually. Please refer to the following code:

```
jatin@puri:~/IdeaProjects/book-examples/chapter-4$ sbt
[info] Loading global plugins from /home/jatin/.sbt/0.13/plugins
[info] Loading project definition from
/home/jatin/IdeaProjects/book-examples/chapter-4/project
runAll
[info] Set current project to chapter-4 (in build
file:/home/jatin/IdeaProjects/book-examples/chapter-4/)
> runAll
--- (Running the application, auto-reloading is enabled) ---
--- (Running the application, auto-reloading is enabled) ---
[info] p.c.s.NettyServer - Listening for HTTP on
/0:0:0:0:0:0:0:0:3000
//....
```

Brief overview of the application

On running the application using runAll, you can access the application at http://localhost:3000. There is a simple registration page to register with email and password.

On logging in, you will the following page:

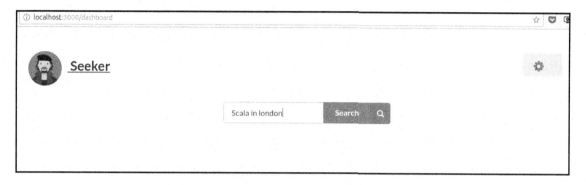

You can search for developers of a programming language in a particular city. Some sample queries are as follows:

- Scala in london
- Java developers in New York
- Scala developers
- Developers in San Jose
- San Francisco

That is, we have our own custom **domain-specific language (DSL)** for the user to be able to search lucidly.

The search works on the tag, which is the programming language, and the location, which is a city. Please refer to the following points:

- Based on the data available at the Stack Overflow microservice and GitHub microservice, the application will obtain the site-specific data for a location and tag
- Rank developers for each corresponding site
- Generate a sorted list based on our ranking engine and displays on top

We will do a brief anatomy of all our microservices in their implementation and the role they play.

Security

There are two parts to this:

- The authentication and authorization of the user accessing the application
- Authentication of inter-microservices communication

Here is the workflow of the authentication mechanism:

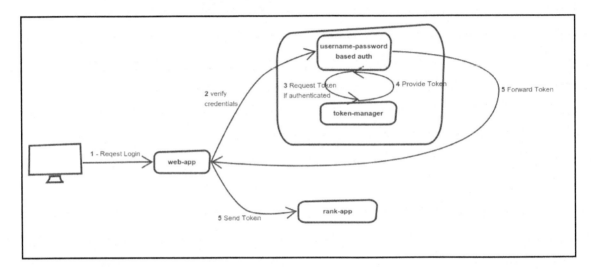

1. The user logs in with a username and password.
2. The **web-app** sends the credentials to the `auth-app`.
3. The `auth-app` verifies the credentials, please refer to these points:
    - If the credentials are invalid, it responds back to the request initiator on the failure
    - If the credentials are valid, it requests the **token-manager** for a token

4. The **token-manager** generates a unique token and provides back. This token can be used by other microservices to verify if the initiator of the request is from a valid source. Please refer to this point:
    - The tokens are also persisted in a database (H2 database in this case) to maintain history

5. The token is provided back to the **web-app** file.

6. Once authenticated successfully, the **web-app** file will request **rank-app** to get the result for the user-asked query. The token generated will have to be provided to the **rank-app** microservice, please refer to these points:

   - The **rank-app** microservice will then validate the token. Only if the token is a valid token, will the **rank-app** microservice proceed.
   - The **time to live (ttl)** of the token is one day. Though, on each usage of a valid token, the duration of the token is increased to one day from that exact moment.

We have segregated the logic and implementation for the authentication and the token manager. Although both are part of the same microservice `auth-app`.

In our setup, if, when going forward, we introduce other auth mechanisms, such as authenticating using Facebook or Google, we can easily modify our architecture in the following way:

- Have a separate microservice that takes care of the `facebook-auth`, `google-auth`, `github-auth`, and so on, or introduce that logic in our `auth-app` project code base itself

- In any case, once the authentication succeeds based on either username-password, `facebook-auth`, or `google-auth`, they will all request **token-manager** for tokens

Our application architecture remains scalable with this design. Maybe an improvement would be to have **token-manager** as a standalone application as it is important for the **token-manager** to be highly available and performant.

Inter-microservice authentication

The token help authenticate inter-microservice communication in our application. However, there are several other ways of implementing authentication during inter micro-service communication. If you can obtain the expertise, Kerberos is one such excellent alternative. Please visit `https://web.mit.edu/kerberos/`.

> **Kerberos** *is a network authentication protocol. It is designed to provide strong authentication for client/server applications using secret-key cryptography. The Kerberos protocol uses* **strong cryptography** *so that a client can prove its identity to a server (and vice versa) across an insecure network connection. After a client and server has used Kerberos to prove their identity, they can also encrypt all of their communications to assure privacy and data integrity as they go about their business.*

Windows 2000 and later uses Kerberos as its default authentication mechanism. Many UNIX and UNIX-like operating systems include software for Kerberos authentication of users or services. Kerberos is quite well-known as a security mechanism at large corporations.

JSON Web Token (JWT) is another alternative for an authentication mechanism across microservice communication. It works very similar to our setup where the token is generated and provided to a client microservice for verification. The client could then use that token to prove that the request initiator is a valid source. The token is an encrypted JSON (hence the name JSON Web Token).

JWT is a JSON-based open standard (RFC-7519 `https://tools.ietf.org/html/rfc7519`):

> **JSON Web Token** *(JWT) is a compact, URL-safe means of representing claims to be transferred between two parties. The claims in a JWT are encoded as a JSON object that is used as the payload of a* **JSON Web Signature** *(JWS) structure or as the plaintext of a* **JSON Web Encryption** *(JWE) structure, enabling the claims to be digitally signed or integrity protected with a* **Message Authentication Code** *(MAC) and/or encrypted.*

There are good open source Scala implementations for JWT available (`https://jwt.io/`). In our application, I haven't used JWT for the sake of simplicity. However, in a real-world application, it would be wise to use JWT as it's a well-known standard.

The auth-app microservice explained

The `auth-app` microservice takes care of everything to do with the following:

- Authentication based on username and password
- Token manager

It uses H2 database (`http://www.h2database.com/`) to persist username, password, and the respective tokens. H2 database is a relational database with a tiny footprint of 1.5 MB only.

Once the user registers in our application, the `web-app` will send the user credentials to the `auth-app` microservice. The `auth-app` microservice will persist the user information, such as their username, password (in encrypted form using Blowfish password hashing), and `creationTime` in the database. Here is the project structure of the `auth-app` microservice:

```
jatin@puri:~/IdeaProjects/book-examples/chapter-4/auth-app$ tree
.
├── app
│   ├── auth
│   │   ├── UserController.scala
```

```
|   |   ┌──── UserDao.scala
|   |   └──── UserService.scala
|   ┌──── tokens
|   |   ┌──── TokenController.scala
|   |   ┌──── TokenDao.scala
|   |   └──── TokenService.scala
|   └──── utils
|   └──── Contexts.scal
┌──── conf
|   ┌──── application.conf
|   ┌──── evolutions
|   |   └──── default
|   |   └──── 1.sql
|   └──── routes
┌──── project
```

For the user to login, an HTTP call needs to provide the username and password, please refer to the following code:

```
POST /v1/auth/login auth.UserController.login
```

The login implementation when the user provides email and password is implemented in `UserController.scala` as follows:

```scala
//User is defined in `commons` project
case class User(email:String, password:String)

implicit val executionContext = contexts.cpuLookup
//UserController.scala
def login = Action.async(parse.json) { implicit request =>
  request.body.validate[User].fold(
    error => Future.successful(BadRequest("Not a valid input format:
      "
    + error.mkString)),
    user =>
    userService.validateUser(user.email, user.password)
    .flatMap { validated =>
      if (validated)
        tokenService.createToken(user.email)
        .map(x => Ok(Json.toJson(x.token)))
      else Future.successful(BadRequest("username/password
        mismatch"))
    }
  )
}
```

It is an HTTP POST call. Please refer to the following points:

- The first interesting thing to notice here is that we have used Action.async and not just Action. Action.async signifies that we want the Action body to be run by our own provided thread pool rather than the default Play one. We will see more on this in the next section.
- In Action.async(parse.json), the parse.json argument signifies that we expect the body of the HTTP call to be of JSON format.
- We will validate if the body of the request is valid JSON in the request.body.validate[User] call, please refer to these points:
  - In case it is not valid JSON, we return suggesting a bad request
  - In case of valid JSON, we verify if the username and password match
  - If success/validated, we create a token using TokenService and reply to the initiator of the service with the token
  - In case of failure, we respond with BadRequest

The validateUser method in UserService is implemented as follows:

```
//UserService.scala
def validateUser(email:String, password:String)
(implicit exec:ExecutionContext): Future[Boolean] = {
  userDao.getUserByEmail(email).map {
  case Some(auth) => checkPassword(password, auth.passwdHash)
  case None => false
  }
}
```

It calls userDao.getUserByEmail to obtain the user information and then verifies the password by calling checkPassword. userDao internally makes a call to the H2 database to obtain results.

Action.async

As we observed in Chapter 3, *Asynchronous and Non-Blocking*, Play is fast, thanks to its work stealing. There is a Play default pool that manages all incoming requests. This same pool of threads also executes our Action body when a request is received. So, Play is asynchronous at every possible level.

Because the same pool is used to handle HTTP requests and execute the Action body, it is important for the Action body execution to be very fast. If not, it would have direct consequences on the net response rate of the Play framework (this is a classic scenario when developer complain that Play is slow). Of course, it's slow because the Play threads are busy executing the Action body and do not take any new requests from the user.

The default thread pool size of Play default pool is the number of cores of processor, which is not a small number usually. Hence, we need to very carefully observe our Action bodies.

In case there is a blocking call as part of the Action body, or you expect that the Action body does a non-trivial operation, as suggested in the *Mixing synchronous and asynchronous code* section of Chapter 3, *Asynchronous and Non-Blocking*, we can offload the time-expensive Action body to another thread pool. Because this is a very common operation, Play provides a way in its API:

```
implicit val executionContext = contexts.cpuLookup
def login = Action.async(parse.json) { implicit request =>
(....)
 //expects a Future response
}
```

Our body will now return a Future object that will contain the time intensive computations. We also import an ExecutionContext that signifies that our Future object must implicitly use the provided thread pool for performing database calls.

When the future is completed, Play will respond back to the user with a completed value of the Future object.

To know more about Action.async, refer to https://www.playframework.com/documentation/2.6.x/ScalaAsync.

Brief introduction to Slick

There are numerous libraries to make SQL calls to database using JDBC, which is the gold standard on the JVM world to access relational databases. In this project, we have used the Slick library to access database.

Slick is like LINQ of the Microsoft world. It adheres to the Reactive Manifesto (`http://www.reactivemanifesto.org/`) (you will learn more about Reactive Manifesto in Chapter 5, *Reactive Manifesto*). Slick lets you access data from a relational database, and the experience is like dealing with collections rather than a database. We deal with tables as if they are collections in reality. Although, in the background, it auto-generates SQL queries.

For example, consider the following lines of code:

```
val q = for {
  user <- users if user.name == "***@gmail.com"
} yield (user.name, user.creationTime)
```

This will generate an SQL command in the background as follows:

```
select .name, user.creationTime from users
where user.name='***@gmail.com'
```

 To know more about Slick, refer to `http://slick.lightbend.com/`.

There are advantages in modeling data in the preceding manner as the code is less verbose. However, I personally prefer the plain old SQL way, as I have realized that as the project grows bigger, it is easier to maintain and configure SQL rather than the automatic generator. Although Slick has evolved over time to be performant, there can be situations where the query generated in the background is not very optimized.

To Slick's credit, it also provides an API to access a database using plain old SQL. The implementation for the `getUserByEmail` method in `UserDao.scala` is as follows:

```
//UserDao.scala
case class UserAuth(email:String, passwdHash:String,
creationTime:Long)

@Singleton
class UserDao @Inject()(protected val dbConfigProvider:
DatabaseConfigProvider) extends
HasDatabaseConfigProvider[JdbcProfile]  {
  import profile.api._
  implicit val getUserResult = GetResult(r =>
   UserAuth(r.nextString, r.nextString, r.nextLong()))

   def getUserByEmail(email:String): Future[Option[UserAuth]] = {
     db.run(sql"select email, passwdHash, creationTime from users
     where email = $email".as[UserAuth].headOption)
```

```
    }
    //...
}
```

`UserDao` takes one constructor argument:

- `DatabaseConfigProvider`—This is a means to access `DatabaseConfig`. `DatabaseConfig` helps us access the driver and the database.

For the dependency injection to work to obtain `DatabaseConfigProvider` in our class, it is required that our class extends the `HasDatabaseConfigProvider` trait. The dependency injection will not work if we do not mix in this trait.

Inside the `getUserByEmail` method, we write our plain old SQL query using the **sql** interpolator.

The **sql** interpolator is special; it automatically creates a `PreparedStatement` out of our query and sets the value.

In our case, it would generate a prepared statement: `select email, passwdHash, creationTime from users where email=?`, and then set the value in `PreparedStatement` with an `$email` value.

It is advisable to use `PreparedStatement` when querying a database as it prevents SQL injection attacks. If you do not use `PreparedStatement`, but rather proceed with string appending, then one could be prone to attacks where the value of the preceding `$email` could rather contain a subquery that could drop the table instead of being a legitimate email string.
With `PreparedStatement`, the value would be verified to match the expected datatype of the column.

To learn more about the SQL injection and the means to prevent it using `PreparedStatement`, refer to `https://en.wikipedia.org/wiki/SQL_injection` and `https://en.wikipedia.org/wiki/Prepared_statement`.

Coming back to our code, once the `PreparedStatement` is executed, we map the result row to `UserAuth` by doing `as[UserAuth]`, please refer to the following command:

```
db.run(sql"select email, passwdHash, creationTime from users where email =
$email".as[UserAuth]
```

`as[UserAuth]` let's easily convert the `ResultSet` (database row) that the driver provides to our `Scala` objects. For this to happen, we need to tell Slick about column mapping of the response row to the field in our Scala class. This happens via the implicit `GetResult` parameter that is provided as an implicit argument to the `as[UserAuth]` method. We provide the column mapping of the response to our `Scala` class as follows:

```
implicit val getUserResult = GetResult(r =>
UserAuth(r.nextString, r.nextString, r.nextLong()))
```

In our query, when we provide the order of columns in the `SELECT` statement, `select email, passwdHash, creationTime`, we need to adhere to the same order while extracting the data from the row by doing `r.nextString, r.nextString, r.nextLong()`, ultimately constructing the `UserAuth` object.

Slick evolutions

If you notice, we have not provided the table creation queries of our schema. To do this automatically on application start-up, we use the `play-slick evolutions` plugin.

Our folder structure looks like:

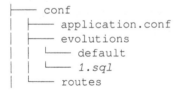

```
├── conf
│   ├── application.conf
│   ├── evolutions
│   │   └── default
│   │       └── 1.sql
│   └── routes
```

By convention, we will create the `1.sql` file in the `conf/evolutions/{database-name}/` directory. In our case, it is in the `conf/evolutions/default/` folder.

The `default` folder signifies the *database namespace* to be used while executing `1.sql`. The tables created in `evolutions/default/1.sql` will be persisted in the `default` database. Please refer to the following code:

```
# --- !Ups

create table users (email VARCHAR NOT NULL PRIMARY KEY,passwdHash
```

```
VARCHAR NOT NULL, creationTime BIGINT NOT NULL );

create table tokens(key VARCHAR NOT NULL  PRIMARY KEY , token
VARCHAR NOT NULL UNIQUE , validTill BIGINT NOT NULL)

# --- !Downs

drop table users;
drop table tokens;
```

The !Ups contents of this file will be executed **only the first time the application starts**. It will not be executed if the application restarts in the future (unless the file content gets changed).

The way it works is as follows:

- Play creates a meta-table PLAY_EVOLUTIONS in our database where it maintains the meta information
- In future, if we create the 2.sql file in the evolutions/default folder, then, during the next start-up of the application:
  - It will execute the !Ups section of the 2.sql file.
  - Suppose, in later releases, the contents of 2.sql have changed. In such cases, play will execute the !Downs section of the 2.sql file and then !Ups on 2.sql to ensure that the database is in sync with the codebase.
  - If the contents of 2.sql do not change, no query will be executed from the file.

The Play evolution plugin will execute 3.sql in case it is created in future.

To summarize:

- !Ups describes our DDL and DML
- !Downs describes how to revert them

With the help of PlaySlick Evolutions, these database queries become part of the application lifecycle. For this to happen, the following things need to be configured:

```
slick.dbs.default.driver="slick.driver.H2Driver
$"slick.dbs.default.db.driver="org.h2.Driver"
slick.dbs.default.db.url="jdbc:h2:~/h2"
slick.dbs.default.db.user=saslick.dbs.default.db.password=""
```

In our `application.conf`, we provide the driver and database settings to PlaySlick. Notice the word `default` in the preceding statements, which represent the connection to the `default` namespace of db.

We have provided a brief description of all the things we have used in building the preceding `auth-app` microservice. You can browse through the full codebase at `https://github.com/scala-microservices-book/book-examples/tree/master/chapter-4/auth-app`.

Slick is asynchronous

Another wonderful thing about Slick is that it is asynchronous. Our `db.run(sql"select ....as[UserAuth]` query returns a `Future` instance rather than waiting on the database to reply back with the rows.

In reality, Slick is not asynchronous down to the driver level due to lack of asynchronous driver support across multiple database vendors. So, the driver is still synchronous in nature. In `Chapter 3`, *Asynchronous and Non-Blocking,* you learned a design technique to handle such scenarios where it is very difficult to be non-blocking. In such cases, you learned to segregate such blocking calls to an independent `ExecutionContext` and let that be fine-tuned to perform better.

Slick adopts a similar tactic where it manages database connections, schedules blocking threads in their own thread pool, and provides us with a `Future` object for our tasks.

The web-app microservice

The `chapter-4/web-app` is the `frontend` application. It takes care of the following things:

- It contains the user-interface HTML, JavaScript, and CSS files
- It takes care of session management of the user accessing the application
- It parses the user query submitted in the search box
- It makes REST calls to other microservices and obtains the final results
- Its results are sent back to the browser

The tree of the `web-app` folder looks like this:

```
├── app
│   ├── assets
│   │   ├── javascripts
│   │   └── stylesheets
```

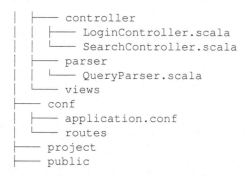

```
|   ├── controller
|   |   ├── LoginController.scala
|   |   └── SearchController.scala
|   ├── parser
|   |   └── QueryParser.scala
|   └── views
├── conf
|   ├── application.conf
|   └── routes
├── project
├── public
```

The user interface is written using ReactJS (https://facebook.github.io/react). All the React related JavaScript and CSS files are placed in the app/assets/ folder. It is a very simple UI code.
The other static JavaScript and CSS files are placed in the public/ folder.

- The app/controller contains our Scala code. Please refer to the following points:
  - The app/controller/LoginController takes care of the login/logout and sessions
  - The app/controller/SearchController contains code dealing with searches
- The app/parser/QueryParser contains the logic of parsing the user query

LoginController.scala, when requested with a username and password, makes REST calls to the auth-server to authenticate and obtain a token. This token is stored as a cookie that is reused during subsequent search calls. We use Play's excellent `WS` module to make asynchronous HTTP calls to external microservices.

After logging in, the user enters the search query in our search box. We need a mechanism to parse the user query and generate a Scala object that could be used in a typesafe manner. See the following Scala case class:

```
case class SearchFilter(location: Option[String], tech:
Option[String])
```

We wish to generate the Scala instance SearchFilter(Some("Scala"), Some("london")) from the string—Scala in london.

Moreover, the user could search in so many different ways:

- Scala in London
- Scala IN London
- Scala Developers in London
- Scala
- Scala developers
- Developers in London

To have the flexibility to cater to so many kinds of queries, we need to parse the input effectively. We have used Scala's Parser Combinator library to parse using search queries (`https://github.com/scala/scala-parser-combinators`).

The rank-app microservice

The `rank-app` is our core microservice that ranks developers available on different platforms. Please refer to these points:

- It uses tokens and `auth-server` to validate tokens
- In the application configuration (`application.conf`) file, we provide the list of microservices that `rank-app` must rely on to obtain the rank of developers across all platforms

For all the microservices registered in the `application.conf` (`so-app`, `github-app`), the `rank-app` will send the serialized JSON of the following `case class` to all the registered microservices:

```
case class SearchFilter(location: Option[String], tech:
Option[String])
```

And, in return, it will expect the response to be JSON deserialized to the `List[SOSearchResult]` format, where `SOSearchResult` is defined in the `commons` project as follows:

```
// SUserResult = SearchUserResult
abstract class SUserResult {
  require(score >= 0 && score <= 1, s"score must be in range of [0-
1]. passed: $score")

  /**
   * value in range of 0-1 absolute
   */
```

```
def score: Float
def tag: String
def location: String
//...
}
```

The class signifies the data associated with one developer. The variable `score` represents the score of that developer with respect to that tag. This score will be in the range of [0-1], where zero represents poor performance and one represents high.

Once it obtains `List[SOSearchResult]` from the `so-app` microservice and `github-app`, it simply has to consolidate the respective results by looking at `score` and normalizing the `score` of that developer across multiple platforms, if any.

This way, in the future, if we introduce a `linkedin-app` or a `topcoder-app` to gauge developer on those platforms, we simply need to add to the configuration in `application.conf` with their URL and everything else will simply work. The reason it works is because `so-app` and `github-app` are designed like functions where they take an input of the same format (`SearchFilter`) and reply back with the same object structure `List[SOSearchResult]`.

The stackoverflow-app (so-app) microservice

The `so-app` takes care of everything to do with Stack Overflow. In our application, we have already pre-fed the data in the database. Although, you can scrape the data from their monthly archives (`https://archive.org/details/stackexchange`) in a batch manner and persist them in a database. Please refer to the following points:

- All the user data is already persisted in the database
- Each developer on the Stack Overflow is ranked internally, based on the tag (such as Java and Scala) and allotted a score in the range of [0-1]
- This rank is used to sort the developers corresponding to a programming language
- In case of search related to location, we simply filter the preceding results based on location

The implementation uses the following:

- H2 database to persist all the Stack Overflow-related data. H2 is not an adequate database for larger data sizes. However, I have used it for two reasons—simplicity and ease of running. There is no need to explicitly install the database and set the admin credentials, like we would have to, in the case of PostgreSql or MySql.
- Play Evolutions to manage our database schema evolutions.
- Cache's most used queries for faster response.

The JSON form of the `case class` from the `commons` project, `com.microservices.search.SearchFilter`, is used to send while making search calls. We use Play JSON to easily convert from a Scala object to JSON and back again.

The following is the `searchPost` method from `SearchController.scala`. The method expects `searchFilter`, validates the format, obtains the result, and responds back:

```
def searchPost = Action.async(parse.json) { implicit request =>
  val body = request.body
  val loc = (body \ "location").validate[String]
  val tag = (body \ "tag").validate[String]

  if(loc.isError || tag.isError){
    Future.successful(BadRequest(s"Not a valid input: $body"))
  }else{
    val filter = SearchFilter(Option(loc.get),Option(tag.get))
    search(filter).map(x => Ok(Json.toJson(x)))
  }
}
```

Most of the code in this project is self-explanatory.

github-app (github-app)

The `github-app` is very similar in implementation and design to the `so-app` microservice, just that the data form is of course, GitHub specific.

The commons project

Mostly, case classes that are used during inter-microservice communication are declared here. This helps in keeping consistency in the expected format of the microservices.

In general, it may not be a clever idea to share a common project across microservices as it adds to dependency on a common thing and our intention is to remain independent. This will be a bigger problem in the future, because, as the microservice evolves, there could be multiple versions of the commons library where different microservices rely on different versions of `commons-lib`. These are usually not a problem if we do not alter the class structures. Moreover, if we do, it maintains the backward compatibility with the previous versions.

However, irrespective of the versioning, any change in the signature of a microservice will, of course, impact other microservices. It's easier to find bugs with static typing of the class rather than relying on documentation in case of changes. So, in many cases, sharing a common signature via a class is an acceptable pattern.

Pitfalls

We now have a working application that seems to work reasonably well. Each microservice is an independent autonomous unit that does one thing and does it well. Nothing is shared across microservices, and they seem to remain independent.

Our microservices are all non-blocking and asynchronous in their internal implementation and communication with external services. We have adequately handled implicitly-blocking database calls by letting Slick take care of all the pain, and in turn, providing us with an asynchronous API.

So, we have fundamentally executed everything we learned up until now in this book, in this chapter. However, are we still good enough?

Service locator: If the `rank-app` microservice needs to make an HTTP call to so-app, it needs to have the URL of the `so-app` microservice. Currently, this URL is provided by the `config` file to `rank-app`. This is a fragile model because we will need to update this URL if the actual URL of the `so-app` changes.

The `so-app` microservice could have different URL's in the development atmosphere, staging, production, and so on. Even in production, if the URL gets changed (during disaster recovery or relaunching on another machine), then the `rank-app` microservice would have to be restarted/notified of the change in URL. This adds to the Dev Ops task.

Tight integration: In our architecture, we have tight integrations across services. Please refer to the following points:

- `web-app` is dependent on `auth-server` and `rank-App`
- `rank-app` is dependent on `auth-server`, `so-app`, and `github-app`

If any of the microservices are down, it has a direct impact on the dependent microservices. Hence, making it a very fragile system. This is analogous to splitting one application across multiple applications where a method call is replaced with a network call.

Domain Modeling : Extensibility

The advantage of microservices lies in the ability to provide space in building up newer functionalities without a considerable change in the existing infrastructure.

For example, in our current application, let's say we wish to build a new microservice `dev-mapping`, the role of which is to consolidate all the developer's meta-information available across all platforms.

The reason this is needed is to merge data available across multiple sites—a user can have an account on Stack Overflow and GitHub. In such a case, it gives more confidence on the capability of the developer if we merge the scores of a developer's GitHub and Stack Overflow profile. So, we need to map information of every platform with every other platform.

To do this, we will need to modify our architecture for the following diagram:

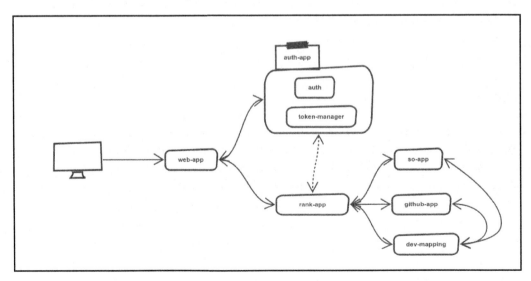

The **dev-mapping** server will interact with other platforms, such as `so-app` and `github-app`, to consolidate. The `so-app` will need to send all its user information to the **dev-mapping** microservice. This will have the following consequences:

- The `so-app` microservice will need to be modified, where, as soon as it scrapes data of the developers, it will need to also send this data to **dev-mapping** server. So, the code will need to be modified.
  This adds complexity with respect to the design as there can be many failure scenarios—what happens if the **dev-mapping** server is down? The `so-app` microservice will need to retry later. Further updates/modifications of the Stack Overflow users data would need to be relayed to dev-mapping server and so on.
- Duplicacy of data on `so-app` and **dev-mapping**.
- The data will need to be synced on both the sides.

The same logic will need to be incorporated inside the GitHub app as well.

Even though our applications are split, which has provided us with advantages such as development ease and working with smaller applications, it adds a new headache.

Other issues, such as deployment, managing logs, and monitoring.

Hence, we now need to explore ways to tackle these problems. In the rest of the book, we will be dealing with the issues specified earlier, in the preceding specified order.

Summary

In this chapter, we have a built a working application that is a combination of six different microservices. Everywhere, each microservice is an independent autonomous unit and communicates with each other in an asynchronous and non-blocking manner using HTTP. You learned about building a multi-project under a single umbrella project in SBT with the ability to configure each one of them individually. Later, we looked into `Action.async` in Play Framework, Slick to query database, and Play evolutions to manage evolutions of schema changes in each application. Also, we went through the basic authentication for the users, as well as inter-microservice communication.

Although, we have also seen how our application is still vulnerable to failures and the pitfalls associated with our architecture. In the next chapters, we will jump to newer concepts that will help us with the issues tackled so far.

5
Reactive Manifesto

The word reactive has been used in many different contexts lately. Although it sounds exciting and fresh, we need to understand its precise definition and benefits when applying the philosophy to microservices.

In this chapter, we will cover the following topics:

- Introducing Reactive Manifesto
- Learning the significance of being reactive

Reactive hype?

Over time, there have been buzzwords in the software industry with their own rise and falls. However, independent of the duration of their presence, they always provide richer insights into the way we program. By learning about them, they provide insights that help us build good software. Even better, we get better equipped to avoid faulty software.

Although there are a few that are more powerful and eternal, as they are backed by strong fundamentals as they say, form is temporary, class is permanent, and functional-programming is another such paradigm that has not only stood the test of time, but we have spent decades trying to realize its wonders and give it the hype it truly deserves.

A well-known quote by humanitarian Sri Sri Ravi Shankar says:

Broaden your vision, deepen your roots.

As much as this applies in our worldly affairs for global peace, its gist is also valid in programming. The book by Andrew Hunt and David Thomas, *The Pragmatic Programmer: From Journeyman to Master*, introduced a quote that has been revered globally. It says:

> *Learn at least one new language every year.*
> *Different languages solve the same problems in different ways. By learning several different approaches, you can help broaden your thinking and avoid getting stuck in a rut. Additionally, learning many languages is far easier now, thanks to the wealth of freely available software on the Internet*

Learning different programming paradigms empowers us with greater wisdom and a richer toolset, which can be used to solve a local problem in our job. The saying *Learning functional programming makes you a better programmer,* is a perfect example of this belief. Where, in a day job, it may be required to code in Perl, Java, and so on, but a collective knowledge of different paradigms empowers us to write our code better in that respective language.

Similarly, being reactive, Reactive Manifesto, and so on, could also be considered marketing terms or newer software industry hype. However, it is also an opportunity to be optimistic about them and learn their core essence. In my humble opinion, they bring along a paradigm that sounds fundamentally right in distributed computing and can be considered a decent starting point to build our applications. Roland Kuhn, one of the authors of the *Reactive Manifesto*, puts it well:

> *Another way to look at the Reactive Manifesto is to call it a dictionary of best practices, some of which have been known for a long time. Its benefit is to collect a consistent and cohesive set of principles and to define names for them and their key building blocks to avoid confusion and facilitate ongoing dialog and improvement.*

So, we don't have to be strict about complying with all the principles mentioned in the manifesto, but, just like any other good practices, they bring some goodness with them.

Reactive Manifesto

The Reactive Manifesto was first introduced by Jonas Bonér (@jboner) in his blog post (https://www.lightbend.com/blog/why_do_we_need_a_reactive_manifesto%3F) in 2013. It has been updated in its second version and the full text can be accessed on http://www.reactivemanifesto.org/.

Reactive Systems have the following traits:

- They react to their users (responsive)
- They react to failures and fully recover (resilient)
- They react to variable loads (elastic)
- They react to inputs (message-driven)

As the manifesto puts it, systems built as Reactive Systems are more flexible, loosely-coupled, and scalable. This makes them easier to develop and amenable to change. They are significantly more tolerant of failure, and when failure does occur, they meet it with elegance rather than disaster. Reactive Systems are highly responsive, giving users effective interactive feedback.

You can access the full glossary of different terms used on http://www.reactivemanifesto.org/glossary.

Manifesto explained

The following diagram summarizes the Reactive Manifesto

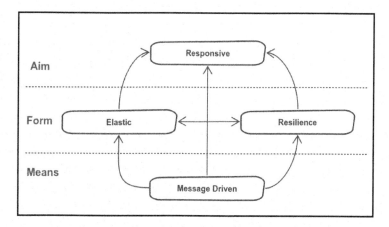

The main aim of a Reactive System is that the system must always be responsive. Synchronous, asynchronous, non-blocking, scalability, and isolation is all immaterial if the application is not responsive. Systems should respond to user input in a timely fashion under all circumstances and must even respond during failures. Failures can be of different kinds, both expected and unexpected--program bugs, outages, disturbances in the network connectivity of interdependent systems, and varying load.

To reiterate, Reactive applications are responsive, which means they always respond to user requests for all kinds of failures and ensure a consistent, positive user experience.

For the application to remain responsive under all conditions, it needs to be:

- Elastic
- Resilient

Moreover, a means to achieve being elastic, resilient, and responsive is by using messages as the mode of communication across systems.

 Responsive web design (https://en.wikipedia.orq/wiki/Responsive_web_design) is another feature that modern websites try to cater to. Where, depending on the size of the display interface (desktop, mobile, or tablet), the view restructures to make it look good on any device. So, the user always has a good viewing experience with a responsive website.

Elastic

An application that is elastic has the following traits:

- The system stays responsive under varying workloads.
- Reactive Systems can react to changes in the input rate by increasing or decreasing the resources allocated to servicing those inputs. This implies designs that have no contention points or central bottlenecks, resulting in the ability to shard or replicate components and distribute inputs among them.

From an architecture perspective, elasticity helps an application respond to sudden spikes in traffic or data and shrink back under reduced traffic to save costs. We have already seen an example of this trait in Chapter 1, *Introduction to Microservices*, while discussing scalability where we have a load balancer in front of multiple instances of the application server and instances being spiked up or removed depending on the traffic. This is only possible due to the statelessness of the microservice.

Ideally, microservices do not share a single common state (persistent storage) among each other, so there is no blocking of one by another (no common transactions on the same database). The same philosophy is valid even within an instance in a shared memory state, where we spawn new threads for higher throughput and are careful about synchronization as it affects the concurrency aspect. Transactions and synchronization are of course very similar, where the former happens in the persistent storage and the latter on shared memory. The former impacts multiple processes and the latter impacts multiple threads.

So, the application has to be elastic at many different levels to be truly responsive. Not only from a macro architectural perspective, where a microservice interacts/shares state with other microservices, but also on the implementation specifics of each microservice.

 The first version of the Reactive Manifesto used the term scalability. It was replaced with elasticity in the second version. The reasoning was that Reactive Systems react to changes in input rate by increasing or decreasing the resources allocated to service those inputs, not just by expanding according to its usage, which is the definition of scalable.

Resilience

To help us better understand the term resilience, let's consider the term **fault tolerance** first. Wikipedia defines fault tolerance as follows:

> *A fault-tolerant design enables a system to continue its intended operation, possibly at a reduced level, rather than failing completely, when some part of the system fails.*

So, if a part of the system breaks, then, instead of the application falling down completely, it still functions, but at a reduced level. So, maybe the application responds slowly, or a part of the application may be unresponsive, but the overall application as such would still be alive.

Resilience goes beyond fault tolerance. A resilient system is not only fault tolerant, but also has the capacity to fully recover itself from failure.

To help explain this, consider the metaphor of a professional boxer. In a boxing match, if a boxer gets hit left, right, and center but has still not given up, this state can be correlated to fault tolerance. The boxer has been physically hit and is in pain with mild consciousness, limping and hanging in there, but hasn't been knocked out. So, at this point, the boxer is fault tolerant, as the boxer is still performing under failure and hasn't fallen over.

Resilience is the ability of the boxer to refresh/inspire himself, and to gain full consciousness and fight back as though nothing happened. It allows us to regain full functionality and not just limp around.

In material sciences, resilience has a very important place in determining the elasticity of a material. Resilience is the ability of a material to absorb energy when it is deformed elastically, and release that energy upon unloading. The following is a diagram of a strain curve on the material when a stress is applied on it:

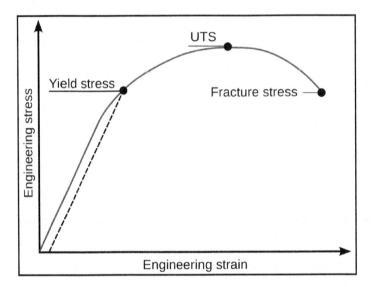

So, a material (for example, steel, iron, copper, bone, nylon, carbon fiber, and so on), when applied with stress, will generate a strain. As the stress is eventually removed, the material will return to its original shape. The material will have gone elastic deformation for a temporary phase and will return back to its original state. So, it was able to resist a distorting influence or deforming force and regain shape when that influence or force was removed.

Although, this physical behavior of recovery has an upper limit called the **Yield Stress**, as seen in the preceding diagram. If the stress applied on the material is more than the Yield Stress of the material, then the material begins to deform plastically and a fraction of the deformation will be permanent and non-reversible. The next significant state is the **Ultimate tensile strength (UTS)**. Beyond this point, the material ultimately fractures. Brittle materials such as glass and stone fracture at the ultimate strength levels.

Aramid fibers are a class of heat resistant and strong synthetic fibers that have a very high Yield Stress value. They are used in aerospace and military applications, for ballistic-rated body armor fabric and ballistic composites.

With respect to our application design, we intend to have this kind of material-like behavior, to be resilient under applied stress and failures, and then recover back fully on its own. Resilience allows it to regain full functionality and not just limp around and actually restore and continue as though nothing just happened.

 Reactive Systems are resilient, which means they remain responsive in the event of failures.

Message-driven

An asynchronous message-driven architecture is the foundation of reactive applications. Message passing forms the means and core enabler for applications to exhibit elasticity and resilience and, hence, remain responsive.

Inter-communication between humans is, by default, message-driven. When a child asks his dad, *can you play Tennis with me?*, the child has sent a message to his father. The father, upon hearing the statement, analyzes it briefly, checks his availability, and replies back to the child, *Yes*. The child then receives the response message from his father and takes the appropriate action.

It is important that the message passing be asynchronous. By asynchronous, we mean that when an application sends a message to another application, it does not wait for the message to arrive at the destination, nor does it remain blocked until the time it receives a message back from the destination. So, as soon as the message is sent by the sender, the sender can continue to execute the next part of the code instead of waiting for the message to arrive at the destination. Of course, the underlying framework would take care of delivering the message, but the whole experience of using the framework perspective remains asynchronous.

Being message-driven is crucial to remaining reactive. The manifesto puts it as:

> *Reactive Systems rely on asynchronous message-passing to establish a boundary between components that ensures loose coupling, isolation and location transparency.*

There are many open-source toolkits that are fantastic for message passing--Apache Kafka, RabbitMQ, **Amazon Simple Queue Service (SQS)**, JMS-based implementations, such as ActiveMQ; actor-based toolkits such as Akka; and so on. Each has their own flavor and you must choose the one that fits your programming model the best. The decision to choose one among the numerous message-passing frameworks depends on the desired features you need from the framework--is it needed to persist the messages, delivery semantics of at least once delivery, or, at most once delivery, rerun the messages in a pipeline later for some analytics, topics versus queue, message passing within the application, or to remote applications, and so on. So, there is no clear winner. Something such as Amazon SQS may fit you well if you do not wish to manage your own infrastructure (as it would be maintained by AWS). For RabbitMQ, you will need your own instances running RabbitMQ broker; hence, its maintenance will be done by you.

Another great aspect of being message-driven is that your client and the sender can be implemented using different programming languages, provided the framework you use supports the respective programming language.

A point to consider is that the message passing does not necessarily have to be across applications, but it can also be within the application, where different parts of the code interact with each other via messages. This is usually referred to as **local routing**, where the sender and the receiver are the same process. The message framework you chose may not support optimizations for local routing. If your tech stack is purely JVM based, Akka is a great alternative.

Asynchronous message passing does not have to be only across inter-applications, but it can also be for a single application, where different modules of the code interact among each other via messages.

Brief overview of Akka

Akka is an actor model (`https://en.wikipedia.org/wiki/Actor_model`) implementation for JVM. The actor model was first defined in 1973 by Carl Hewitt. The inspiration was to build a strong abstraction for massive concurrency and parallel systems. Erlang is a very famous example of actor model implementation. The actor model fits very well in places where large-scale concurrency is needed without worrying about dealing with lower-level threads and explicit locking. WhatsApp, the famous messaging mobile application, is known to have its servers implemented in Erlang.

In an actor model, there are actors. Actors can be thought of as an individual computational unit. Actors communicate with other actors via messages. They send messages to each other to communicate. Each actor is equipped with a message queue that gets occupied with messages if the actor receives any messages. The actor will extract a message from the queue and process it. Once processing of the message is finished, the actor will pull out the next message from its queue and process it.

To help explain the concept better, consider the metaphor of a child asking his father, can *you play tennis with me?*. The child is an actor and so is the father. The child actor has sent the message to his father. The father actor will receive the message, analyze the message contents, and try to make a decision whether to play tennis or not (maybe it's not alright to play, as it is too late and it's time for bed), and ultimately reply back to the child actor.

Actors have the following properties:

- Process only one message at a time.
    - So, we do not need to worry about synchronization as an actor will only process one message at a time. The internal state of the actor is thread-safe as its state is accessed and manipulated only by itself. This concept is technically also called **Thread-Confinement**.
- They can send a finite number of messages to other actors.
- Actors can create other actors.
- They are very lightweight. You can have millions of actors in a few megabytes of memory.

An important part to notice here is that the actors can send messages to other actors. The receiver actor may be an actor on the same JVM or on a remote JVM. If it is the same JVM, Akka will simply transfer the message reference to the receiving actor internally. For a remote process, Akka will serialize the message and send it over the network (TCP/UDP based on configuration) to the target actor.

The great part about this abstraction is that, as a developer, it is extremely easy to scale out. Because our code logic simply deals with actors communicating with each other, a mere configuration change means we can go from *all the actors on the same JVM* to *each actor on different JVMs*. And this can be done literally with no code change; just a change in configuration. This philosophy unlocks massive potential to write distributed software with great ease.

Akka is designed for scalability and fault tolerance from the ground up. You can scale from a single VM to multiple VMs without considering any code changes.

To learn more about Akka, please refer to `http://akka.io/`.

Akka versus message brokers

There are significant differences between a toolkit such as Akka and broker-based systems such as ActiveMQ. In the latter, the broker acts as an intermediary, where the sender sends a message to the broker and then the broker forwards it to the receiver. Akka is peer-to-peer, where the sender directly sends the message over to the client. Each one has its own advantages.

Using Akka, you can create millions of actors and each actor can send thousands of messages to other actors with a very small memory footprint. So, you can have millions of actors with minimal latency, but at the expense of reliability. In Akka, as there is no intermediary broker, the message is not guaranteed to be received by the consumer. This can happen if the consumer is not alive at that moment due to network breakdown. So you will need to handle cases of message loss. Akka does have numerous modules to help you out with various use cases such as persistence of messages, Akka cluster, and so on.

For broker-based systems such as RabbitMQ and ActiveMQ, one gets reliability (and message persistence) at the expense of latency. This concept is an implementation of **Transactional Persistent Queues** and is not considered lightweight. Moreover, the routing is mostly done over the network, so there is clearly high latency if the application is itself the sender and the receiver. With Akka, this is super-efficient, as passing the message locally is equivalent to passing the message reference.

In the truest sense, Akka and RabbitMQ as solutions cannot be compared. Akka is a concurrency toolkit, whereas RabbitMQ is an **Advanced Message Queueing Protocol (AMQP)** implementation (`https://en.wikipedia.org/wiki/Advanced_Message_Queuing_Protocol`). Though you can use both as a mode of being message-driven.

Isolation

Message passing provides with Isolation in Time. By being isolated in time, it helps us in being isolated by space.

We have already covered Isolation with respect to microservices in Chapter 1, *Introduction to Microservices*, where we witnessed the advantages of obtaining Isolation in Time and space with respect to our demo example.

To reiterate:

- It is not necessary for both the sender and the receiver to be active at the same time.
  - The sender could send a message and the message could be persisted by the intermediary broker. The client would retrieve the message once it was alive or free.
  - No preconceived expectation that the messages would be processed immediately.
- This is Isolation in Time.

 This behavior can also be implemented in Akka, where there is no broker. The receiver, on obtaining a message, can reply back to the sender with a success message. The original sender will keep track of the success messages and retry sending the messages in future in case the message was not delivered to the client.

Isolation is a core benefit that we obtain by being message-driven. The sender and receiver are completely isolated from each other, as the intermediary message broker is the only piece of contact common to each other. Another advantage of this setup is the ability to scale.

With a message broker in place, under a heavy load, we can scale up the number of instances of producers or the consumers. The producers will simply need to keep sending the messages to the broker (let's say Apache Kafka Broker) and the increased number of consumers can start picking up. There is no change in our architectural setup, and yet we are able to handle higher loads. This gives us the ability to scale horizontally.

Isolation is also needed for a system to self-heal. When Isolation is in place, if a part of the system goes down, it does not affect the other parts, that is, if the consumer or the producer of the messages goes down, it does not impact the other. Let's say the consumer is faced with failures of some kind, or is burdened by a heavy load where it's going to take a considerable amount of time for it to process further messages. In the meantime, the producer does not have to worry about what's happening on the other side and can continue to behave normally and send messages. All the intermediary messages would be managed by the message queue service.

This gives the chance for the failed component to self heal and the component can again start from where it left off in the previous state. So, failure in one isolated component won't impact the responsiveness of the overall system. Neither is there any loss of data.
This capacity to scale and yet have the ability to self-heal helps our system be elastic and resilient.

Flow control

In TCP implementation, flow control is of very high importance. TCP uses a flow control mechanism where the sender sends data at an adequate rate which the receiver can process.

Imagine a scenario where you are trying to Google search for a term from your mobile device. The Google server will quickly generate the response and push it back to you. But because you may be on a slow internet connection, your network would be overwhelmed with its network buffers overfilled, resulting in a drop of data packets. And because TCP is a reliable transmission protocol, it will again have to request for the lost data packets, resulting in duplication of work.

Using the **Sliding Window Flow Control** implementation of TCP (https://en.wikipedia.org/wiki/Sliding_window_protocol), the receiver signals to the sender the amount of additional data that it is willing to buffer. The sender would then only send the amount of data that the receiver can manage.

Reactive Systems need to be equipped with a flow control mechanism so that the producer only sends message volumes which the client can comfortably handle. This phenomenon is also called **back-pressure** in Reactive Systems where the sender experiences back-pressure. Akka Streams (http://doc.akka.io/docs/akka/2.5.1/scala/stream/) is a well know streaming API that implicitly provides back-pressure.

In the absence of back-pressure, the consumer would get overwhelmed with the messages and would need to drop them. An alternative could be to increase the size of the queue on the consumer side. But this could result in an out of memory error or overfilling the buffer with too large a content of practical usage. With back-pressure, the application does not do unnecessary extra work by losing messages or filling up resources with them, but rather restores sanity by requesting the sender decreases the pace. An interesting and impressive part of Akka Streams is that this logic is taken care of by the framework and does not creep into the API. Which means there is nothing much to be done by the developer when the framework takes care of it.

Though, sometimes, your message broker might not provide this provision for back-pressure. Under these situations, an alternative strategy could be adopted. If the destination queue is full, you could either drop the new message, or drop the oldest message in the queue, or sort them in a priority queue and drop the least preferred message. Of course, it depends on your precise use case.

Location Transparency

Two separate modules communicate with each other via messages. The modules in action could either be part of the same process or be running on multiple VMs spread across different continents.

- This is also called Location Transparency
- Akka is a very good example of this behavior

I feel the Reactive Manifesto truly does justice to the definition of Location Transparency in its glossary (`http://www.reactivemanifesto.org/glossary#Location-Transparency`):

Elastic systems need to be adaptive and continuously react to changes in demand, they need to gracefully and efficiently increase and decrease scale. One key insight that simplifies this problem immensely is to realize that we are all doing distributed computing. This is true whether we are running our systems on a single node or on a cluster of nodes (with independent machines communicating over the network). Embracing this fact means that there is no conceptual difference between scaling vertically on multi-core or horizontally on the cluster.

If all of our components support mobility, and local communication is just an optimization, then we do not have to define a static system topology and deployment model upfront. We can leave this decision to the operations personnel and the runtime, which can adapt and optimize the system depending on how it is used.

This decoupling in space, enabled through asynchronous message-passing, and decoupling of the runtime instances from their references is what we call Location Transparency.

Message passing often provides an excellent boundary to scale an application horizontally by moving the receiver to a different process, and also gives us the ability to scale vertically if the application itself is the sender and receiver of the message. So, the application can scale horizontally by expanding to run on more computers, and yet also have the ability to run the entire system on a single computer when desirable.

Immutability

Reactive Systems are message-driven. When different components interact with each other via messages, it is important for the messages to be immutable.

Consider the case of an email. When you send an email to someone, you definitely know that the contents of the email are not going to change. It is expected and guaranteed that the email you have sent will be the one which the receiver will receive. And the contents of the email will not change. It does not matter if the receiver checks his email the same day, or the same month, or in a different year, or maybe decades later. The email is always immutable.

This confidence that the contents of the email are never going to change is golden. Imagine that the email contents automatically changed, that is, either your mail server altered it or you yourself changed the contents of the mail. Tracking the changes would then require extra effort. Or worse, if you did not keep track of the changes, it could give rise to confusion, where the sender and the receiver do not agree to the common message transferred.

Just as in programming, where the immutability of objects has many advantages, it is easy to reason that the value of the object will never change, since it is defined. This causes lesser bugs. Moreover, it is safer to write thread safe code, as there would be no need for synchronization across threads when accessing the same object. This is because the state of the object cannot be changed. The same advantages also apply when dealing with inter-process communication as well.

Immutability has many other unseen advantages. If the changes are propagated between modules by way of events, which are immutable facts that describe state changes that have occurred we can persist the messages in the same order the client received; we can replay the same objects in the same order in future to replay the same set of events. This can be used to run analytics engines, or find the cause of bugs, if any. This replaying of events would only work if the objects are immutable. We will cover deeper aspects of this strategy in Chapter 8, *Effective Communication*.

Event driven versus message-driven

The first version of the Reactive Manifesto used the term event driven. It was replaced with message passing in the second version. Both of them may sound equivalent, but there is considerable difference between them.

An example of an event-based system are the UI toolkits such as Swing, QT, Android UI toolkit, and so on. In these, every action generates an event and the event is added to the event queue which is processed by the single event processing thread. For example, if a button is clicked on the screen, then this button click event is added to the event queue. The event processing thread would enqueue from the queue on a first come first serve basis, and execute the necessary action set for the button click.

So, behaviors are attached to every event, and when the event is received, the mapped behavior is executed. This behavior is usually provided as a callback (a callback is an anonymous procedure).

Another example of an event-based system is our web browser. When we make an Ajax GET call to the server, we provide it with a set of callbacks (a success callback and failure callback) that must be executed once the HTTP GET calls is completed. The success callback would be called in the event of a success event and the failure callback otherwise. In either case, we provide the callback to our event thread which executes the respective one on arrival of an event.

This model is also employed by single threaded runtimes such as Node.js. Please refer to the following code snippet:

```
//event thread
while(event = queue.extractHead){
  //process the callback associated with the event
}
```

In an event-driven system, notification listeners are attached to the sources of events such that they are invoked when the event is emitted.

In contrast, in a message-driven philosophy, the callbacks are completely replaced with the recipient. A message is sent to the recipient and the recipient takes the necessary action associated with the message. So, the anonymous callback is replaced with the addressable recipient.

Significant differences are:

- In an event driven system, the callbacks attached are mutually exclusive with other callbacks. In a message-driven system, the recipient has all the flexibility to mutually associate them and club responses. The recipient may wish to batch messages into groups and process them together, or may wish to ignore some messages.

- In message systems, the consumer may be directly referenced by the producer. In such cases, the message would only be processed by the addressed consumer. In such cases, the consumer can sequentially process those messages in a thread safe fashion without the need for synchronization. Akka is an example of this. In multi-threaded event systems, there is no control on which thread would process our callback. This is because the consumer cannot be directly addressed. Though, of course, in a single threaded event system such as Node.js or the web browser, just the event thread would process those messages.
- Handling of failures resilience is more difficult to achieve in an event-driven system due to the nature of event consumption queues. Once the event callbacks or event listeners are provided, they are only called on occurrence of the corresponding event. These listeners typically handle success or failure directly and may report back to the original client. In the event of failures, in order for the system to recuperate, it is necessary that the system behaves so as to achieve overall component health rather than typical handling of the failure callbacks of each event.
- The recipient of the message may not have access to the sender. In cases where it is possible, flow control can be implemented where the sender is signaled to send the messages at an appropriate pace. This clearly is not easily possible in event-based systems.

Summary

We have learned about the Reactive Manifesto. We have also seen that message passing enables us to be elastic and resilient, and together we aim to achieve responsiveness under all situations. Message passing needs some discipline with immutable messages and gracefully dealing with message loss.

In the next chapter, we will learn about the Reactive Microservices Framework Lagom and how Lagom was designed to adhere to being reactive.

6
Introduction to Lagom

Lagom is an opinionated microservices framework. By convention, it adopts a few design principles that it considers appropriate to gracefully build applications based on microservice architecture.

In this chapter, we will provide a brief overview of Lagom and several design philosophies that it adapts. Of course, our focus will be on understanding the framework specifications, but, more importantly, the design principles it adapts.

We will cover the following topics in this chapter:

- Introducing Lagom and the concepts it gets on the table
- Learning about the Lagom Service API

Why Lagom?

In the first few chapters, we took a look at the Play Framework and its internals. We stressed the importance of asynchronous and non-blocking ways of how to write internal code, but also how to make external API calls in a non-blocking way using an asynchronous IO. This was done using the Play WS API
(`https://www.playframework.com/documentation/2.5.x/ScalaWS`).

So, by using the Play WS API, our microservice was calling other web services. On receiving the response, if the response had a reasonable schema such as JSON, we would deserialize it to a Scala object and use it accordingly. When making an HTTP POST call to another web service, we would serialize our object likewise.

Thankfully, due to the lucid Play API, this did not result in much boilerplate code. However, a few things do come up:

- The protocol used in the communication
- The URL in which to connect

For example, consider the following piece of code:

```
import play.api.libs.json._
val data = Json.obj(
  "firstName" -> "Lionel",
  "lastName" -> "Messi"
)
val url = "http://someip/users/getUser"
val futureResponse: Future[WSResponse] = ws.url(url).post(data)
//eventually validate the response object and convert it to a
`User` object
```

When our microservice is making a call to other microservices of our own, what we are intending to achieve is a **Remote Procedure Call (RPC)** (`https://en.wikipedia.org/wiki/Remote_procedure_call`) behavior over the network. From a coding perspective, we want the experience of calling other microservices with an argument to be simply like calling a method. Something along the lines of the following code snippet, for example:

```
val userService = clientFor[UserService]
val response:Future[User] = userService.getUser()
//This would back a HTTP call in the background to the server,
get
//the response and convert the json to a User object
```

So, when compared to the previous case where we deserialized our object, made an HTTP POST/GET call to a URL, obtained the response, and serialized it to a Scala object, we can simply call the foreign microservice in the preceding fashion like any other method call. It's important to note, however, that internally, it would perform all the mentioned operations, but they will not be exposed in the API. The protocol used (such as TCP/UDP or higher-level protocols using JSON/XML/Protocol buffers, streaming, and so on) would be hidden at the framework level and could be configured.

For this to work seamlessly, however, we would need to wire the microservices in some magical fashion, where a microservice is aware of services being exposed by other microservices. This facility needs to be available at compile time for the experience to be seamless.

Another point to notice here is that we were previously providing the URL of the service exposed (In `ws.url(url)`). In complex systems, this is not a simple problem to overcome, as there can be multiple duplicate microservices running, systems being migrated to other hosts or even continents, migration to a disaster recovery mode, application upgrades, and the handling of calls during network failures.

This needs a design of its own. It would also be great if the framework was aware of the function. We will dive into the *Service Discovery* section in greater detail in `Chapter 10, Production Containers`.

There are a few things that could aid in improving the experience of building applications in a microservices architecture—build and deploy, testing of services, development environment and production environments, inter-communication across microservices, and so on.

Lagom is an opinionated microservices framework where its design is inspired to solve the usual problems faced in building applications, such as earlier in microservices architecture.

> Note that the Play Framework is a fantastic framework. Play is a web framework and is great to build web applications. It is also alright to use Play to build microservices.
>
> Lagom, on the other hand, solves a different problem; it has been designed to build microservices and to tackle common issues faced when building them. So, it is not fair to compare Play with Lagom. Instead, we would say that they complement each other so that an application can have a Play application along with Lagom microservices running in the background.
>
> Play and Lagom both come from the same company—Lightbend Inc.

Brief overview of Lagom

Lagom is a Swedish word that means *just the right amount* or *sufficient*. A description on the Lagom website gives the inspiration for the name as:

> *Often, when people talk about microservices, they focus on the micro part of the name, assuming it means that a service should be small. We want to emphasize that the important thing when splitting a system into services is to find the right boundaries between services. A system of right-sized microservices will naturally achieve scalability and resilience requirements and be easy to deploy and manage. So, rather than focus on how small your services should be, design "Lagom" size services.*

Lagom is built on top of Play and Akka. So, some of the Lagom configurations are Play and Akka configurations. Lagom is internally built using Scala, but it exposes a separate Java and Scala API.

The Scala and Java API are sufficiently independent (that is, plainly, one is not a wrapper on top of another), so our experience with the Scala API is very Scala-ish, rather than it being a Java wrapper and vice versa.

The default build tool for Lagom projects is SBT. There is also a Maven plugin available. However, in this book, we will use SBT for our code samples.

Lagom is opinionated. It considers a set of guiding principles as the *de facto* standard and incorporates them in its API. The guiding principles are based on the following points:

- Asynchronous and non-blocking in virtually everything:
    - The inter-service communication uses asynchronous IO and is built on top of Akka Streams.
    - The services exposed via Lagom are plain, standard HTTP for synchronous communication and WebSockets for streaming and asynchronous messages; therefore, it is easy to build polyglot systems and external systems that can directly call Lagom Services over HTTP.
    - When communicating across services, streams are provided as a first-class concept; this way, one can use streams for asynchronous messaging rather than synchronous request-response communication, leading to higher levels of resilience. The streaming support is simply out of the box.
- It adheres to the Reactive Manifesto:
    - This is apparent from the isolation boundaries we will see
    - With the Message Broker API integrated as part of it, it means it is straightforward to use messages as a mode of communication; we will be covering this in `Chapter 7`, *CQRS and Event Sourcing*
    - It prefers distributed persistent patterns in contrast with traditional centralized databases, and its Persistence API offers de facto support for event sourcing and **Command Query Responsibility Segregation (CQRS)**; we will be covering this in `Chapter 8`, *Effective Communication*
    - Location transparency—Lagom has a default implementation for service registry and client-side and server-side service registry
    - In summary, Lagom has been designed to make the process of designing, developing, and deploying microservices great

- Ease of development:
    - One can have multiple Lagom microservices as part of the same build; it is simple to compile, test, and run all of them in a single sentence
    - The development mode supports hot redeployment (just like Play) for developers' productivity gain
- Others:
    - Great ease of inter-microservice communication with flexibility of protocol of communication

Lagom primarily has three APIs, and they are as follows:

- Service API
- Message Broker API
- Persistence API

James Roper (`https://twitter.com/jroper`), the tech lead for Lagom, defines the Service API as follows:

> *The Service API provides a way of declaring and implementing service interfaces. These service interfaces can be consumed by clients and backed by service locator for location transparency. The API supports both synchronous request response service calls as well as asynchronous streaming between services.*

We will be covering the Service API and its details in this chapter. The Message Broker API will be covered in `Chapter 7`, *CQRS and Event Sourcing*
, and the Persistence API will be covered in `Chapter 8`, *Effective Communication*. Lagom also has a Message Broker API (which is currently based on Apache Kafka) and a Persistence API (based on Cassandra). This is why **Kafka** and **Cassandra** are also available by default in the Lagom build itself. In the initial stages, when you don't need them, you will need to manually disable Cassandra and Kafka on application startup.

Lagom has other modules available, most notably clustering support (`https://www.lagomframework.com/documentation/1.3.x/scala/Cluster.html`). It is built on top of the Akka Cluster. Clustering allows you to scale out by forming a cluster of nodes where instances of the same service may be running on multiple nodes in a cluster, thus providing reliability. This is further coupled with support for PersistentEntity (of the Persistence API), where the entities are automatically distributed across the nodes in the cluster of the service. Further, it has default tactics on handling common problems faced by clustering, such as network partitions.

We will not be covering cluster support in this book.

Lagom Service API

In this section, we will build a small application using Lagom. Throughout the application, we will introduce several topics of Lagom to quickly get us started.

Lagom has two APIs—`javadsl` and `scaladsl`. The `javadsl` is, of course, a Java-based API, but it can be very easily used from Scala as well. A lot of examples on the internet are in fact based on the `javadsl` with Scala, as the API is new (it launched in December 2016). In this book, however, we will be using the `scaladsl` API, as that will be the preferred way going forward.

Lagom needs at least JDK 8, so you will need JDK 8 installed on your machine. Lagom has an SBT plugin and, hence, you will need at least SBT 0.13.5 to build Lagom projects. You will also need at least SBT 0.13.13 to create new Lagom projects using Lagom's supplied templates (examples), though this is optional. In this book's examples, we will be using SBT 0.13.13.

 You can find more details regarding the basic setup (including the proxy setup)
at `https://www.lagomframework.com/documentation/1.3.x/scala/Insta llation.html`.

Minimized chirper application

In this section, we will build a tiny Twitter-like application using Play and Lagom, which will contain the following features:

- Simple signup, login, and logout pages
- Ability to tweet
- Ability to follow friends
- A feed page containing our own tweets as well as our friends, this page is updated in real time when our friends tweet

The following diagram is a small overview of our desired application.

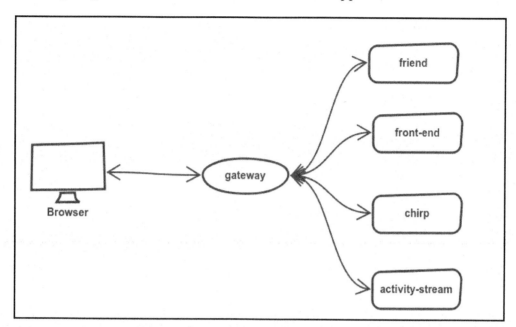

A couple of components are missing in the image and we will introduce them at a later stage. A quick summary of each microservice is as follows:

- **front-end**: This is a Play-based web application. It contains all our UI code. In this example, we are not doing server-side session management.
- **friend**: The friend microservice takes care of all the users in our system. It also contains information about the friends a user follows.
- **chirp**: The chirp, or tweet (we will be referring to tweets as chirps from now on), microservice contains all the chirps of our system. It, of course, also contains information about the timestamp and the user who chirped a chirp.
- **activity-stream**: The activity microservice provides a live stream of chirps of a user and their friends. This is fundamentally a user's feed page.

All the data that each microservice stores is in memory for simplicity. The friend, chirp, and activity-stream microservices are based on the Lagom framework.

You can find the source for the code on `https://github.com/scala-microservices-book/book-examples/tree/master/chirper-app-primer`

Anatomy of a Lagom project

In our chirper application, we have a single SBT project that contains all the microservices as subprojects. Here is the top-level view:

```
jatin@puri:~/IdeaProjects/book-examples/chapter-6$ tree -L 1
.
├── front-end/
├── chirp-api/
├── chirp-impl/
├── friend-api/
├── friend-impl/
├── activity-stream-api/
├── activity-stream-impl/
├── project/
│   ├── build.properties
│   ├── plugins.sbt
├── build.sbt
```

Each Lagom microservice is defined by two projects—API and its **implementation (impl)**. The significance of each will be covered shortly.

The sbt build information is, of course, provided in build.sbt. Note that we will need to add the following lines in project/plugins.sbt to include the Lagom plugin:

```
addSbtPlugin("com.lightbend.lagom" % "lagom-sbt-plugin" % "1.3.7")
```

The Lagom plugin is lagom-sbt-plugin. Our project/plugins.sbt further contains other sbt plugins that will be used by our application—ReactJS (used by front-end), sbteclipse (for Eclipse), and Conductr.

The build.sbt file is a standard sbt file declaring our projects and their dependencies. An overview of the file is as follows:

```
organization in ThisBuild := "sample.chirper"

scalaVersion in ThisBuild := "2.11.8"

val macwire = "com.softwaremill.macwire" %% "macros" % "2.2.5" %
"provided"

lazy val friendApi = project("friend-api")
.settings(
  version := "1.0-SNAPSHOT",
  libraryDependencies += lagomScaladslApi
)
```

```
lazy val friendImpl = project("friend-impl")
.enablePlugins(LagomScala)
.settings(
  version := "1.0-SNAPSHOT",
  libraryDependencies ++= Seq(
  lagomScaladslTestKit,
  macwire
 )
)
.settings(lagomForkedTestSettings: _*)
.dependsOn(friendApi)
```

Dependency injection in Lagom

In Chapter 2, *Introduction to Play Framework,* we presented alternative ways of performing a **dependency injection (DI)** in Play—Runtime DI using Google Guice or any JSR 330 compliant framework, or Compile time DI (Macwire is a strong option). Our previous chapters used Guice for DI in their examples.

The Lagom Scala API is built on top of the Play Framework, and uses Play's compile time DI support to wire together a Lagom application. Macwire is thus the de facto standard to be used while building Lagom applications with Scala API. We will use Macwire for a compile time dependency injection in our example.

 To know more about a dependency injection and its requirements when building applications in Lagom, refer to https://www.lagomframework. com/documentation/1.3.x/scala/DependencyInjection.html.

API and Impl

We will also define two modules from the preceding snippet, and they are as follows:

- **friendApi**: This project *only defines our services*. It contains traits defining our services.
- **friendImpl**: This project is an implementation of the services defined in friendApi and, hence, depends on friendApi. Here, you will also need to explicitly enable the LagomScala plugin.

There is a lot more than what meets the eye here. If any external services wish to access `friendImpl web-service`, we can provide them the JAR of `friendApi`. Lagom will magically provide a client so that the external services can directly call `friendImpl web-service` as a method call rather than manually making a call over HTTP.

The `friendApi` also has a dependency, `libraryDependencies += lagomScaladslApi`. `lagomScaladslApi`, which provides a nice API to declare our services. This can be thought of as an alternative to the `routes` file in the Play framework, which is used to define all our calls.

We have also added the following lines in our `build.sbt` file:

```
lagomCassandraEnabled in ThisBuild := false

lagomKafkaEnabled in ThisBuild := false
```

Lagom, by default, comes with the Cassandra database and Kafka message broker enabled. So, when the application starts up, the Cassandra database and Kafka are also started. Because we are not using Cassandra nor Kafka in our application, we need to manually disable them.

Defining services

Let's consider the case of the `friend-api` project where we *define* our service to create users, add friends, and get the followers of a user.

We define our services in the trait `sample.chirper.friend.api.FriendService.scala`:

```scala
trait FriendService extends Service {

def getUser(id: String): ServiceCall[NotUsed, User]
def createUser(): ServiceCall[CreateUser, Done]
def addFriend(userId: String): ServiceCall[FriendId, Done]
def getFollowers(userId: String): ServiceCall[NotUsed,
Seq[String]]

override def descriptor(): Descriptor = {
  import Service._

  named("friendservice").withCalls(
    pathCall("/api/users/:id", getUser _),
    namedCall("/api/users", createUser _),
    pathCall("/api/users/:userId/friends", addFriend _),
```

```
            pathCall("/api/users/:id/followers", getFollowers _)
      ).withAutoAcl(true)
   }
}
```

Our trait `FriendService` extends the
`com.lightbend.lagom.scaladsl.api.Service` trait. The `Service` trait primarily
declares a single method:

```
def descriptor: Descriptor
```

A descriptor primarily describes a service. It explains the HTTP path, the HTTP parameters,
and headers. It also describes the behavior to be executed when a service call is made. It can
also provide information about the service versions, circuit breaker strategies, and much
more.

In our trait `FriendService`, we override `descriptor` to provide an implementation. Let's
understand the `descriptor()` implementation presented earlier:

- `named("friendservice")`: `friendservice` is the name that we have given to
  this descriptor:
    - The significance of the name is that it is used by the service locator;
      by using the service locator, the consumers of the service will be
      able to access it. We will cover the significance of the service locator
      in this chapter.
- `namedCall("/api/users", createUser _ )`: We provide a given name,
  `/api/users`, and we provide the behavior that must be executed when the
  service call is made. The behavior is provided by the Scala eta expansion `*`
  `createUser _`
    - `createUser _`: The Scala compiler will convert the statement to a
      function object `() => createUser()` thanks to eta-expansion.
      Hence, the type of that function object would be `() =>`
      `ServiceCall[CreateUser,Done]`.
      This function object would be used by Lagom to process HTTP
      request when it receives. `* http://scala-lang.org/files/`
      `archive/spec/2.11/06-expressions.html#method-values`.
    - If our function did not take any parameters, then we could also
      define it as:
      `namedCall("/api/users", createUser)`
    - If our function took zero parameters, then we would have defined
      it as:
      `namedCall("/api/users", createUser())`

- **Path-based identifier:** `pathCall("/api/users/:id", getUser _)`—The ID is extracted from the URL and passed as a method argument to `def getUser(id: String)`:
  - For example, if a call is made to http://ip:port/api/users/Jon, then the `getUser` function would be called with `Jon` as the argument
  - `:id` earlier is called as a dynamic path parameter; dynamic path parameters are prefixed with a colon

If someone wanted to provide query parameters, they could instead define the service as `pathCall("`**`/api/users?id`**`", getUser _)`. In this case, a call made of the pattern http://ip:port/api/users?id=mike would make a call to `getUser("mike")`. To provide multiple query parameters:

```
def get(firstName:String, lastName:String)
//we would then use
pathCall("/api/sample?firstName&lastName", get _)
```

Towards the end we declare `.withAutoAcl(`**`true`**`)`. We define whether this service should automatically have all its service calls made publicly routable by the service gateway.

It roughly means that the mechanism to access this service (the IP and port, and so on) is outsourced to a service gateway.

We will cover this in a later section of this chapter.

Note—You will rarely need this information, but we have included it for reference purposes. When we provide `pathCall("...", getUser _)`, a lot of magic happens to convert `getUser _` to the precise argument expected of type `ScalaMethodServiceCall`. This conversion happens via implicits available in `ServiceSupport`.

ServiceCall

Once we have defined our `Descriptor`, we also declare our behaviors as:

```
def getUser(id: String): ServiceCall[NotUsed, User]
def createUser(): ServiceCall[CreateUser, Done]
```

`com.lightbend.lagom.scaladsl.api.ServiceCall` is defined as:

```
trait ServiceCall[Request, Response] {
  /**
```

```
 * Invoke the service call.
 *
 * @param request The request entity.
 * @return A future of the response entity.
 */
 def invoke(request: Request): Future[Response]
}
```

`ServiceCall` takes two types of parameters:

- **Request**: This is the input type.
  Based on the HTTP body, the body is parsed and automatically converted to the `Request` type specified.

    For example, in the case of the **def** `createUser():`
    `ServiceCall[CreateUser, Done]` function, the browser would send a JSON in the HTTP body and Lagom would automatically convert that JSON to a `CreateUser` Scala object.

- **Response**: The response type.
  For example, in the case of **def** `getUser(id: String):`
  `ServiceCall[NotUsed, User]`, the `getUser` `ServiceCall` implementation would simply return a `User` Scala object and Lagom would automatically convert that to JSON (by default) and respond back to the browser.

    Note--To help you better understand:

    ```
    def createUser(): ServiceCall[CreateUser, Done]
    ```

    An implementation of `createUser` returns a function (`ServiceCall` is a function; it takes an input and returns an output).

    When an HTTP request is received,
    Lagom would call `createUser()`, which would return a function (`ServiceCall`). Lagom would then execute this function with the `CreateUser` object (the `CreateUser` object would be created from HTTP body JSON).

In the case of **def** `createUser(): ServiceCall[CreateUser, Done]`,
`akka.Done` signifies that there is no actual value to be returned. So, the browser would display `HTTP 200 (Ok)` with an empty response body.

When defining **def** `getUser(id: String): ServiceCall[NotUsed, User]`, there are two parts to consider:

- It takes an argument (`ID: String`). The argument of such functions is derived from the HTTP route path. In our case, `Jon` would be extracted from `http://ip:port/api/users/Jon.ty./`.
- Its return type is `ServiceCall[NotUsed, User]`.
- `akka.NotUsed`—signifies that the input is of no importance. This input is based on the HTTP request body.
- Similarly, we define other methods in our `FriendService` trait.

 Note—Service descriptors not only define the service, but also define the underlying transport protocol. It could be REST, WebSockets, and so on. In our earlier case, both calls would be REST-based.

Before looking at `friend-impl`, which implements `friend-api` as defined earlier, let's now look at Macwire. Macwire is the preferred tool in Scala for compile time dependency injection.

Brief overview of Macwire

Macwire is a compile time dependency injection framework. If you are coming from a Spring background, it differs from Spring as Spring is a runtime Dependency Injection framework.

Compile Time DI offers a few advantages, mainly Type Safety.

In runtime DI, an invalid injection would result in a runtime error. With Macwire, illegitimate injections are caught at the compile time itself, thus providing a greater degree of safety net. Also, compile time DIs are known to be relatively lightweight, providing a slight start-up time benefit over runtime DI, which must scan the classes and inject at runtime.

At the same time, Macwire replaces most of the handwritten boilerplate, which would have been the case with manual DI. This is done using Scala Macros. Let's consider a simple example:

```
case class JdbcSession
case class UserDao(jdbcSession: JdbcSession)
case class UserService(userDao: UserDao)
case class UserController(userService: UserService, userDao:
```

```
  UserDao)

  object Prac {
    def main(args: Array[String]): Unit = {
      import com.softwaremill.macwire._
      val session:JdbcSession = null

    lazy val userDao = wire[UserDao]
    lazy val userService = wire[UserService]
    lazy val userController = wire[UserController]
    println(userController)
    }
  }
```

We declare our service and controllers in a usual fashion, expecting constructor arguments. (We don't mark controllers as case-class, but we have done that here to get a printable string when printed.)

When we do `wire[UserDao]`:

- At compile time, it searches for an instance of `UserDao`.
- If it is not yet created, it attempts to create it:
    - It observes that `UserDao` expects a `JdbcSession` argument, so it looks up an instance of `JdbcSession` in the scope. We already have an object session, `JdbcSession`, in the scope.
    - Using `session` as the constructor, it initializes `UserDao`.

Therefore, it is equivalent to:

```
lazy val userDao = new UserDao(session)
lazy val userService = new UserService(userDao)
lazy val userController = new UserController(userService,
userDao)
```

The bytecode at runtime in both cases would be similar.
A few points to take note of are as follows:

- If any dependencies are missing or not available in the current scope, this would result in a compile time error. You can test for this by commenting `userDao`.
- Usage of the `wire` macro can be mixed with creating new instances by hand like we did with the `session` object above.

- The `wire` macro works in the following fashion to determine the dependencies needed:
  - In a class, the `wire` macro first tries to find a constructor annotated with `@Inject` (`javax.inject.Inject`)
  - Then it will find the non-primary constructor
  - Finally, an `apply` method in the companion object
- If there are multiple dependencies of the same type in scope, then it results in compile time failure.
  - For example, if there were multiple instances of `userDao` in the scope:
    ```
    lazy val userDao2: UserDao = null
    ```
    then initialization of `userService` and `userController` would fail.

- In our example, all the objects defined would be singletons in the scope of usage. Of course, they aren't singletons in the global sense because we can create multiple copies, but because the same object is injected at multiple places. If we wish to create new instances of a dependency for ease of usage (dependent scope), we can declare our variables as `def` instead of `lazy val`.

 There are many more features available, such as dealing with implicit parameters, interceptors, wiring using factory patterns, and so on. To learn more about Macwire, please refer to `http://di-in-scala.github.io/`. It's a quick read.

Implementing friend-impl

In the preceding post, we explained `friend-api`, which was a declaration of the service. We will now look at the implementation of the `friend-impl` module in the source code.

`FriendServiceImpl` contains the implementation of `FriendService`:

```
class FriendServiceImpl()(implicit ec: ExecutionContext) extends
  FriendService {
    val userMap = new ConcurrentHashMap[String, User]()
    val friendsMap = new ConcurrentHashMap[String,
    ConcurrentLinkedQueue[User]]()
```

Our implementation is quite simple:

- `userMap`: contains the mapping of the user ID and the respective user
- `friendsMap`: contains a mapping of the user ID and all the user's friends

The following function takes a user ID as argument and returns the corresponding User object

```
override def getUser(id: String): ServiceCall[NotUsed, User] = {
request: NotUsed =>
val user = userMap.get(id)
if (user == null)
  throw NotFound(s"user $id not found")
else {
  Future.successful(getUser(user.userId, user.name))
}
}
//getUser(id: String) returns a ServiceCall[NotUsed, User]. And
as discussed in
previous section, ServiceCall is ultimately a function `NotUsed
=>
Future[Used]`
```

The logic is straightforward. We search in our map for `userId` and return the `User` object for the requested `userId`. The implementation and logic for other methods is plain Scala code and is skipped here.

In our `friend-api` module, we defined our services. The `friend-impl` module is an implementation of the `friend-api` module, so we need to explicitly tell Lagom about this *relationship*. This is done with the following:

```
abstract class FriendModule (context: LagomApplicationContext)
extends LagomApplication(context)
  with AhcWSComponents {
    override lazy val lagomServer: LagomServer =
    serverFor[FriendService](wire[FriendServiceImpl])
  }
```

The `LagomApplication` class performs quite a few Lagom-centric things. The one relevant at this moment is:

- `LagomServerComponents.lagomServer`: This binds our *service declaration* with its *implementation*:

    ```
    override lazy val lagomServer = serverFor[FriendService]
    (wire[FriendServiceImpl])
    ```

- By performing `serverFor`, we provide a binding of the friend service and its descriptor with its implementation

In regards to our class `FriendModule`, apart from extending `LagomApplication`, it also mixes in the trait `AhcWSComponents`. `AhcWSComponents` is a Play Framework trait and it gives us `WSClient` to make HTTP calls.

Service locator

The role of a service locator is to provide the ability to discover application services and communicate with them. For example, if an application has five different microservices running, then each one would need to know the address of the other for the communication to be possible.

The service locator takes the responsibility of keeping the information regarding the address of the microservices concerned. In the absence of this service locator, we would need to configure the URL of each microservice and make it available to each microservice (this can be achieve via a properties file).

To know more about service locator, please refer:
https://www.lagomframework.com/documentation/1.3.x/scala/ServiceLocator.html

Our class `FriendModule` is an abstract class (not fully complete) because we have not yet provided it with the service locator (`LagomServiceClientComponents.serviceLocator`). A default implementation of the service locator is available in the trait `LagomDevModeComponents` for development usage, and in `ConductRApplicationComponents` for production usage.

```
class FriendApplicationLoader extends LagomApplicationLoader {
  override def loadDevMode(context: LagomApplicationContext):
  LagomApplication =
  new FriendModule(context) with LagomDevModeComponents

  override def load(context: LagomApplicationContext):
   LagomApplication =
  new FriendModule(context) with ConductRApplicationComponents
  override def describeService =
  Some(readDescriptor[FriendService])
}
```

Finally, we need to build `play.api.ApplicationLoader`. `ApplicationLoader` loads a context and instantiates the application. We provide two things in `FriendApplicationLoader`:

- A fully instantiated `LagomApplication`. Our subclass `FriendModule` is still abstract as we haven't provided it with a service locator (`LagomServiceClientComponents.serviceLocator`). We provide that using `LagomDevModeComponents`, which contains a simple implementation for a service locator in order to access other microservices.
- We read the descriptor of `FriendService`.

Last but not least, we need to tell Lagom to use our defined `FriendApplicationLoader` to load our application. This is done via a property in the `src/main/resources/application.conf` file:

```
play.application.loader =
sample.chirper.friend.impl.FriendApplicationLoader
```

We now have a fully functioning `FriendService` microservice available. We have defined the behaviors and we have also defined a service locator, which other services can use to access our friend service.

Akka Streams

Before we proceed, I will introduce some basics regarding Akka Streams. Lagom uses Akka Streams comprehensively, hence a basic understanding of Akka Streams is needed.

Akka Streams is a stream processing API. Simply put, with Akka Streams we write a set of functions where the output of one function is the input of another. We then simply flow the data through these functions. Akka Streams has three classes—Source, Sink, and Flow.

- **Source**: Source is a data creator. It creates data and passes it on to the downstream. A simple metaphor would be the case of a water tap. The tap provides water to whoever wishes to take it. To create a Source:

```
Source(List(1, 2, 3))

// Create a source from a single element
Source.single("element")// Create a source from a Future
Source.fromFuture(Future.successful("Hello!"))
```

- **Sink**: Sink is the opposite of Source. It consumes data. Please refer to the following code:

```
// A Sink that consumes a stream without doing anything with
the elements
Sink.ignore

// A Sink that prints every element of the stream
Sink.foreach[String](x => println(x))
```

- **Flow**: Flow connects a Source and a Sink. It connects the upstream and downstream applications by transforming the data passing through it. A real-life metaphor would be a water purifier. The tap provides water to the water purifier and the purifier purifies the water in real time before pushing it over to another tap (where the water can then be consumed for drinking):

```
import akka.actor.ActorSystem
import akka.stream.scaladsl._
import akka.stream.{ActorMaterializer, ClosedShape}implicit
val
  system = ActorSystem("TestSystem")
implicit val materializer = ActorMaterializer()
val source = Source(1 to 3)
val double = Flow[Int].map(elem => elem * 2)
val sink = Sink.foreach[Int](println)
val runnable = source via double to sink
runnable.run()
//this would print: 2 4 6
```

Akka Streams are reactive. They comply with the reactive-streams API (http://www.reactive-streams.org/). This means that they also offer back-pressure (a Flow control mechanism). In a normal use case, if the producer sends data at a faster rate than the consumer consuming the messages, then the messages may pile up at the consumer side and the buffer may overflow.

With back-pressure, the consumer signals the producer to lower the rate of transmission at a pace the consumer is comfortable with. The producer may have someone else streaming data to it, and hence would signal its producer to lower the data transmission pace, and so on. This leads to stabilization of the load.

To learn more about Akka Streams, please refer to http://doc.akka.io/docs/akka/snapshot/scala/stream/index.html.

Chirp service

The chirp service contains all of our tweets. The API is defined in the `chirp-api` module, which is like the `friend-api` module.

```
case class LiveChirpsRequest(userIds: Seq[String])

trait ChirpService extends Service {
  //(.........) other service declarations

  def getLiveChirps: ServiceCall[LiveChirpsRequest, Source[Chirp,
  NotUsed]]

  override def descriptor(): Descriptor = {
   import Service._

   named("chirpservice").withCalls(
     namedCall("/api/chirps/live", getLiveChirps _)
     ).withAutoAcl(true)
  }
}
```

Most of the services defined here are similar in signature to what we have previously done in `friend-api`. There is a new thing being introduced here:

```
def getLiveChirps: ServiceCall[LiveChirpsRequest, Source[Chirp,
NotUsed]]
```

The `getLiveChirps` service would expect JSON, which adheres to the format of the case class `LiveChirpsRequest` in the HTTP request body. In the response, the service returns a `Source[Chirp, NotUsed]`.

 This is the one place where Lagom simply shines exceedingly well. The `Source[]` here is `akka.stream.scaladsl.Source` from Akka Streams.

So, when we define:

```
def getLiveChirps: ServiceCall[LiveChirpsRequest, Source[Chirp,
NotUsed]]
```

The service returns a Source of chirps, and because a Source keeps creating data and pushing it down the stream until the data is exhausted, it will keep pushing chirps to the client. WebSockets are used to transmit the *source* of data. Please refer to the following points:

- If the request to a microservice was from a browser, Lagom will keep pushing chirps to the browser via a Web Socket
- If the request was from a Lagom Service, then the client would receive a Source and the client can then use Akka Stream operations over this source of stream
- If the request was from an external service (like a Ruby or Python service) via HTTP directly, then they can still access the stream contents using the web-socket API

In the `chirp-impl` module, which is an implementation of `chirp-api`, we again need to provide `LagomApplicationLoader`, as we did with the `friend-impl` module.

`ChirpServiceImpl.java` contains the implementation of `chirp-api`. We simply maintain all the chirps of all users in a single list:

```
private var allChirps = List[Chirp]()
```

The implementations of other service calls are pretty straightforward:

- Once we receive a chirp, we add it to our list and *publish* the chirp to all *subscribers* of that user
- When a call is made to `getLiveChirps` with a list of user IDs, we obtain a Source of chirps, chirped by the user, and live concatenate them with other users; this provides a live stream of all the chirps the user requested.

Activity Stream

We finally need to club our friend and chirp microservices together to have a working application. When a user logs in to his account and accesses his feed, the user expects the feed to contain all of the user's chirps and chirps of the user's friends. This live Source of the feed is provided by Activity Stream.

`activity-stream-api` needs to access `FriendService` and `ChirpService`. It needs to access `FriendService` to get the user's friend list, and it needs `ChirpService` to access chirps of respective users.

Because it would be making service calls to the preceding microservices, we need to declare this dependency in its dependency list in `build.sbt` file:

```
//build.sbt
lazy val activityStreamImpl = project("activity-stream-impl")
.enablePlugins(LagomScala)
.settings(
  version := "1.0-SNAPSHOT",
  libraryDependencies ++= Seq(
    lagomScaladslTestKit,
    macwire
  )
)
.dependsOn(activityStreamApi, chirpApi, friendApi)
```

This represents its reliance on the service declarations of `chirp-api` and `friend-api`.

Here is the service declaration:

```
trait ActivityStreamService extends Service {

def getLiveActivityStream(userId: String): ServiceCall[NotUsed,
  Source[Chirp, NotUsed]]

def getHistoricalActivityStream(userId: String):
  ServiceCall[NotUsed, Source[Chirp, NotUsed]]

override def descriptor(): Descriptor = {
  import Service._

  named("activityservice").withCalls(
  pathCall("/api/activity/:userId/live", getLiveActivityStream
  _),
  pathCall("/api/activity/:userId/history",
  getHistoricalActivityStream _)
  ).withAutoAcl(true)
  }
}
```

`getLiveActivityStream` expects a user ID and returns a live Source that would generate chirps corresponding to all the user's chirps and the user's friends.

`activity-stream-impl` contains the implementation for the preceding service, defined as follows:

```
class ActivityStreamServiceImpl (
friendService: FriendService,
chirpService: ChirpService) (implicit ec: ExecutionContext)
extends
ActivityStreamService {

  override def getLiveActivityStream(userId: String):
  ServiceCall[NotUsed, Source[Chirp, NotUsed]] = {
  req =>
   for {
     user <- friendService.getUser(userId).invoke()
     userIds = user.friends :+ userId
     chirpsReq = LiveChirpsRequest(userIds)
     chirps <- chirpService.getLiveChirps.invoke(chirpsReq)
    } yield chirps
  }
 }
```

A few interesting things to note are as follows:

- `ActivityStreamServiceImpl` expects constructor arguments to access `FriendService` and `ChirpService`.
- In the implementation for the `getLiveActivityStream` method:
  - To obtain the `User` object from `FriendService`, we invoke the API with the following:

    `user <- friendService.getUser(userId).invoke()`
    In the background, an **HTTP call is made to the Friend Microservice**.

- We obtain the live chirps for all the friends of the user and the user itself with the following:
  `chirps <- chirpService.getLiveChirps.invoke(chirpsReq)`
  `chirps` is of type `Source[Chirp,_]` as `getLiveChirps` returns us a Source of chirp.

We need to provide the class `ActivityStreamServiceImpl` with the client for `FriendService` and `ChirpService`. This is provided via a dependency injection in `ActivityStreamModule.scala`:

```
abstract class ActivityStreamModule (context:
LagomApplicationContext)
```

```
extends LagomApplication(context)
with AhcWSComponents {
  lazy val friendService : FriendService =
  serviceClient.implement[FriendService]
  lazy val chirpService : ChirpService
  = serviceClient.implement[ChirpService]

  override lazy val lagomServer = serverFor[ActivityStreamService]
    (wire[ActivityStreamServiceImpl])
}
```

By performing *serviceClient*.implement[FriendService], we obtain a handle to access the Friend Microservice programmatically in a RPC-like manner. Finally, we ultimately wire up the service defined with its implementation using serverFor.

Frontend

We now have all our microservices defined. We simply need to expose our UI application. The UI application that exposes our website is written in Play.

We have defined our front-end project here. Because this is a Play project, we need to include the PlayScala plugin:

```
build.sbt
lazy val frontEnd = project("front-end")
.enablePlugins(PlayScala, LagomPlay)
.settings(
  version := "1.0-SNAPSHOT",
  routesGenerator := StaticRoutesGenerator,
  libraryDependencies ++= Seq(
  "org.webjars" % "react" % "0.14.3",
  "org.webjars" % "react-router" % "1.0.3",
  "org.webjars" % "jquery" % "2.2.0",
  "org.webjars" % "foundation" % "5.3.0",
  macwire,
  lagomScaladslServer
  ),
  ReactJsKeys.sourceMapInline := true
)
```

We also need the LagomPlay plugin for our Play application in order *to access other microservices using the service locator, as well as register itself with the service registry in Lagom's dev mode.*

Another line of importance in the previous snippet is `routesGenerator :=`
`StaticRoutesGenerator`. By default, Play 2.5 uses `InjectedRoutesGenerator`, which
is based on Guice for dependency injection. Because we are using Macwire for DI, we need
to explicitly provide `StaticRoutesGenerator`. You wouldn't need to do this if you were
using Guice.

Our UI code is based on ReactJS (`https://facebook.github.io/react/`).

Through chapters 2-4 in our book, we were using Guice for dependency injection. With
Lagom, we used Macwire for compile time dependency injection. Our *frontend* is a Play
application that uses Macwire for DI instead of Guice. (It is important to use Guice because
we need to integrate our Play app with Lagom apps, which are based on Macwire.)

If we were using Macwire for DI in building Play applications, then we would need to
manually provide `ApplicationLoader`:

```
abstract class FrontEndModule(context: Context) extends
BuiltInComponentsFromContext(context)
with I18nComponents
with AhcWSComponents
with LagomServiceClientComponents {

  override lazy val serviceInfo: ServiceInfo = ServiceInfo(
  "front-end",
  Map(
   "front-end" -> immutable.Seq(ServiceAcl.forPathRegex("
   (?!/api/).*"))
  )
 )

  override implicit lazy val executionContext: ExecutionContext =
  actorSystem.dispatcher
  override lazy val router = {
    wire[Routes]
  }
}
```

The first difference is the `serviceInfo` defined. This provides the name of the service,
which is **front-end**. It also provides the **Access Control Rules (ACL)** that only allow us to
make calls with the `/api/` prefix.

We then explicitly set the `router` by accessing `router.Routes`. Our `ApplicationLoader` is provided in the following way:

```
class FrontEndLoader extends ApplicationLoader {
  override def load(context: Context) = context.environment.mode
    match {
      case Mode.Dev =>
      (new FrontEndModule(context) with
      LagomDevModeComponents).application

    //(......)
    }
  }
```

Last but not least, we need to tell Play to use our custom loader. This is done by adding a property in the `application.conf` file:

```
play.application.loader = FrontEndLoader
```

Running the application

Now that we have seen all our microservices, let's run the application using the following command:

```
sbt runAll
```

The application will be accessible at the default port `http://localhost:9000/`.

On running the application, you will observe similar logs to those in the following screenshot:

```
> runAll
[info] Kafka won't be started because the build setting `lagomKafkaEnabled` is set to `false`
[info] Cassandra won't be started because the build setting `lagomCassandraEnabled` is set to `false`
2017-08-25T20:12:33.059Z [info] akka.event.slf4j.Slf4jLogger [] - Slf4jLogger started
2017-08-25T20:12:39.465Z [info] com.lightbend.lagom.discovery.ServiceLocatorServer [] - Service locator can be reached at http://localhost:8000
2017-08-25T20:12:39.467Z [info] com.lightbend.lagom.discovery.ServiceLocatorServer [] - Service gateway can be reached at http://localhost:9000
[info] Service locator is running at http://localhost:8000
[info] Service gateway is running at http://localhost:9000
01:42:51.769 [info] play.core.server.NettyServer [] - Listening for HTTP on /0:0:0:0:0:0:0:0:51855
01:42:51.803 [info] play.core.server.NettyServer [] - Listening for HTTP on /0:0:0:0:0:0:0:0:60399
01:42:51.849 [info] play.core.server.NettyServer [] - Listening for HTTP on /0:0:0:0:0:0:0:0:57143
01:42:51.932 [info] play.core.server.NettyServer [] - Listening for HTTP on /0:0:0:0:0:0:0:0:54485
01:42:58.084 [info] akka.event.slf4j.Slf4jLogger [] - Slf4jLogger started
01:43:02.439 [info] akka.event.slf4j.Slf4jLogger [] - Slf4jLogger started
01:43:03.134 [info] play.api.Play [] - Application started (Dev)
```

A few points to note:

- Each microservice is running on a different port, so these microservices can't always be directly accessed, as they don't have a stable port.
- The main service gateway will be running on port 9000. All the incoming requests will be routed via port 9000. The HTTP call would be forwarded to the respective microservice depending on the URL.
- Service locator is running on port 8000. Service locator is needed for microservices in order to access other microservices (using the client).

Multi project builds

In our application, we had a single project that defined multiple sub-projects, so a single project contained definitions and implementations of all our microservices. This has a few advantages—it is much easier to include the Lagom Service API's definitions of a microservice as dependencies with other microservices.

However, if there are more people working on the same project, then it can become tedious for multiple developers. In which case, each microservice can be a separate independent SBT project of its own. However, the `service-api` definition's JARs would need to be uploaded to a Maven repository and shared with other teams.

With Lagom, you can take any approach. You can start with a single project approach and later split it to multiple projects if the need arises. If you split your application into multiple builds, the following doc might be helpful—`https://www.lagomframework.com/documentation/1.3.x/scala/MultipleBuilds.html`.

Summary

In this chapter, we gave you an overview of Lagom by building a simple Twitter-like application. We had a look at its service API, and the mechanism to call other Lagom microservices using its service client.

We also had a brief look at the importance of service gateway and service locator, and how Lagom makes life easier by integrating them as part of the framework.

In the next chapter, we will learn on how to model data for highly interactive applications by using CQRS and Event Sourcing.

7
CQRS and Event Sourcing

In this chapter, we will learn about modelling data with a design pattern called **Command Query Responsibility Segregation (CQRS)** and Event Sourcing. We will introduce these concepts in a general fashion so that they could be applied directly or by using some other API and not Lagom.

In the second half of the chapter, we will introduce the Lagom Persistence API. Lagom Persistence API is a Lagom API for Event Sourcing and CQRS implementation.

CQRS and Event Sourcing have a lot of literature associated with them and it is beyond the scope of this book to cover them in depth. Hence, we would only be providing a reasonable overview to help us get started. For more information on CQRS, please refer `https://cqrs.files.wordpress.com/2010/11/cqrs_documents.pdf`.

In this chapter, we will be covering the following topics:

- Data modelling
- Event sourcing and CQRS
- Lagom persistence API

Data modelling

We all love **Create Read Update Delete (CRUD)** system (`https://en.wikipedia.org/wiki/Create,_read,_update_and_delete`) when dealing with persistent storage. It is simple, easy to understand and maintain. It has stood the test of time and it works.

There is nothing wrong with CRUD and it should be used if the solves the problem in an elegant manner. But there are scenarios when data modelling with CRUD does create problems and we need to equip ourselves to use the appropriate design to fix our need.

Bounded context

As a small project grows bigger, the domain that was initially modeled starts meaning different things in different scenarios. Each domain model is only sensible in certain limits within a system. For example, in an e-commerce application, during the initial stages of the company, the website sold products online. So, the information associated with the product was--barcode, price, product details and other meta information.

As the company grew bigger, the word product started getting associated with multiple domains. And in each context, it needed to be modelled as per the business rules of that context. For example:

- **Sales context**: Sales teams need extensive product information and pictures. The product could be made part of a bonus program or associate a coupon with that product. The **Key Performance Indicators** (**KPI**) of the product and its marketing and advertisement on social media platforms or newspaper advertisements. Sales teams could have their job bonus associated with the sales of a product.
  The delivery mechanism of the product via respective couriers.
  All the preceding scenarios would need modelling when dealing with a Product
- **Accounting context**: Modelling with respect to billing, tax rates, tax concerns of the place being delivered to. If the sale was due to a referral program, then referrer needs to be modelled as part of the context.
  The delivery address of the customer and the preferred delivery service to account to any region taxes.

The rich product information is not needed by this context. Neither is the promotion related information as was needed by the Sales context.

- **Support context**: Any refund requested for the product or a complaint raised. Manufacturing defects and associating the product from its procured warehouse.
- And others

The product is intended to be used and modeled differently in each context. And the same would apply for things such as Customer. The billing, sales, support team would need to model `customer` as per their own domain and each context would have their own set of rules and schema. In object-oriented sense, a different `customer` and `order` class *may* be needed in each different context.

It's not simple to just create a product table in a relational data store and build foreign keys to it. Different domains need their own modelling so that the domain is effectively modeled. Different teams in the company will have different vocabularies as part of their domain. And the precise meaning of each entity will start to mean different things to different teams, usually leading to confusion.

Having a single unified model that covers all domains is hard to build and scale. In finance, the word *trade* often means differently. It could mean an equity trade, a bond trade, a swap agreement (there are hundreds of different swap types), currency trade. Each division in a company will have different meaning associated with a trade. And even the same equity trade would mean differently to the front office desk, compliance team, back office and accounting team.

Eric Evans who coined the term Domain Driven Design puts it in his book *Domain-Driven Design: Tackling Complexity in the Heart of Software*:

> *To communicate effectively, the code must be based on the same language used to write the requirements-the same language that the developers speak with each other and with domain experts.*

This means that the business must be effectively modelled for the success of the software. He further adds as:

> *Total unification of the domain model for a large system will not be feasible or cost-effective.*

Because it is difficult to have a single model for large systems, we divide our modelling into multiple **bounded contexts.**

Bounded context--The term *bounded context* comes from Eric Evans' book. In brief, Evans introduces this concept as a way to decompose a large, complex system into more manageable pieces; a large system is composed of multiple bounded contexts. Each bounded context is the context for its own self-contained domain model, and has its own ubiquitous language. You can also view a bounded context as an autonomous business component defining clear consistency boundaries--one bounded context typically communicates with another bounded context by raising events.

Source--https://msdn.microsoft.com/en-us/library/jj591575.aspx

We define our bounded contexts and explicitly specify the inter-relationships between them. Like in our e-commerce example earlier, we had multiple bounded contexts-- accounting, sales, support and each modeled its data as per its business definition. And they interacted with each other in a well-defined manner. They could all be part of a single application or be different and that is immaterial, till the time they are modeled as per their business requirement rather than one gigantic model.

We have already been following this approach by building microservices where microservices are formulated by their bounded context. Each bounded context might be implemented in different architectures. One may use a two-tier CRUD and the other microservice may use CQRS design pattern.

 Note--There is no direct relation between bounded contexts and microservices. Microservices are about architecture and bounded contexts is about classes, objects and the interaction between them. One could have a one to one mapping in between them, or a bounded context could be implemented by multiple microservices, or have a single application dealing with multiple domains.

Domain-driven design

Bounded contexts has its origins in the paradigm Domain-driven design. There are a few simple terminologies that we need to become aware of (as they would be frequently used by Lagom Persistence API):

- **Entities**: Entities are objects that are defined by their identity. For example, in an e-commerce site, a user is an entity.
  Many of the user attributes could change with time (address, payment details), but each user is a unique identity.
- **Value objects**: Objects that are completely defined by their attributes. For example--Date, Money, Address. Usually these are immutable.
  A specific Date is a value object as it is entirely defined by the value of the date it represents. A different date has a different value and, therefore, is a different object. And therefore, they are usually immutable. Changing the value of a value object turns it into a different object.
- **Services**: An operation within the context of domain. For example, a payment service that takes user credit card information and obtains money. Usually the services are stateless (unlike entities and value objects)

- **Aggregate**: Aggregate is a cluster of domain objects that can be treated as a single unit. For example, a music playlist, an e-commerce order.
  We usually load or save aggregates. A user wishes to see its order history and we provide a list of orders (aggregates) where each order would contain information like: the delivery address, mode of delivery, payment details, cancellation charges.
  Eric Evans puts it as:

An aggregate is like grapes, in the sense that you have something you think of as a conceptual whole, which is also made up of smaller parts. You have rules that apply to the whole thing. So, every one of those grapes is part of a grape bunch.

- **Aggregate root:** Each aggregate has a root and a boundary. The boundary defines what is inside the aggregate. The root is a single, specific entity contained in the aggregate.
  Evans describes it as:

The stem is the root of an aggregate, berries are objects in the aggregate but the grape as a whole is an aggregate. The weight of the grape is a property of the whole aggregate (grape), not of the aggregate root (stem).

In case of an order from e-commerce site, an order by a customer would have the payment information associated with it. It would not make sense from outside to just gain access to this payment information without the overall picture that the payment was associated with that order by a customer. So, the customer entity associated with the payment entity (along with other entities) constitute to form an aggregate (order) with the customer being an aggregate root.
Using the customer entity, if it is root of other aggregates (customer settings for example), one can access the aggregate using the root.

These are simple concepts with complex terms (Just like many things in computer science). And they are extensively used in the DDD literature and in Lagom Persistence API

Now that we understand the basic terminologies of domain driven design, lets introduce another uncomplicated design pattern (but with a complicated name) called Event Sourcing.

Event Sourcing

Simply put Event Sourcing is:

Storing a series of events and rebuilding a state within the system by replaying that series of events

So, we maintain an event store (either in a relational database or a document store like Mongo or some other NoSQL database) and keep appending the events generated by the system to the same store. Hence to calculate the current state, we play all the events generated.

For example, in the case of an airline ticketing system, that keeps track of the tickets sold and available for an airline, if a user requests to book tickets on a flight, the system would check the current tickets available. And if there are spare seats available, it would book them for the user. The system would also keep track of the cancellations. There can be two ways of designing such a system:

- We maintain the current spare seat count in an integer (or in a row in database). When a ticket is sanctioned, we decrease the count and update the variable (database row). When a ticket is cancelled, we read the count from the database (or variable) and increase the count.
  In short, we maintain the final summary of the count and keep updating it.
- Alternative way could be to--store all the booking and cancellation events for the flight and then calculate the number of spare seats available by replaying all the events and ultimately generating the spare seat count.
  Suppose the system received 3 events for the same flight:

Book 1 Ticket for seat 1A
Book 2 Tickets for seat 1D, 1E
Cancel 1 Ticket for seat 1A
Now if a new command is received as Book 1 Ticket for seat 1A, the system would replay all the events received till now, understand that the seat 1A is available and append the newly received event in the same order.

In short, the system will query events by an aggregate id (the flight id in this case), and append the newly received event to it. (Every aggregate has a unique id)

Note--As an optimization, we don't need to replay all the events every time and we could cache them and preserve the final state of the aggregate in memory. When a new event is received, we append the event to our event store, and play that event to the existing cached in-memory state. Hence the application state gets updated.

But from the persistence layer side, the modelling is quite simple. We don't update/delete any entry but simply keep appending logs.

All the state changes in your aggregates are recorded as events. By replaying stream of events (associated with an aggregate), you can recreate the latest state of aggregate.

By doing this, our data model is simple as we only append events. To generate the current state, we simply must replay all the events.

Advantages of Event Sourcing

The advantages are:

- **Simplicity of data model**: No need to maintain complex objects and updating relationships between them. Even from the relational tables side, there isn't a need to build tables with complex relationship constraints in between them.
- **No need of ORM**: With ORM, once the variable is updated in the object, the value is pushed down to the database. Without ORM, this needs to be managed manually where we first update the value in database and then read it back. In both the cases, the values need to be kept in synced across the object state and the database persisted value. The synchronization/locking would be needed. With event sourcing, this gets eliminated.
- Intact complete history. The audit of all booking/cancellations requests are available for free.
  In the case of first scenario (updating the count), this is not freely available as we don't maintain audit trail. And even if we maintained, we would need to mechanically make sure that the audit trail matches with the final update counter that we maintained. So, there is duplication involved.
  With the second case (storing events), the audit trail is the golden source of truth

With bank accounts, for modelling accounts and all the transactions, event sourcing is usually preferred.

> *The primary benefit of using event sourcing is a built-in audit mechanism that ensures consistency of transactional data and audit data because these are the same data. Representation via events allows you to reconstruct the state of any object at any moment in time.*
>
> *-Paweł Wilkosz (Customer Advisory Council)*

- **Writes performance**: Because we only append events, the writing to the storage is fast when compared to complex relational storage mechanisms
- **Scalability**: We append to the event store. There is no need to run transactions, and update multiple tables when making an entry.

- **Integration with other subsystems**: Once the event is appended, we communicate the event to other systems to update application state.
  One can use an event raised by an aggregate to notify interested parties that a transaction (consistent set of updates) has taken place on that group of entities.
- **Analysis**: We can analyze the audit trail to obtain interesting business insights based on the events at any given point of time.
  Secondly by storing events as and when we receive, we are not losing any information that may be lost when persisting in relational models (as we may not persist some information not required then but may be needed in future).
  With event sourcing, we obtain the above both for free.
- **Debugging**: If there is an application bug in production, generating a skewed state. It is simple to debug as we just must replay the production events in a test environment and obtain the cause for incorrect state.
  Post the bug fix, when we redeploy the application, the application can come back to the latest state by replaying all the events received.
- **Testing**: All the state changes in your aggregates are recorded as events. You can test expected effect by a command on an aggregate simply checking for the event

The Event Streams can be persisted in any form. They can be persisted in a SQL table or as a JSON in Mongo DB.

A few notes on Event Sourcing:

- Event Sourcing provides fast update speeds. But we also mentioned that we maintain the current state in memory by playing events. And when a system reboots/object-loading, it replays all the events to obtain latest state. But this can be a time-consuming process.
  One way of dealing with this problem is to store snapshots. One can preserve snapshots in some timely fashion (daily/weekly). During bootup, one can access the latest snapshot and replay all the events post the snapshot to obtain the latest state.
- Because the data is simply stored as a queue of events, one can't directly query: get me all orders greater than 10$ on 13th May for an aggregate.
  We would need to build services, to obtain such data. CQRS can be helpful in such scenarios and we will witness this shortly.

Event

Qualities of an Event:

- Events must be immutable
- Events are one-way messages. They have only one source. One or multiple recipients can receive them
- Events should be complete and thoroughly describe business information
- Events have some standard metadata associated with them such as aggregate id (in case of airline ticketing system, the aggregate id would be an id associated with a flight number on a date), version number of event (for updates) and the event information itself.
  So, if you are storing events in a SQL table, the aggregate id would be the key.
- Consistency--When an event is received, we append to our store and publish the event to update the application state. So, both the operations must succeed. If the appending succeeds but publishing fails, then this can lead to inconsistent state. We would need to make both the operations part of a transaction to remain consistent. Though not many technologies offer such a transaction mechanism spanning across data store and message publisher. We will deal with these scenarios in `Chapter 8`, *Effective Communication*.
  A good read on this topic can be found at: *your coffee shop doesn't use two-phase commit* `http://www.enterpriseintegrationpatterns.com/docs/IEEE_Software_Design_2PC.pdf` by Martin Fowler.

To learn more about Event Sourcing, I suggest reading the below references:

- Greg Young's `http://codebetter.com/gregyoung/2010/02/20/why-use-event-sourcing/` is a very quick and simple read on Event Sourcing
- `https://msdn.microsoft.com/en-us/library/jj591559.aspx` provides an extensive and a very satisfying explanation of Event Sourcing and its challenges

Now that we have covered Event Sourcing briefly, let us look at another design pattern called **CQRS**. Note--CQRS and Event Sourcing have no relation with each other and are distinct design patterns.

CQRS

CQRS stands for **Command Query Responsibility Segregation**. Greg Young has coined this term and most of the literature on the internet regarding CQRS would be associated with him.

In the simplest sense, consider the following scenario:

```scala
UserService.scala
trait UserService{
  def createUser(user: User): Unit
  def editUser(details: UserDetails): Unit
  def deleteUser(user:User): Unit
  def getUser(userId: Int): User
  def getUserFromName(name: String): User
  def getUserPreferences(userId:Int): UserPreference
}
```

We have a `UserService` that declares calls to `create/get/update` users. Applying CQRS would result in splitting `UserService` into two separate services:

```scala
trait UserReadService {
  def getUser(userId: Int): User
  def getUserFromName(name: String): User
  def getUserPreferences(userId: Int): UserPreference
}

trait UserWriteService {
  def createUser(user: User): Unit
  def editUser(details: UserDetails): Unit
  def deleteUser(user: User): Unit
}
```

We have fundamentally segregated the write calls with read calls. We have segregated commands with queries.

- **Command:** Command changes the state of an object and does not return any data. Command is any method that mutates state.
  Example: Book Seat A1, A2 on flight XX 1234.
- **Query:** Queries return data and does not alter the state of the object.
  Example: Get available seats on the flight XX 1234.

The essence of CQRS is to split our service based on commands and queries. In short segregating based on reads and writes.

> *CQRS is simply the creation of two objects where there was previously only one. The separation occurs based upon whether the methods are a command or a query (the same definition that is used by Meyer in Command and Query Separation: a command is any method that mutates state and a query is any method that returns a value).*
> *-Greg Young,* http://codebetter.com/gregyoung/2010/02/16/cqrs-task-based-uis-event-sourcing-agh/

CQRS is fundamentally a very simple pattern. We segregate reads and writes. When we perform reads, no side effects occur. In REST terminology, a query corresponds to a GET call and a command corresponds to PUT, POST and DELETE requests.

This simplicity of segregating commands and queries enables us to build richer and scalable applications.

CQRS example

Consider the following scenario:

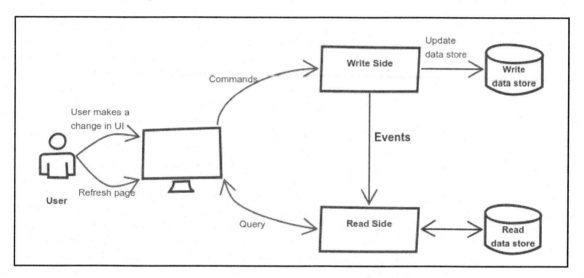

1. The user updates the UI and does an operation that demands a mutation of state
2. A command is sent to write side
3. The write side:
   - Updates its data store regarding the *command*. It may be using a schema model best suited for its needs like a relational storage. The schema usually chosen is decided for faster writes
   - The write side, will generate an *event*/notification like Seat 1A has been booked by Foo for flight XX 1234. The event is forwarded to the read side

4. The read side receives the event and persists the event information in any data model that would make any subsequent reads faster. Note that the role of read side is to process all queries and respond with requested data. So, it is extremely important that the reads are efficient and the data model must be designed accordingly.

When an event is received, the information is persisted in its store

Event: Events are notifications that report something has already happened. Events are a way of syncing the changes on the write-side (effects generated due to a processing commands) with the read-side. When a write side pushes an event, the read side should update data on its side.

An event is an undisputed fact. Just like in the world, events occur irrevocably.
The state of the world is the consequence of the events.

We send commands to A. And A gets a new state

Events can be processed multiple times by multiple consumers.

Later when a user refreshes the page or requests for latest information, a Query call is made to the read side. (In our case, once the read side receives an event, it could even push the UI change directly to the user instead of relying on the user to refresh)

In case of both read sides and the write sides:

- Each data store is optimized for its own respective use case. Write side for faster writes. Read side for faster reads. Each side is optimized for its respective role. For example, write side may store data in 3rd Normalized Form and the read side in denormalized form to avoid joins.
  Moreover: the read side could be separately scaled to support faster reads (launching multiple instances?) without affecting the write side
  Note: In usual CRUD based applications, reads and writes effectively happen on the same set of tables. If there are more writes happening (may be as part of transactions), then the reads are affected. It is difficult to design tables to achieve both: faster reads and writes in CRUD based applications.
- Commands involve complex business level operations. To ensure consistency of data, the operation may be wrapped as part of transactions and may involve updating multiple tables. Whereas the read side may have an uncomplicated design structure. By segregating them, it is easier to design and maintain systems. In case of CRUD, transactions can significantly impact the read side. In CRUD systems, read and writes are not mutually exclusive.

So, it is apparent that this newer design looks more efficient from a performance perspective. Here are some further advantages:

- **Scale**: In many systems, the number of reads outperform the number of writes. By designing for faster reads on the read side, it is faster to respond back to queries.
- **Modelling complex domains**: Designing large data models to comprise reading and writing can be very complex. With CQRS we are splitting the data modelling based on reads and writes separately making it easier to reason about in each respective case. Martin Fowler, explains it as (`https://martinfowler.com/bliki/CommandQuerySeparation.html`)

    - *The really valuable idea in this principle is that it's extremely handy if you can clearly separate methods that change state from those that don't. This is because you can use queries in many situations with much more confidence, introducing them anywhere, changing their order. You have to be more careful with modifiers.*

- **Faster functionalities**: By segregating reads, if a requirement arises to build a new query service, then it would be quick to build it without impacting the business logic. The same applies on the write side.
- **Distribution**: Larger applications can be split across multiple machines with reads and writes on different machines and events are transmitted via message brokers.
    For scalability, there can be multiple instances of reads side servers and each one would receive an event from the write side. This makes the read side scalable and highly available. (Lagom provides this ability and we explore this concept in `Chapter 8`, *Effective Communication*)

 Note--Performance should not be the only reason is choosing CQRS. Modern SQL vendors like MySQL, SQL Server, PostgreSQL offers replication and one can add horizontally more database servers to support more users.

Pain points with CQRS

Of-course the advantages that come with CQRS also come with additional costs.

- There is additional complexity associated with maintaining separate read side and write side. And the communication from the write side to the read side
- What happens when the write side persists the data but fails in forwarding to the read side? Or the medium via which the events are transferred (may be broker) is down
- What if there is a delay in transfer of events from the write to read side
- And other human related costs like: Steep learning curve.

Some of these problems can be solved with **Eventual Consistency.** We say that the read side will be eventually consistent over time with the write side. In case of delays, they may be out of sync but eventually would get synced.

CQRS is not cheap and should only be used when appropriate.

When should CQRS be avoided?

Not every bounded context needs to be modelled in CQRS fashion.

> *So, when should you avoid CQRS?*
>
> *The answer is most of the time.*
> - *Udi Dahan* (http://udidahan.com/2011/04/22/when-to-avoid-cqrs/)

In most systems, most bounded contexts will not benefit from CQRS pattern. One must only use when one can the see clear benefits. In most of the cases such as simple domains, CRUD should be good enough.

> *In general, applying the CQRS pattern may provide the most value in those bounded contexts that are* **collaborative, complex,** *include* **ever-changing business rules,** *and deliver a significant competitive advantage to the business. Analyzing the business requirements, building a useful model, expressing it in code, and implementing it using the CQRS pattern for such a bounded context all take time and cost money. You should expect this investment to pay dividends in the medium to long term. It is probably not worth making this investment if you don't expect to see returns such as increased adaptability and flexibility in the system, or reduced maintenance costs.*
>
> - https://msdn.microsoft.com/en-us/library/jj591573.aspx

A simple example could be a social networking site, where people may like other posts, comments, share their own images and so on. It is highly collaborative across bunded contexts, with multiple concurrently accessing and mutating state at the same time, scaling at massive levels.

> *"In a collaborative domain, an inherent property of the domain is that multiple actors operate in parallel on the same set of data. A reservation system for concerts would be a good example of a collaborative domain; everyone wants the good seats."*
> -*Udi Dahan,* `http://udidahan.com/2011/10/02/why-you-should-be-using-cqrs-almost-everywhere/`

The benefits of CQRS is that it enables to focus on bounded contexts that are complex, subject to ever-changing business rules.

A final crucial point regarding CQRS:

CQRS is not a top level architectural approach that encompasses the whole application. It is rather associated with a **bounded context**. So CQRS should be applied within a specific bounded context, rather than at the entire system level, unless the entire system is just one single bounded context.

So, an application can have multiple bounded contexts and one of them could be based on CRUD and the other on CQRS.

Another point to note is that: The read-side and write-side could use different persistence storage mechanisms. Or they could both use the same database server. The only thing relevant is that their data should be in different schema's and not dependent on each other.

Event Sourcing and CQRS

Event sourcing and Command Query Responsibility Segregation are frequently mentioned together. Although neither one necessarily implies the other, but they do complement each other.

In our CQRS explanation, we had observed the following diagram:

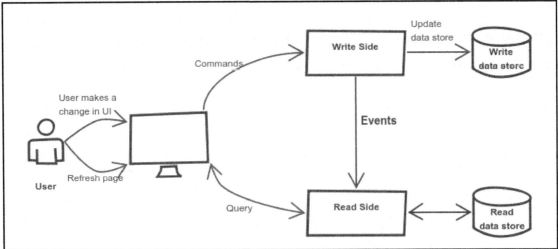

Events in a way act as synchronization of data on the write-side with the read-side. Once the data is synced with the read side, the read side stores the data in a fashion that makes it very fast to read (denomalized data?).

We could improvise our model by including Event Sourcing in the picture. On the write side, when a command is received, instead of persisting data in its own data model. The write side would generate events, append it to its event store and finally push it towards the read side.

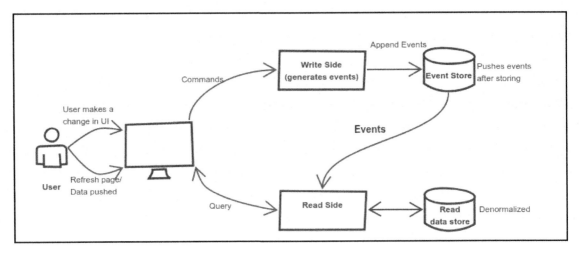

The write side manages the event side, and pushes all the updates made on the write-side as events towards the read side so that the read side could be in sync.

> *Using Event Sourcing does not change the architecture above much, the primary difference is that we have an Event Store holding the events to rebuild an object behind the domain as opposed to something storing the current state.*
> *- Greg Young* http://codebetter.com/gregyoung/2010/02/20/ why-use-event-sourcing/

As you can observe, event sourcing is not the only way to act as a sync between the write side and the read side.

The read side will be in sync in almost real time. One can also rebuild the read side by replaying the events from the event store on the write-side. Replaying is sometimes helpful in cases when the read side ran out of sync or the read side went down or the read side was manually updated. This is only possible by the fact that the write side is the sole source of truth, and the read side is just a projection of it to the outside world.

Though you would need to be careful with *replaying* if the read side is a source of data to other bounded contexts. As the other bounded contexts may treat it as duplicate events. So it all depends on how we set the contract.

There is no constraint on what technology you use to persist your data. The write side and the read side are isolated to use the persistence storage of their own preference. Or they could both be part of the same storage under different schemas.

Conclusion

CQRS and Event Sourcing nicely complement each other. And they could be implemented using no special framework using a general-purpose programming language. Microsoft developer network has comprehensive literature on this topic: https://msdn.microsoft. com/en-us/library/jj591560.aspx

Lagom comes with Lagom Persistence API that lets us implement CQRS and Event Sourcing in a simple fashion. In the next section, we will explore this API to have a simple implementation up and running.

Lagom Persistence API

The Lagom Persistence API offers us a framework to implement CQRS with Event Sourcing lucidly, and it is backed by a persistence storage to store events.

To persist data (event store), Lagom provides support for Cassandra database out of the box. For faster development, Cassandra is started when Lagom applications starts. Though you are free to use other databases--PostgreSQL, MySQL, Oracle & H2 with Lagom. To use a relational database instead of Cassandra, refer to `https://www.lagomframework.com/documentation/1.3.x/scala/PersistentEntityRDBMS.html`.

We will continue with the `chirper-app` we built in the previous chapter. You can find the full source of this chapter in the git branch of the repository in chapter-8 (`https://github.com/scala-microservices-book/book-examples/tree/chapter-8/chirper-app`).

In this chapter, we will use Cassandra for persistence.

Getting started with setup

You would need to make changes in the `build.sbt` file. The dependency `lagomScaladslPersistenceCassandra` would need to be added. For example, in case of `chirp-impl`:

```
//build.sbt
lazy val chirpImpl = project("chirp-impl")
    .enablePlugins(LagomScala)
    .settings(
      version := "1.0-SNAPSHOT",
        libraryDependencies ++= Seq(
          lagomScaladslPubSub,
          lagomScaladslTestKit,
          lagomScaladslPersistenceCassandra,
           macwire
        )
    )
```

Similarly, the dependency is added in other modules wherever needed. We also need to enable Cassandra on startup (this is by default, but we had disabled it in previous chapters):

```
lagomCassandraEnabled in ThisBuild := true

// do not delete database files on start
lagomCassandraCleanOnStart in ThisBuild := false
```

Managing Friends with CQRS

We'll implement the **friend-impl** microservice to use CQRS and Event Sourcing. The role of `friend-impl` is to create users and provide facility to add friends.

Previously, we were maintaining the user's information along with their friends simply in a Map data structure. Now, we will preserve this information as an Event Store in Cassandra and segregating our read and write side activities.

Here is a brief flow of the behavior:

1. When Lagom receives a command (for example, create user):

   - If it was a valid command, a respective event is generated. And another response object (success) is sent back to the caller.
   - If it was an invalid command, the caller is responded with a failure message

2. Once the event is generated, the event is persisted in the event store

   The preceding operation corresponds to the write-side activity we learnt in previous sections:

   - The generated event is then used to update the application state.

So there are 3 data types that we need to declare--**Command**, **Event** and **State**

Command

We will define all our commands as follows:

```
sealed trait FriendCommand

case class CreateUserCommand(user: User) extends
  PersistentEntity.ReplyType[Done] with FriendCommand
case class GetUser() extends
  PersistentEntity.ReplyType[GetUserReply] with FriendCommand

case class AddFriend(friendUserId: String) extends
  PersistentEntity.ReplyType[Done] with FriendCommand
//query
case class GetUserReply(user: Option[User])
```

Lagom, for example, will receive `CreateUserCommand(user)` from the caller (as a JSON and later deserialized to object by Lagom). `CreateUserCommand` extends `PersistentEntity.ReplyType[Done]`. This represents that:

- When a create user command is received, then the caller needs to be sent a message `Done` if the operation was a success

- This is primarily for compiler type checking. When the service returns, the compiler type checks to see if the correct type was returned

Similarly, we will create other commands--`GetUser` and `AddFriend`.

We also create a `case class GetUserReply` that is responded back when a request is made for the command `GetUser`. Of course, `GetUserReply` does not extend `FriendCommand` because it is only used to reply and it is not a command.

Events

We define the events objects that are generated when a command is received. These events would be persisted in event store based on Cassandra.

```
import com.lightbend.lagom.scaladsl.persistence.AggregateEvent
import com.lightbend.lagom.scaladsl.persistence.AggregateEventTag

object FriendEvent {
  val Tag = AggregateEventTag[FriendEvent]
}

sealed trait FriendEvent extends AggregateEvent[FriendEvent] {
  override def aggregateTag(): AggregateEventTag[FriendEvent] =
    FriendEvent.Tag
}

case class UserCreated(userId: String, name: String,
  timestamp: Instant = Instant.now()) extends FriendEvent

case class FriendAdded(userId: String, friendId: String,
  timestamp: Instant = Instant.now()) extends FriendEvent
```

`AggregateEvent` are events that are persisted and made available for read side processing. Because these events are persisted and available on the read side, a tag is needed to identify the events. One way of identifying is based on the class name. Like in this case `FriendEvent`. This is simple and the tag based on the class name is returned by `AggregateEventTag[FriendEvent]`.

Though note that because the data is persisted and sort of immutable. If the class name changes then this disturbs the semantics. So, an alternative could also be to instead provide the tag name manually:

```
sealed trait FriendEvent extends AggregateEvent[FriendEvent] {
  override def aggregateTag(): AggregateEventTag[FriendEvent] =
    new AggregateEventTag[FriendEvent](classOf[FriendEvent],
```

```
  "StableFriendEvent")
}
```

Where the string `StableFriendEvent` would be used as a tag. In our example case, we would be using the class name as originally shown earlier.

State

As mentioned before, state of the world is the consequence of the events; we send a new event to someone and they change their state.

 State is needed for validation of commands.

State is maintained by our application and is Lagom agnostic. We define our class as:

```
case class FriendState(user: Option[User]) {
  def addFriend(friendUserId: String): FriendState = user match {
    case None => throw new IllegalStateException("friend can't
    be added before user is created")
    case Some(x) =>
    val newFriends = x.friends :+ friendUserId
    FriendState(Some(x.copy(friends = newFriends)))
  }
}
```

A single instance of `FriendState` is created for each user and maintained in memory by our application.

PersistentEntity

Lagom has a class called `PersistentEntity`. Each instance of this entity has a unique identifier. This identifier is generated and maintained by Lagom directly. Persistent Entity corresponds to an Aggregate Root.

In our case, our Aggregate Root is a single user. This user can choose to have multiple friends the user follows. We will define our class as follows:

```
class FriendEntity extends PersistentEntity {
  override type Command = FriendCommand
  override type Event = FriendEvent
  override type State = FriendState
```

```
override def initialState: FriendState = FriendState(None)

override def behavior: Behavior
//type Behavior = (FriendState) => Actions
```

We defined our `FriendEntity` class, which is a `PersistentEntity`. We defined the types of our commands, events, and state. We then implemented two crucial functions: `initialState` and `behavior`:

- `initialState` is the initial state of the application. Of course it is none where the user has not been created or any friend has been added.
- The `behavior` is defined as a set of actions given a state. The actions are functions to *process* incoming *commands* and generated *events*.
  To help explain, behavior defines the logic to be run when a command or an event is received, knowing the current state of the application.
  In our airline example, this would mean that when a new ticket booking command is received, we need to check our *state* to verify if the flight has any empty seats left.

Actions are fundamentally the logic containing the action to be taken when a command or event is received. The question may arise on why the Behavior is defined as `(FriendState) => Actions`. This is because, when a command is needed then it may be important to access the state, to validate if the incoming command is a valid command. For example, if the balance in an account is zero, then a withdraw of money should be cancelled.

```
override def behavior: (FriendState) => Actions = {
  // No state exists yet. Because the user has not been
     created till now
  case FriendState(None) => userNotCreated
  // user object exists and it receives commands
  case FriendState(Some(x)) =>
   Actions()
     .onCommand[CreateUserCommand, Done] {
       case (CreateUserCommand(user), ctx, state) =>
         ctx.invalidCommand(s"User $x is already created")
         ctx.done
     }
     .orElse(addFriend)
     .orElse(getUserCommand)
}
```

Case1: User not yet created

In the first case, we see if the current state suggests that the user has not been created yet. In such a case, we return the actions as defined by the userNotCreated variable:

```
val userNotCreated = {
  Actions()
  .onCommand[CreateUserCommand, Done] {
    case (CreateUserCommand(user), ctx, state) =>

      val event = UserCreated(user.userId, user.name)
      ctx.thenPersist(event){ _ =>
       ctx.reply(Done)
      }
    .onEvent {
      case (UserCreated(userId, name, ts), state) =>
        FriendState(User(userId, name, List()))
    } .onReadOnlyCommand[GetUser, GetUserReply] {
        case (GetUser(), ctx, state) =>
          ctx.reply(GetUserReply(None))
    }}
```

- The onCommand: suggests the code to execute when a CreateUserCommand is received.

```
val event = UserCreated(user.userId, user.name)
 ctx.thenPersist(event){ _ =>
   ctx.reply(Done)
 }
```

When CreateUserCommand is received, then the preceding code creates a new event and persists it. If the persistence was a success, then the ctx.reply(Done) code gets executed, which returns akka.Done back to the caller.

- The onEvent suggests the code to be executed to update the state provided in event.
  This is called once the event has been **generated** and **persisted**.
- The onEvent expects the latest state of the application to be returned.
  In our case, because the current state of the application was FriendState(None), which means that the user object does not exist yet, we simply create a new FriendState object that contains the user created, and, of course, he doesn't have any initial friends.

- `onReadOnlyCommand`: This is exactly like `onCommand`, but with a different name for readability purpose.
  The `onReadOnlyCommands` suggests that the block will not persist any events. This is useful in cases where the request is for a read query or is an invalid command and the request should not change the state of the application.
  In our example, we receive a request to obtain user details, and we reply as None because, as per the current state, no user object exists).
- All the preceding code is related to the scenario when the current state suggests that the user object does not exist yet. We will now discuss when the user object already exists:

Case2: User has been created.

- The user has been created and we now need to define behavior when receive commands:

```
// user object exists and it receives commands
case FriendState(Some(x)) =>
  Actions()
    .onCommand[CreateUserCommand, Done] {
      case (CreateUserCommand(user), ctx, state) =>
        ctx.invalidCommand(s"User $x is already created")
        ctx.done
    }
    .orElse(addFriend)
    .orElse(getUserCommand)
```

- **Case-1**: when the user already exists and a command is received to create a new user of the same user details. This is an invalid command.
  In such a case we do:

```
ctx.invalidCommand(s"User $x is already created")
ctx.done
```

In this case. We reply with a negative acknowledgment. `InvalidCommandException` would be provided to the user.
`ctx.done` represents that we don't need to generate any event in this case. Secondly, we could have also used `onReadOnlyCommand` instead of `onCommand` here.

- Else we do `.orElse(addFriend)`, which means to handle if the commands were to add a friend.
- `.orElse(getUserCommand)` if it was a command related to get user details

- The `orElse` is used to chain multiple Actions. We could either append multiple `onCommand`, `onEvent`, or so on, to a single action, or we could write multiple actions and then combine them together for the sake of better readability `addFriend` variable provides Actions containing a set of `onCommand` and `onEvent`:

```
Actions().onCommand[AddFriend, Done] {
    case (AddFriend(id), ctx, FriendState(Some(user))) if
    user.friends.contains(id) =>
    //already a friend. Nothing to be done
    ctx.reply(Done)
    ctx.done

    case (AddFriend(friendUserId), ctx,
    FriendState(Some(user))) =>
      ctx.thenPersist(FriendAdded(user.userId, friendUserId))
      (evt => ctx.reply(Done))
}
.onEvent {
    case (FriendAdded(userId, friendId, ts), state) =>
    state.addFriend(friendId)
}
}
```

We verify if the friend command sent is already a friend. If not, we reply success and do nothing. If yes, we add him as a friend and persist it.

Finally, `getUserCommand` is a read-only command that replies back to the user with complete information about them, such as their name, and a list of their friends.

```
private val getUserCommand = Actions().onReadOnlyCommand[GetUser,
GetUserReply] {
    case (GetUser(), ctx, state) =>
    ctx.reply(GetUserReply(state.user))
}
```

The preceding code is plainly simple. We reply to the user with the user's information. So, we have implemented the `FriendEntity` that defines the behavior when faced with commands. We will now implement the service that receives HTTP requests from users and invokes our entity.

Implementing FriendService

Please refer to the following code:

```
class FriendServiceImpl(persistentEntities:
 PersistentEntityRegistry,
  db: CassandraSession)(implicit ec: ExecutionContext) extends
  FriendService {
    private def friendEntityRef(userId: String):
     PersistentEntityRef[FriendCommand] =
      persistentEntities.refFor[FriendEntity](userId)

    override def getUser(id: String): ServiceCall[NotUsed,
    User] = {
      request =>
       friendEntityRef(id).ask(GetUser())
        .map(_.user.getOrElse(throw NotFound(s"user $id not
        found")))
    }
    (...)
}
```

The `FriendServiceImpl` class takes `PersistentEntityRegistry` as an argument. This is used to obtain the instance of our `FriendEntity` that we declared in the previous section.

```
private def friendEntityRef(userId: String):
 PersistentEntityRef[FriendCommand] =
  persistentEntities.refFor[FriendEntity](userId)
```

The `persistentEntities.refFor` returns an instance of a `FriendEntity` for the corresponding `userId` requested. As mentioned earlier, every aggregate has a unique ID. So, when a call is made to `friendEntityRef` with a `userId`, then Lagom will create a new object of `FriendEntity` in case no entity existed previously for the given userId, or else, it returns the already existing entity object.

When a `getUser` call is made:

- The `friendEntityRef(id)` returns the `PersistentEntity` associated with the user ID

- The `ask(GetUser())` sends a `GetUser()` command to the entity. It returns a Future that will get completed with the `ReplyType` of `GetUser`. If you remember, `GetUser` was declared as follows:

```
case class GetUser() extends
PersistentEntity.ReplyType[GetUserReply] with FriendCommand
So ` ask(GetUser())` will return a `Future[GetUserReply]`
```

- We map over the future and return the user information or throw an exception:

```
Other service methods are also implemented in a similar fashion.
```

ReadSide

In our friend-service example, once the events are generated, we update the state. And then, we are also using the same state to respond back to users, in case there is a query from a user. This may serve our purpose, but may not fully solve it in more complex examples.

The events generated could be forwarded to a special read-side registry that would receive these events. The read side may choose to persist this data in its own schema and use it to reply to read queries.

This is especially needed in cases where one must deal with data corresponding to multiple entities and not a single entity. For example, if there was a request to get all users who have more than 1 million friends. Such queries can't be responded back in our current form. So, there is a legitimate need for the read side to model its data in a manner that reads are fast.

Lagom provides two approaches to build this:

- As part of the same application, we build a read-side event processor. This event processor would receive events and may choose to persist it.

  To learn more about this approach, refer to `https://www.lagomframework.com/documentation/1.3.x/scala/ReadSide.html`.
  In our example, a read-side event processor is implemented as part of the `sample.chirper.friend.impl.FriendEventProcessor.scala` class for reference purposes.

- The events could be forwarded to another application. We would be considering this approach in the next `Chapter 8`, *Effective Communication*

Snapshots

When the application starts, then the application state is recovered by replaying stored events. Replaying all the events is a time expensive process and may not always be possible. To reduce this recovery time, the entity may start the recovery from a snapshot of the state, and only then replaying the events that were stored after the snapshot for that entity.

Such snapshots are automatically saved by Lagom, after a configured number of persisted events. The snapshot, if any, is automatically used as the initial state, before replaying the events that were generated post the snapshot creation.

You can configure the snapshot related settings in your configuration file:

```
(application.conf, in our example case)
lagom.persistence {

  # Persistent entities saves snapshots after this number
    of persistent
  # events. Snapshots are used to reduce recovery times.
  # It may be configured to "off" to disable snapshots.
    snapshot-after = 100

}
```

Summary

In this chapter, we introduced Event Sourcing and CQRS to model data. We also observed that they complement each other very well. The Lagom Persistence API was used to implement them in our application.

In the next chapter, we will explore the effective means of communication across microservices.

8
Effective Communication

In this chapter, we will look at the significance of the asynchronous mode of communication using message passing across microservices. We will also understand that the secret to being resilient to failures is communication via message passing.

We will explore Apache Kafka and see its usage for different purposes, including as a message broker and for a publish-subscribe model.

Lagom provides a message broker API (on top of Apache Kafka) for ease of access from our microservices. The message broker API is a continuation of the Persistence API, and we will see how together they let us do solid engineering with a few lines of code.

We will cover the following topics in this chapter:

- Asynchronous mode of communication and its significance
- Apache Kafka and its usage-message broker
- Lagom message broker API

Isolation

In `Chapter 5`, *Reactive Manifesto*, we observed the importance of being message-driven for being resilient. Let's consider a simple real-life scenario while building applications and let's understand the role of messages.

Let's assume we are building an image-sharing social networking site (such as Instagram). Users would upload pictures from their mobile phones and share them with their friends and followers. A simplified view would be as follows:

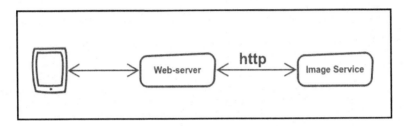

Of course, there would be many other background services, but let's consider a cropped-down version for simplicity.

Once the user shares a picture on his mobile app, the following steps will occur:

- The app would upload the image to our web server along with other probable details such as the location and the time of the picture was taken, any post associated with the image, privacy constraints of that post, and so on.
- On receiving the post, the web server has to take a range of multiple actions. As managing images for all the users on a large scale is not a simple task, we have a separate microservice, **Image Microserservice**, that takes care of managing images.
- The web server, based on the request, would make a REST call to Image Microservice, along with the user ID and the image.
  The Image Microservice would persist the image and respond as HTTP 200.
- The web server may do other corresponding actions if needed, deal with other microservices, and finally, respond to the user as a success call.

So, for every image posted on the app by the user, Image Microservice would be hit with a request.

This seems to be reasonable, but is prone to a few things that could go wrong:

- Image Microservice could take a long time to respond, may be because of a sudden burst of higher volumes of traffic or a performance bottleneck around its database.
- This could result in extra time taken in the acknowledgement in the app. The user may think the app isn't working or is slow, leading to bad reviews.
- Even worse, Image Microservice could be temporarily down due to an outrage, in which case the web server would respond as a failure to the app. In such a scenario, this would result in failure of the operation performed by the user.
- If the web server were dealing not just with Image Microservice but with a range of other microservices, then a failure of any of the microservices could result in a net failed operation.
  This is bad because a state of one microservice has had adverse consequences on the complete application, even though the other parts of the architecture are performing sanely.

This design is clearly not resilient to failures. Note that Image Service is just an example shown earlier. It could be any microservice managing user information; any microservice managing user posts, comments, and likes statuses; and so on.

One way of fixing our preceding problem is to add an intermediary layer between the web server and Image Microservice, as shown here:

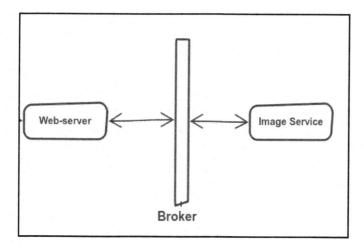

An alternate proposal is to introduce a **Message Broker**
(`https://en.wikipedia.org/wiki/Message_broker`) in between the web server and Image
Microservice. By Message Broker, we mean a highly available instance of software whose
core job is to accept messages from producers and let consumers read from them. The
Message Broker is itself running as a separate process on some machine.

We intend to have the following functionality from our message broker in our scenario:

- The message broker must **persist** our incoming messages. The message contents
  would be the image file along with other meta information of the user in our case.
  We need this behavior of persistence in our case so that if the broker gets
  restarted, we do not lose any data.
- Once the message is persisted on the broker, we want our consumer
  microservice, Image Microservice, to read this data in real time and do the
  necessary operation.
  You could also think of our message broker acting as a persistent queue. We will
  write messages to the tail of the queue and the consumer (Image Microservice)
  will read from the head of the queue.

So, in our new architecture, the flow of logic would be as follows:

1. On receiving an image share request from a user, the web server, instead of
   making a REST call to Image Microservice, would rather send a message with the
   image contents and other user information to the message broker.
2. Once the message has been successfully delivered to our message broker, the web
   server would proceed with other necessary tasks relevant to that request.
3. Image Microservice would read messages from the broker and process them.

This change in architecture gives the following advantages:

- The web server's course of action is no longer dependent on the health of Image
  Microservice. As soon as the web server sends a message to the broker, the web
  server can confidently proceed forward. So, the wait time has drastically reduced.
- It does not have to rely on whether Image Microservice is currently alive or
  responding in a fast/slow manner.
  The only concern for the web server would be to publish a message to the broker.

- Image Microservice would fetch this message from the broker. If there is a higher load of traffic, our message broker would keep filling itself with messages, and Image Microservice would keep fetching messages and work at its own pace.
- So, Image Microservice does not get overwhelmed abruptly with high volumes of request.
- If the traffic volume rises drastically, we can spawn multiple instances of Image Microservice. Each instance would fetch a message from the broker and do its operation.
  So, adding a broker provides an opportunity to scale easily.

 In the case of failures where our Image Microservice is currently down or under a higher load, the application is still functioning normally, thanks to Message broker. This gives us isolation in the true sense as a failure of one part of our architecture does not impact other parts of our application

Note: One can argue that we are offloading the actual problem to the broker. If the broker goes down (just like Image Microservice can go down), then we are in the same position as before. Here, we need to understand that we are using the broker as a persistence storage. The role of broker becomes persistence, the scalability to handle high loads of messages, fast, fault tolerant, horizontal scaling. Thankfully, modern brokers offer these functionalities.

Making brokers highly available is an easier problem to solve compared to applications as the broker has a well-defined functionality. Apache Kafka is a superb example of this, and you will learn more about Kafka in the next section.

Post the user operation where the user has uploaded an image, the user may refresh their page (or pull for the latest page feed). The image uploaded may/ may not appear immediately depending on whether Image Microservice has completed the operation in the background. Under usual traffic, Image Microservice would process the messages in real time, and the user feed call would contain those images.

However, if things go wrong on our server front (a high load or worse failures), then the user feed may appear stale for a few seconds, but it does not destabilize our application and our application would be resilient. Once our Image Microservice catches up (may be by spawning multiple instances), things automatically become normal again.

Let's compare our new architecture to the previous design, that is, using plain old REST for inter-microservice communication versus using messages:

	Direct REST Call	Message Driven
Failures	If Image Microservice goes down, the net call results in failure. **Retry:** Because the call has resulted in failure, the user would need to retry the operation again. Repeated retries would further deteriorate the condition as it would result in duplicate requests and higher traffic, when the application is already suffering.	Uptime of Image Microservice has no impact on success/failure of request. **Retry:** User doesn't have to retry, as the message is persisted with broker. Image Microservice can catch up with time.
Fault Tolerance	Under higher load, Image Microservice may not cope up with the traffic. It may result in deteriorated experience or, worse, may end up in OutOfMemoryError's or in shortage of CPU.	Image Microservice would work at a pace stable to itself, without falling.
Resilience	If the traffic eases, Image Microservice may / may not come back to a normal state.	Resilient as Image Microservice would keep functioning normally.
Response Time	Response time of Image Microservice has impact on net response time.	Instantaneous. The message just has to be delivered to the broker (and brokers such as Kafka are quite good at this).

This change in design has advantages, but it also results in extra infrastructure to learn and maintain. In my experience, in the long run, it is worth the effort.

The broker can be configured to retain the messages for a few days and clear them post the duration (say, a week).

Isolation - part 2

There is another scenario commonly faced in designing applications, and message broker is a good fix to the problem.

Let's assume that in our existing Instagram-like social networking site, we have another microservice called *user-service* that manages all the user's information such as name, preferences, and privacy settings. When a person accesses the mobile app, the web server, on receiving a request, would, of course, need the user information of the person who has requested and may be the information of the person's followers/friends:

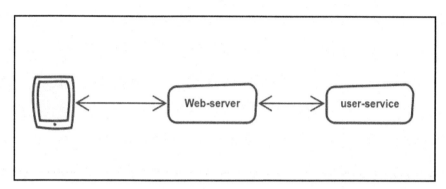

So, when the request is made, the web server would need to access user-service to obtain user-related information. This results in tight coupling of the two servers (web server and user service) even though they are separate applications. Hence, they are not completely isolated in the true sense as the availability and response rate of the user service have a direct impact on the response of web server.

Note: This situation is different from the Image Microservice scenario. In the Image Microservice scenario, the web server would simply push data towards Image Microservice (via the broker) without expecting any response. In this case, the web server also expects a response spontaneously.

To avoid tight coupling of the web server and the user service, one solution is to keep this user-related data to be highly available in a separate infrastructure that stores that data for some predefined period. This infrastructure could be a part of the web server instance or as a standalone server.

- The web server instance could maintain a local cache on its side containing user information.
    - It is important for all the user-related data to be accessible at the web server as well.
    - The user-service microservice would keep pushing any changed user data or new user information to a *message broker*.
    - The web server instance would keep pulling the data from the message broker, and it's in-memory cache would be updated.
    - If the web server restarts, it would attempt to re-fetch all the data.

- Another dignified way of solving this problem is to dump all the user data on a separate infrastructure such as Redis Cache (https://redis.io/) or MongoDB. The user service would push all data directly to Redis, and other microservices could directly read it from there.

Any of the two solutions would help solve our isolation problem. The former is normally quick and useful. However, if the data tends to get much bigger in volume and you think it is becoming a pain to keep so much in-memory data, then in such conditions, one may opt for the latter solution.

In our preceding scenario, user-service was just an example. *There can always be scenarios where data owned by one microservice would always be desired with others in real time.* In the finance industry, the meta information of a stock would be needed by many other microservices. If every stock-related information (like its ISIN) has to be accessed by making a REST call each time, this would make the service a bottleneck for everything we do.

Making a direct call can seem to be an easy solution for a problem. However, in reality, it may not be a wise choice.

Lagom summarizes the need for this design change as follows:

The system can be architected so that data owned by a service, but needed by other services, is published to an infrastructure component that stores the data for some pre-defined amount of time. This additional component allows publishing and consuming to happen at different times, effectively decoupling services, and hence enabling services to communicate asynchronously.

A sole reliance on synchronous communication between microservices is an architectural smell. A microservices architecture has many moving parts, and this means there is more opportunity for failure. The word synchronous literally means "happening at the same time", synchronous communication implies that both the sender and receiver have to be running at the same time. This means in the face of failure, synchronous communication fails too. This can lead to consistency problems if messages get missed, and can result in a system that is brittle, where a failure in one component leads to the whole system failing.

Message brokers

There are multiple frameworks/vendors in the market that can be used as a message broker. You could choose enterprise JMS (http://docs.oracle.com/javaee/6/tutorial/doc/bncdq.html), specification-based message brokers such as ActiveMQ, or open source alternatives such as RabbitMQ (https://www.rabbitmq.com/).

Each broker service follows different semantics and excels in different scenarios, and you may wish to go through them in detail before deciding on one. Usually, the factors that matter are as follows:

- **PAAS versus SAAS**: With **PAAS (Platform as a service)**, you would need a solution such as Amazon SQS (https://aws.amazon.com/sqs/) where AWS would manage the broker infrastructure.
  With SAAS, you would need to manage it yourself.
- **Replication and fault tolerance**: Depending on your need, you may wish to scale your broker to multiple instances so that even if one of the instances goes down, the broker is still available.
- **Persistence**: You may / may not wish to persist messages. A solution such as ActiveMQ provides both options.
- **Ordering**: Should the order of messages be maintained? For example, Simple Queues in Amazon SQS does not provide strict ordering.
- **Atmost once versus Atleast once versus Exactly once**: This is a very touchy topic in the broker world. The terms are explained briefly here:
    - **Atmost once**: The producer sends a message, and the consumer application may / may not receive it
    - **Atleast once**: The producer sends a message, and the consumer may process duplicate instances of the message
    - **Exactly once**: The producer sends a message exactly once, and the consumer processes it exactly once

Exactly once is a very difficult task. It is far more difficult in a distributed world where there are multiple replicated brokers. It is all about trade-off. If you deeply think about it, exactly once is a very complex problem to solve. Think of the following scenarios:

- Producer sends a message to the broker. The broker sends an acknowledgement to the producer on the success of the call, but the producer dies before receiving it. The broker would have persisted the message, but the producer may retry with the same messages the next time, as the producer thinks that the last operation was a failure.

  The consumer, broker, or network may die during the transmission of the ack for a message, thus causing retransmission of the message.

- On receiving a message successfully, the consumer would process the message, but fail during the last steps. In such a scenario, when the consumer restarts, it wouldn't receive the same message from the broker as, from the broker's perspective, the previous call was a success.
  However, it needs to receive the previous message as it would result in a message loss (atmost once).

- To avoid the preceding problem, the consumer would not like to acknowledge back to the broker, until it has done the computation associated with the message completely.
  Suppose it has done the computation and, just before, it tries to acknowledge the broker of the success, the consumer or the broker dies. In such a case, post a restart, the consumer would re-request for the message, resulting in a duplicate re-process (atleast once).

> The RabbitMQ mailing list has an interesting discussion along the same lines for reference at https://lists.rabbitmq.com/pipermail/rabbitmq-discuss/2010-August/008272.html.

Different messaging platforms solve these problems differently. RabbitMQ and ActiveMQ provide atleast once and atmost once guarantees (https://www.rabbitmq.com/reliability.html), but not exactly-once. The solution that these frameworks suggest is to make our consumer **idempotent**.

> **Idempotence**: Consumers on re-processing the same message must have the same outcome of processing the original message.

If idempotence is taken care of, the atleast-once scenario fits the bill well. In this book, we will be using Apache Kafka as the message broker solution that provides atleast-once semantics. Kafka also provides exactly-once at the expense of some throughput.

Apache Kafka

Apache Kafka (`https://kafka.apache.org`) is a blazingly fast distributed transaction log. It can be used as a message broker, as a publish subscribe model, and for real-time reactive streams. Kafka has its origins in LinkedIn, and it is written in Scala and Java. Kafka has a very simple model and does not take much time to get started with.

Think of Kafka as a file system. All the operations are directly done on disk. It doesn't need much memory for the job it does.

Kafka is a disk space where messages are sequentially stored on disk based on a first-come basis, like a queue. A message sent is simply appended next to the previous message.

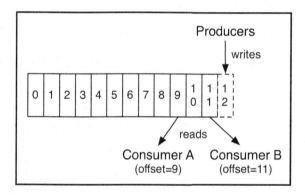

Image source: `https://kafka.apache.org/documentation/`

In the case of the consumer, Kafka uses a pull-based mechanism rather than a push-based mechanism. In other words, the consumer would decide to read the messages in a sequential order based on the offset. You could think of offset as the index of the element. So, the consumer could either start from the beginning (offset 0) or could start from an intermediary position based on the offset number. Kafka also provides a provision where the consumer can store its offset automatically in Kafka, and if the consumer restarts, it can start from the previously committed offset (`http://kafka.apache.org/0110/javadoc/org/apache/kafka/clients/consumer/KafkaConsumer.html#commitSync()`).

In Kafka, the queue concept we explained earlier is called a **Topic.** A Topic can contain multiple partitions, as shown here:

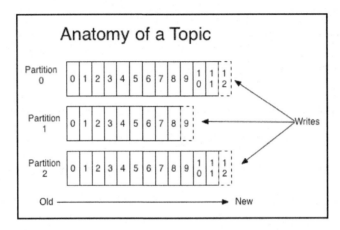

Each partition is a sequential queue like persistent storage. Partition is the unit of parallelism in Kafka. On both the producer and the broker sides, writes to different partitions can be done fully in parallel. On the consumer side, Kafka always gives a single partition's data to one consumer thread. Therefore, in general, the more partitions there are in a Kafka cluster, the higher the throughput one can achieve. Of course, more partitions come at a cost. To know more, refer to `https://www.confluent.io/blog/how-to-choose-the-number-of-topicspartitions-in-a-kafka-cluster/`.

You can create multiple topics, and each topic could contain multiple partitions. Order is maintained within each partition of a Topic.

So, if the order of the messages matters to you, you would have to manually make sure to *send messages of the same type to the same partition.* Partitions are provided an ID starting from zero. So, you can manually provide the partition ID while sending a message. If you do not care for ordering, you could send a message to Kafka, and Kafka will automatically forward it to one of its partitions.

Multiple consumers can read the contents from a topic in parallel. As the consumer decides the partition and the offset, the handle is with the consumer, and there is no synchronization involved on the server side. This makes both writing and reading from Kafka very fast.

Kafka is also distributed. In other words, you can spawn a Kafka cluster with multiple nodes (say three). It would automatically decide on a leader (Kafka uses Apache Zookeeper https://zookeeper.apache.org/ for this job) and uses the other two nodes as a replicated store. If the leader dies, one of the backups would automatically become the leader. From the official spec:

The partitions of the log are distributed over the servers in the Kafka cluster, with each server handling data and requests for a share of the partitions. Each partition is replicated across a configurable number of servers for fault tolerance.

Each partition has one server that acts as the leader and zero or more servers that act as followers. The leader handles all read and write requests for the partition, while the followers passively replicate the leader. If the leader fails, one of the followers will automatically become the new leader. Each server acts as a leader for some of its partitions and a follower for others, so the load is well balanced within the cluster.

Kafka is fault-tolerant. Because of its simple data model, a high frequency of reads and writes can happen in parallel at a very fast rate. Linked has shared its results for Kafka running in production with a 6 GB allotted heap (-Xmx6G):

- 60 brokers
- 50k partitions (replication factor 2)
- 800,000 messages/sec in
- 300 MB/sec inbound, 1 GB/sec+ outbound

As mentioned earlier, because most of the operations it does are disk-related, it is not very memory-intensive. In my personal experience, Kafka is very reliable as a data store and highly performant with over 500k messages/sec throughput observed in our production instances. However, it hogs on disk space and needs a lot of disk.

Overall, Kafka has a very simplistic model and implements it well. We have covered the basics of Kafka earlier, and it is sufficient enough to start building on top of it. You can read more about Kafka at https://kafka.apache.org/documentation/.

Lagom comes with Kafka by default. So, it can manage Kafka instances for us. However, if you chose to manage it yourself (frankly, it is always advisable to manage it yourself and not rely on Lagom; though initially, it's not a bad option to use the default Lagom setup to quickly get started), you can refer to the getting started guide at https://kafka.apache.org/quickstart. The guide will help you run Kafka, create a Topic with partitions, and send and receive messages from the Kafka broker.

It is highly recommended that you go through the quickstart guide before proceeding. You may go through steps 1 to 5 to understand the basic Kafka setup.

 Before the 0.11.0 version, Kafka provided at least once semantics. Post 0.11.0 version, Kafka provides the exactly-once option. Though exactly-once is a slightly more expensive operation when compared to exactly once. `https://www.confluent.io/blog/exactly-once-semantics-are-possibl e-heres-how-apache-kafka-does-it/` provides more details on its internal implementation.

If you want to get a quick feel for how to send messages to Kafka using its official Java API, follow these steps:

1. Download Kafka from `https://kafka.apache.org/downloads`. Unzip it and `cd` to its folder.

2. Kafka needs Apache Zookeeper running. To start Zookeeper, use the following line of code:

   ```
   bin/zookeeper-server-start.sh config/zookeeper.properties
   ```

3. To start Apache Kafka, run the following command from a new terminal:

   ```
   bin/kafka-server-start.sh config/server.properties
   ```

4. To create a new topic, use the following lines of code:

   ```
   bin/kafka-topics.sh --create --zookeeper localhost:2181
       --replication-factor 1 --partitions 1 --topic testTopic
   ```

5. To send a message to `testTopic` using simple Scala code, you would need to add the following sbt dependency in your project:

   ```
   libraryDependencies += "org.apache.kafka" % "kafka-clients" %
       "0.11.0.0"
   ```

A very simple Scala code to send a message to `testTopic` in Kafka is as follows:

```scala
import java.util.Properties
import org.apache.kafka.clients.producer.{KafkaProducer,
ProducerRecord, RecordMetadata}


object ProducerExample {

def main(args: Array[String]): Unit = {
```

```
val props = new Properties()
props.put("bootstrap.servers", "localhost:9092")
props.put("key.serializer",
  "org.apache.kafka.common.serialization.StringSerializer")
props.put("value.serializer",
  "org.apache.kafka.common.serialization.StringSerializer")

val producer = new KafkaProducer[String, String](props)

val rec = new ProducerRecord[String, String]("testTopic",
  "key", "hi")

val future: Future[RecordMetadata] = producer.send(rec)
future.get(5, TimeUnit.SECONDS)
  }
}
```

You can verify that the message was persisted by Kafka using the following command:

```
bin/kafka-console-consumer.sh --bootstrap-server localhost:9092 --topic
testTopic --from-beginning
```

Conclusion

We have seen that it is a promising idea to use messages as the mode of communication. It offers us isolation across different modules of our application and gives us the ability to be resilient. This can be done using any technology and a broker of your choice.

In Chapter 7, *CQRS and Event Sourcing*, we had explored the Persistence API. Lagom expands it by providing a message broker API to send *events* generated across microservices.

There isn't a need to use the Lagom Message API if you are not using Lagom Persistence API. In such cases, you could directly access the Kafka broker from the Kafka API. If you wish to take this route, you may want to look at https://kafka.apache.org/documentation/#api. The link provides the dependencies you need with the link to the java docs. The Internet contains many examples to quickly get started with Java/Scala code to access Kafka from the API they have provided.

In the earlier versions of Kafka, Kafka used to provide an official Scala API. Post version 0.8.0, they have stopped providing the Scala client and only provide the Java-based client. There are a few third-party Scala-based wrappers available on top of the Java API for Scala (https://github.com/cakesolutions/scala-kafka-client/). Akka Streams also has a Kafka API wrapper called Reactive Kafka (https://github.com/akka/reactive-kafka).

Lagom Message Broker API

Lagom Message Broker API provides the functionality to forward the *events generated* by Persistent Entity to other microservices via a broker.

PersistentEntity briefly had the following flow:

- Receive commands.
- Generate events. Persist them in the event store.
- Use events to update the state.
- The events are then available on the read side (CQRS).

The last operation, of forwarding the events to the read side, can be further enhanced by forwarding it to another microservice spontaneously. The other microservice would receive the events and do its respective operations based on the events. In fact, the application can be split by carving out the read side as a separate microservice.

Currently, there is only Apache Kafka-based implementation available for Lagom Message Broker API. API implementations for other messaging brokers are currently a work in progress.

Lagom comes with a Kafka in built (just like with Cassandra). Launching a plain Lagom application would also launch Apache Kafka (though this is optional). To enable Kafka, add the following line in your `build.sbt`:

```
lagomKafkaEnabled in ThisBuild := true
//to set a custom port:
lagomKafkaPort in ThisBuild := 10000
```

You can find further details about the Lagom Message Broker API at `https://www.lagomframework.com/documentation/1.3.x/scala/MessageBroker.html`.

On a side note: To view all the Lagom specific sbt tasks and settings, you can view the source of LagomPlugin.scala file from the Lagom sbt plugin. You can also access it at: `https://github.com/lagom/lagom/blob/1.3.x/dev/sbt-plugin/src/main/scala/com/lightbend/lagom/sbt/LagomPlugin.scala#L259`

Friend Recommendation

We will now continue from where we left off in Chapter 7, CQRS and Event Sourcing. In that chapter, we had a working chirper application where the friend-service was implemented using Event Sourcing and CQRS.

Now, we wish to build another microservice that recommends new friends to a user. The recommendation would be done based on the current friends a user already has. It would look at a social graph of friends of friends and try recommending new contacts to the user.

You can access the full example source at https://github.com/scala-microservices-book/book-examples/tree/master/chirper-app-complete

 The friend-recommendation microservice would rely on friend-service to obtain information on the current users and their friends. The friend-service would stream live events via the broker.

build.sbt

Because the friend-service would need to stream the events (for example: user-added, friend-added events) to the friend-recommendation-service via the broker, the Lagom Message API and Kafka-related dependencies would need to be added in friend-service:

```
lazy val friendImpl = project("friend-impl")
    .enablePlugins(LagomScala)
    .settings(
version := "1.0-SNAPSHOT",
libraryDependencies ++= Seq(
lagomScaladslTestKit,
lagomScaladslPersistenceCassandra,
lagomScaladslKafkaBroker,
    macwire
  )
 )
    .settings(lagomForkedTestSettings: _*)
    .dependsOn(friendApi)
```

The only new dependency added in the preceding bunch of code is lagomScaladslKafkaBroker. This represents the dependency on the Lagom Broker API and Apache Kafka.

We declare the dependencies of the friend-recommendation-api as follows:

```scala
lazy val friendRecommendationApi = project(
  "friend-recommendation-api")
  .settings(
    version := "1.0-SNAPSHOT",
    libraryDependencies += lagomScaladslApi
  )

lazy val friendRecommendationImpl = project(
  "friend-recommendation-impl")
  .enablePlugins(LagomScala)
  .settings(
    version := "1.0-SNAPSHOT",
    libraryDependencies ++= Seq(
      lagomScaladslTestKit,
      lagomScaladslKafkaClient,
      macwire
    )
  )
  .dependsOn(friendRecommendationApi, friendApi)
```

It has a library dependency on `lagomScaladslKafkaClient`. Note that this is different from `lagomScaladslKafkaBroker` because the friend-recommendation server is just a consumer and does not need access to the full-fledged Broker API. The `friend-recommendationAPi` also depends on `friendApi` to obtain messages.

Friend-api

The friend-service would stream live events via the broker. This needs to be declared by the friend-api:

```scala
sample.chirper.friend.api.FriendService.scala
trait FriendService extends Service {
  (...)

  def friendsTopic: Topic[KFriendMessage]

  override def descriptor(): Descriptor = {
    import Service._

    named("friendservice").withCalls(
      pathCall("/api/users/:id", getUser _),
      namedCall("/api/users", createUser),
      pathCall("/api/users/:userId/friends", addFriend _),
      pathCall("/api/users/:id/followers", getFollowers _)
```

```
    ).withTopics(
      topic(FriendService.TOPIC_NAME, friendsTopic)
      .addProperty(
        KafkaProperties.partitionKeyStrategy,
        PartitionKeyStrategy[KFriendMessage](_ => "0")
      )
    ).withAutoAcl(true)
  }
}
```

We will define a topic (this is a Lagom topic and is not to be confused with the Kafka topic though they mean similar things) to publish the messages:

```
def friendsTopic: Topic[KFriendMessage]
```

 A topic can be used to publish/subscribe messages to/from a message broker.

KFriendMessage is declared as follows:

```
sealed trait KFriendMessage

case class KUserCreated(userId: String, name: String, timestamp:
  Instant = Instant.now()) extends KFriendMessage

case class KFriendAdded(userId: String, friendId: String,
  timestamp: Instant = Instant.now()) extends KFriendMessage
```

So, friendsTopic is declared as a topic of messages where a message could signify either a user creation or a friend-added event.

In the descriptor, we will declare the topic properties as follows:

```
.withTopics(
  topic(FriendService.TOPIC_NAME, friendsTopic)
  .addProperty(
    KafkaProperties.partitionKeyStrategy,
    PartitionKeyStrategy[KFriendMessage](_ => "0")
  )
)
```

We provided the topic name to be used (this would be used by Kafka for its topic name) and we specified the partition strategy to be used in Kafka. For simplicity sake, we specified that all the messages independent of their class type should go to the same topic. You could very well provide a lambda that determines the partition number based on the message here.

Let's now look at the implementation of the function declared. The full source can be found in the file: `sample.chirper.friend.impl.FriendServiceImpl.scala`

```scala
override def friendsTopic = TopicProducer.singleStreamWithOffset {
    fromOffset =>
      persistentEntities.eventStream(FriendEvent.Tag, fromOffset)
      .map(ev => {
        (convertEvent(ev), ev.offset)
      })
  }


  def convertEvent(helloEvent: EventStreamElement[FriendEvent]):
KFriendMessage =
    {
        helloEvent.event match {
          case UserCreated(userId, name, ts) => KUserCreated(userId,
          name, ts)
          case FriendAdded(userId, friendId, ts) => KFriendAdded(userId,
          friendId, ts)
        }
    }
```

- We already know that each event produced by a `PersistentEntity` has a unique offset.
- `singleStreamWithOffset` provides an event stream containing all events that were generated after the offset.
- `FriendEvent.Tag` represents the messages associated with a tag. A tag is like an identifier used to represent similar events (rather than blindly depending on the class name because, if the class name changes, we still wish to remain compliant with existing events in tables).
- Based on the event in the event store, we will then convert the event to the appropriate Scala object and forward it.

`FriendModule.scala`:

```scala
abstract class FriendModule (context: LagomApplicationContext)
extends LagomApplication(context)
with AhcWSComponents
with CassandraPersistenceComponents
```

```
with LagomKafkaComponents
{
  //(...)
  //other declarations
}
```

Note that in all our code until now, we have not used any Kafka API directly, but we integrated with the Lagom Message Broker API instead. In the application loader of our microservice, we mix in `LagomKafkaComponents`, which represents that we intend to use a Kafka-based implementation for the Broker API.

The friend-recommendation-api

The exposed topic of the friend-service is then processed by the friend-recommendation-api:

```
class FriendRecServiceImpl(friendService: FriendService)(
  implicit ex: ExecutionContext) extends FriendRecService {

  val log = LoggerFactory.getLogger(getClass)

  val userMap = new ConcurrentHashMap[String, KUserCreated]()
  val allFriends = new ConcurrentLinkedQueue[KFriendAdded]()

  friendService.friendsTopic.subscribe
  .atLeastOnce(
    Flow[KFriendMessage].map { msg =>
    log.info("KMessage received " + msg)
    msg match {
      case x: KUserCreated => userMap.put(x.userId, x)
      case y: KFriendAdded => allFriends.add(y)
    }
    Done
    }
  )
  (...)
}
```

We subscribe to the topic and process all the messages. The messages could be a new user created or a user might have added another user as a friend.

The flow used earlier is from AkkaStreams. We define the behavior to be executed when a message is received. This object can then store this information, calculate, and recommend friends when a service call is made.

It could internally model friends and their relationship graphs in the best suited model (may be a Neo4J graph database by storing all the users as nodes of a graph and with friends acting as unidirectional edges between them).

For the sake of simplicity, we calculated this in memory and responded to users.

Finally, we declare the application loader by mixing in the appropriate traits:

```
abstract class FriendRecModule (context: LagomApplicationContext)
 extends LagomApplication(context)
 with AhcWSComponents
 with LagomKafkaClientComponents
 {
   lazy val friendService: FriendService =
     serviceClient.implement[FriendService]
   override lazy val lagomServer: LagomServer =
     serverFor[FriendRecService](wire[FriendRecServiceImpl])
 }
```

This is very much like what we have seen earlier. The only new dependency is mixing in the trait LagomKafkaClientComponents.

Finally, when we run all our microservices using runAll sbt command, then the friend-recommendation microservice would also be available. To validate, you can make an HTTP GET call to: http://localhost:9000/api/friends/rec/userId where the userId in the URL is the id of the user. You can of-course also access the friend recommendations by logging into the application from your browser.

Summary

In this chapter, we looked at the significance of our architecture being message-driven and the isolation benefits it provides. We had an overview of Apache Kafka and used it as a message broker for mode of our communication.

Finally, we explored the message broker API to send events across microservices.

9

Development Process

We have reached an interesting point in the book. For the next few chapters, we will switch our developer role to Ops. Having successfully designed a microservice-based architecture for our example application, we need a scalable way to continuously develop, test, and deploy them. In this chapter, we will discuss how such a process would look, and in the process, define an effective development process philosophy. We will call it the **feedback loop**. It is more than just using GitHub for code, Jenkins to build binaries, version control for issues (JIRA), and slack for communication. It is a philosophy about shipping code in small increments with high confidence and flexibility. This philosophy is imperative for large teams working on a myriad of codebases. It is a great fit for microservice-based architecture as well.

Previous chapters talked about the tremendous benefits of creating smaller and business domain-specific microservices. It is also important to note some of the complexities being added because of this approach. Notably, the following:

- More code repositories
- Code/logic sharing across repositories
- Inter-service communication overhead

All of the preceding points make the system more complex, and development can get messy and slow over time. As a result, a team, in order to regain lost speed, may be tempted to make quick decisions, which can lead to poor design, code duplication, and tight coupling. An effective and planned development strategy is therefore essential to regain speed in the right way. It is totally worth spending a few weeks, even months, finalizing a good process.

In this chapter, we will cover the following topics:

- Building an effective development process for engineers
- Learning about the CI/CD pipeline, and how to build one using the Jenkins pipeline
- Learning about containers, and how to create, build, and run Docker containers

Getting to know the key ingredients

A development team is a living organism with moving parts, where engineers join and leave, make mistakes, and hate a lot of processes. How can we ensure smooth functioning of such a team? Let's try to list out the possible ingredients for a good development process for engineers. Think along the lines of collaboration, measurement, and automation. I want to go over a few key areas that might help; it is not a comprehensive list, but it can serve as a starting list that you can build on:

- **Measurement (telemetry)**: This measures anything and everything. It is probably one of the most valuable tasks other than writing code. This needs to be at the core of the engineering culture to be effective. To help you remember this, I want to mention two catchy quotes in the industry:

  "If it moves measure it, if it's important alert it."

  "If you can't measure it, you can't improve it."

  This takeaway is not specific to engineering, it applies well to production, HR, management—you name it. You can either define questions first, or collect data and define questions later. Once the data is getting aggregated, set up dashboards and notifications to act quickly on insights. Remember that this can sometimes be misused by people by selective measurement to help their version of the story. To truly identify trends, measurements should be unbiased and comprehensive.

  Keeping to these basic ideas at every step will go a long way in truly making data-driven decisions throughout the company. It's very hard to excel at this.

- **Peer reviews and feedback**: These help maintain a high quality of logic, design, and style. It is the first line of defense for a code check-in. Usually, the review request is created using a **source control management** (SCM) collaborative tool, such as GitHub, GitLab, and so on. A healthy, open commenting culture in review requests should be established. Criticism should be precise so as to help the reviewee get actionables out of it.
- **Automation**: This minimizes human errors. Use public bots and custom scripts for chores. For example, use Chatbot integration (Hipchat or Slack) to communicate to your team member on a failed build. Some of these automations become obsolete after a while. Pick the ones that work, and improve them constantly. It's a never-ending process.

   If you do a task twice, write a script.

- **Simplicity**: The simplest solution should always be preferred. **Keep it simple stupid (KISS)**, a term coined by the US Navy in 1960, helps us minimize over-engineering problems. It is very tempting to design general solutions that cater to all possible use cases, but some may have very low **return on investment** (ROI) for the business or application in the short term. Also, in the long term, the design or the product might be obsolete. So, keeping KISS in mind will help at times to pick competing design solutions.

Since each team will own microservices that work autonomously in defining their own process, there can be a lot of drift among team processes. I would like to stress the importance of investing time in this step to get it right and share knowledge across teams. The payoff of a good feedback loop is incalculable and poor processes can deter good engineers from joining the team.

The feedback loop

We went over what might be some of the key principles for an effective development process in the last section. In this section, we will try to enumerate and visualize this development process and call it the **feedback loop**. The objective is to provide guidelines and industry-best practices to enable you to define your own feedback loop eventually. Every team is unique, but all good engineering teams have a great amount of overlap.

If you think about it, we can model (almost) every good process into a closed loop system, be it an architectural design, a job interview, or a government health care plan. A **closed loop system** feeds back part of the output signal into the input as an error signal. In case the output is drifting away from the expected output, the error signal will help modulate the input to reduce the difference. The following image shows a closed loop versus an open loop system. Take a look at control system books to see how many devices around you have feedback loops embedded within them:

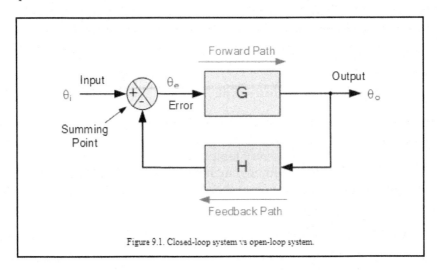

Figure 9.1. Closed-loop system vs open-loop system.

Our feedback loop, a development process for engineers, is also a closed loop system. Any new code addition goes through a predefined set of steps to reach its final place, that is, production servers. We want to add tiny feedback loops at every step to help us stay close to the expected output parameters (for example, build times and test cases). It is important to pay attention to these *predefined* steps because many teams don't plan properly for adverse conditions such as rollbacks. In startups, lead engineers usually, based on their experiences, set up a subset of the feedback loop, albeit mostly incomplete. Over time, they improve it organically. Getting this right will give the team an amazing advantage over others.

The feedback loop relying on the four principles—measure, automate, collaborate, simplify—uses the following components to achieve it. Each component has a clear purpose in helping high quality code check in to reach production servers and its maintenance. Refer to the following points:

- Code versioning
- Continuous integration
- Testing strategies

- Continuous delivery
- Monitoring and metrics

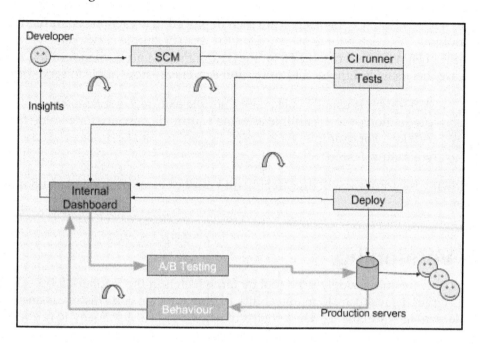

The preceding diagram has a typical feedback loop:

- **CI runner**: Continuous integration runner
- **SCM**: Source code management

Also, you will notice a tiny feedback signal going from almost all steps into the dashboard. There are more feedback signals than the ones shown in the image. The important takeaway here is to identify the most important signals, and measure and take an action on them. New signals can always be found as you build your product.

Let's look at **CI runner**'s feedback signal. Every code check in will trigger a suite of test cases. Metrics, such as duration, success status, and pending build requests, should be reported to the **Internal Dashboard**. It will help identify bottlenecks, high build times, and frequency of failing tests. Now, we can provision the appropriate number of CI server slave machines to reduce cost (unless you are using auto scaling, where slaves are created on demand automatically). At the end, we want the developer to get feedback as soon as possible, whether the code check in is valid or not.

The **A/B Testing** signal in the preceding figure is more to do with product than engineering. I have intentionally added that to highlight how the feedback loop can be improved with other non-engineering features as well. Engineers and managers collectively make a design choice, let's say A, B, and C. All designs are then deployed to a fraction of **Production servers** randomly. The behavior is measured in the form of simple clicks, page views, or more complex behavior patterns. Based on the data, a final choice is made suiting the business case. Let's say design A—all **Production servers** are now made to serve design A.

 A/B testing is usually backed by a simple feature *flag service*. The production code at runtime asks the feature flag service for a value for an A/B key. For example, `FeatureFlag.getValue('signup-button')` will return `'blue'`.

In the following sections, we will dive deeply into most of these components and how they fit together.

Code versioning

This is probably the most widely-used tool by far, which is in the feedback loop. Also, this is the first step in the feedback loop, the ability to time travel in code history is one of the most fundamental requirements. The benefits of using one is just so many to not warrant its use; however, using it to its true potential is not trivial.

There are a few popular **version control systems** (**VCS**), such as SVN, Git, Mercurial, and Perforce. We will be focusing on Git as it has fairly new paradigms and is steadily increasing in popularity.

Linus Torvalds wrote the Git protocol to have a decentralized way of committing code—to remove the politics around who can commit and who can't (`https://www.linux.com/blog/10-years-git-interview-git-creator-linus-torvalds`). Git gives more freedom to developers to commit code, perform resolutions, and make the process very asynchronous. Let's see what it takes to get the most of Git versioning.

First and foremost, a consistent Git workflow needs to be adopted. It doesn't matter how simple or complex it is, discipline trumps everything else. Let's define a simple workflow for developers to follow in a team using Git.

 All code branches should have a suffix (`feat-`, `bug-`, `chore-`, `refactor-`) to indicate its purpose. No code **merge request** (**MR**) will be merged without two reviewers commenting *ship it* on it.

There is no direct MR approval feature in the Git protocol, but there are VCS management softwares, such as GitHub, that offer this ability to approve and comment on MRs.

Surprisingly, this workflow is sufficient for a smooth functioning team, if followed diligently. The idea needs to be simple enough for it to become muscle memory to engineers. Positive reinforcement will help get there faster. Please refer to the following image:

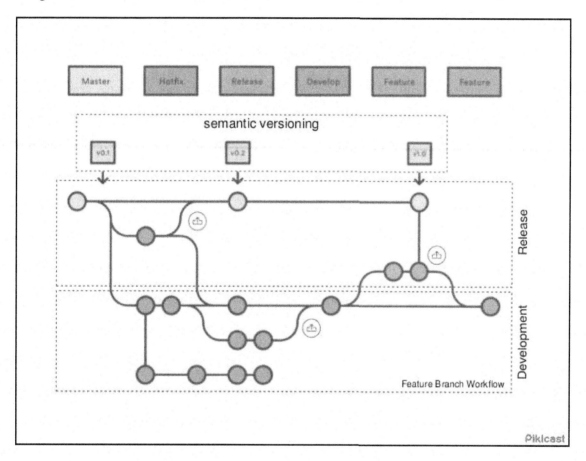

Having said that, there are popular Git models used by teams. The preceding figure shows one of the popular models. There is a clear separation between the **Release** and **Development** phases. Engineers are free to create new feature branches off of the **Develop** branch. Once the feature is complete, with passing test cases, an MR is raised against the **Develop** branch. CI pipeline runs the tests, and on successful code reviews by peers, MR is approved and merged. If there are any issues, the requester is asked to fix it first and reraise the MR. This process happens quite often and features are constantly getting merged upstream to the **Develop** branch.

CI/CD Pipeline: Continuous integration and delivery is a downstream process that tests and deploys the code to production.

After a while, the Develop branch will have enough stable features warranting a production release. The code branches off into a release candidate, **Release**. After successful rigorous testing by the CI server, the code is merged to **Master** and eventually deployed. The merge to **Master** is usually tagged with a release number, such as **v1.4.0**.

```
$ git tag  "v1.4.0"
```

- Pick up a Git workflow that the team agrees with; this is very important as it is one of the most used process by engineers daily.
- *Prioritize code reviews*; some companies such as Amazon are known to measure the number of reviews to promote engineers. Git protocol unfortunately doesn't have a code review feature. Fear not, Google has created an extension (https://github.com/google/git-appraise) that stores code review requests as Git objects. This way, you can version it, store review requests on your own Git server, and not depend on a public cloud Git server such as GitHub or GitLab.
- *Simple clear rules* to keep pull requests sane-manageable code diffs, with clear documentation in code, small enough to be rewritten in a couple of days.
- Branch naming convention and frequent code commits during the day.

 I highly recommend reading the official Git book, https://git-scm.com. I promise, in a few weeks, you will be setting up your own Git server as a backup to your current cloud Git servers.

Testing strategies

Now that our engineers have a way to version code and get peer reviews, we turn our attention toward testing. We talked briefly about peer reviews. They certainly do a lot in challenging and verifying the developer's design. They also help with code heuristics and validity of algorithms, but they fail to tell us if the code is actually correct for all cases and, more importantly, they fail to indicate any adverse impact on existing code until the code is in production, breaking things!

With microservices architecture, there is another reason for doing it. We have broken down the monolith into many smaller microservices for multiple axes of scalability, ease of deployment, and localized changes to business logic without interruption to other services. This partitioning of code introduces lots of services to service network calls over the internet that are inherently flaky. Thus, we need more rigorous testing to help us write resilient code. One of the important preferred styles in programming is called **defensive programming**. You never trust your input, and write code checks so the code dies gracefully when external services or functions fail, improving overall confidence in the code.

Testing improves confidence in code. It helps in identifying problems fast. It also helps maintain development speed throughout the lifespan of the project:

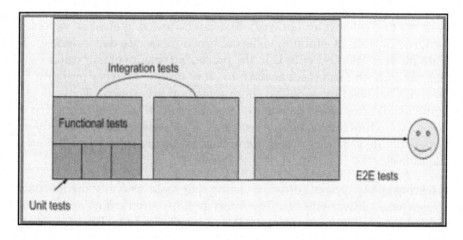

We will look into the four major test phases using an example—**unit, integration, component,** and **end-to-end testing**.

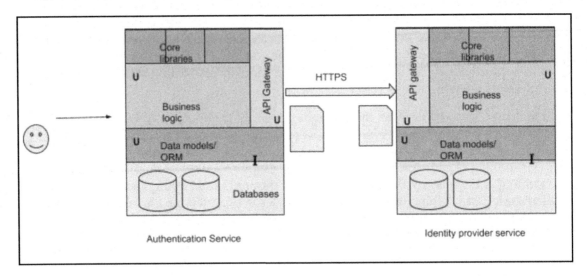

Looking at the preceding image, you can see that the **Authentication Service** depends on an external **Identity provider service**.

Unit test cases are the smallest unit of work that can be tested against an expected output. One of the ways to do so is by stubbing external function/service dependencies. **Business logic** and **Data models** (marked with **U** in the preceding image) of each microservice should have their own unit test cases as they are very unique to every individual service, so investing most of your test time will have high return on investment. To write effective unit test cases, some teams adopt **Test-driven development (TDD)**. Developers first define the expectations of a code function as failing test cases, then write code to make them pass. This helps developers define test cases without any bias, and truly capture the business requirements as tests.

Integration testing is any type of software testing that seeks to verify the interfaces between components against a software design. The interface between the **data access objects (DAO)** and database is a good place to start. The changes made by **Business logic** via **Data models** should interface well with the database schema. There will be some work involved to seed the database with test data, and tearing it down after certain tests.

Unit tests and integration tests alone can't help to ensure correct service contracts. **Component test suites** only mock external (service) dependencies and test the output. In our example, an authorization server exposes an API for the user to invoke. The component tests will be written to test the API and the expected output while stubbing the **Identity provider service** and the **Databases**. They will handle DB failures and network failures gracefully, which are simulated with our stubs.

Finally, it is valuable to write a few highly important user stories (journeys), such as login, signup, and payment, into end-to-end tests. They help identify flaky parts of the flow that cannot be easily caught in the lower levels of the test.

Continuous integration and deployments

Continuous integration (CI) is a concept to integrate small increments of code changes, often to the mainline in a distributed team. Also, it expects clear policies as to what qualifies as a successful code check in. A CI server verifies the code check in against the user-defined policies, which mostly are a suite of tests (written by the developer). The policies are run on every code check in. It reduces the introduction of bugs into mainline by failing fast. Typically, developers should check in often and ensure that the code change passes all checks/policies enforced by the CI server.

 Most important branch: `== mainline (perforce) == master (git) == trunk (svn)`.

There are some clear wins with enforcing CI with your team. The latest code on mainline (master) is always a working and deployable copy of the application. Code errors are caught early as it's a fail fast model. It blocks the other teams from pushing code to the same branch until its fixed; this creates an artificial pressure on the developer to investigate the issue right away, and revert or push a fix.

There are a lot of open source CI server offerings, but the most common and popular is **Jenkins**, created by Cloudbees in 2004. A few notable proprietary tools worth mentioning are AWS CodePipeline, CircleCI, and Travis CI. Use cloud tools such as CircleCI and its ilk, which are essentially managed by Jenkins services, to avoid setup and maintenance overhead. All it needs is VCS credentials to listen on code check ins, optional access to your infrastructure (for example, **Amazon Web Services (AWS)**, **Google Cloud Platform (GCP)**) to run downstream steps. In this section, we will use Jenkins as a CI server and look at some examples on how to define the CI policies as code via a configuration file called `Jenkinsfile` (`https://jenkins.io/doc/book/pipeline/`).

It is a good rule for engineers to check in code regularly into the feature branch and update mainline changes back into it to avoid large code drift from mainline.

Deployments

Let's recap—we now have a good understanding of how development teams push code, write test cases, and continuously integrate into mainline in SCM. The next step of the feedback loop (from the preceding figure) is **Deploy**—pushing the code to production machines automatically.

We need an orchestrator of some sorts that can do rule-based deployments to environments specific to code branches. Traditionally, software development cycles were long and deployments were done sparingly. In many cases, the software was installed on the client side. This did not warrant a continuous delivery setup.

A shift towards cloud-based SaaS software has made it highly valuable to have an automated frequent continuous delivery setup. A code check in, irrespective of its size, needs to pass user-defined checks before it can become an artifact. If it does succeed in doing so, then it automatically gets deployed to end users without human intervention. Continuous integration and deployments are two key concepts we will be dealing with in this regard.

An artifact is a deployment-ready code package (usually a JAR, WAR, `tar.gz` file) with all dependencies resolved.

Continuous delivery helps increase confidence in the quality of service. Any change, however small it may be, has to pass through a CI server to reach production servers. This automated, incorruptible process ensures the same quality of delivery every single time. We will, with the help of examples, see how Jenkins can enable us to deliver code continuously.

Jenkins pipelines

Jenkins recently released the 2.0 version with much awaited pipeline capabilities. A **pipeline** is a configuration file that contains the decision tree for every code check in and rules, and checks to decide what automation step to run.

As Jenkins creator Kohsuke Kawaguchi puts it:

Jenkins Pipelines allows you to describe your chain of automation in a textual form.

We will use it to codify most of our feedback loop (described in the preceding image). It comes in two flavors—scripting and declarative pipeline syntax. The original scripted pipeline uses a DSL based on Groovy, giving almost full imperative language constructs. The execution engine underneath is the same for both. We will stick to the newer declarative syntax as it's easier to write and, in the near future, Jenkins plans to release a GUI editor based on the declarative configuration `Jenkinsfile` file.

In the preceding sections, you learned the importance of continuous integration and deployments. Jenkins Pipelines helps them become a reality.

Jenkins pipeline - In action

Example Setup

Create a new file called `Jenkinsfile` at the root of your versioned project. Your Jenkins server has to watch for this code repository for changes. The configuration file, `Jenkinsfile`, will be picked up by Jenkins to run the pipeline.

Example development

The `agent` directive tells Jenkins where and how to execute `pipeline`. The following example allows the Jenkins master to run this pipeline in any slave it wants to:

```
$ cat Jenkinsfile
pipeline {
  agent any
}
```

Let's add a `stage` block to the pipeline. **Stage** is a logical block in the pipeline. A `stage` block encapsulates a few build commands as a `stage` for clarity. It has no significance to the build process. Since this is a declarative `config` file, we will have to use specific syntax to use a directive:

```
$ cat Jenkinsfile
pipeline {
  agent any
  stages {
    stage('Build') {
      agent { docker 'maven:3-alpine' }
    }
```

```
        }
    }
$ git commit -am 'updated jenkinsfile'
$ git push
```

When the code is pushed to remote repository, Jenkins starts the pipeline on the new commit. The result will be a Docker image Maven running and Jenkins' job will succeed. Now, let's add steps to the stages. Steps are the actual commands that execute, stages are just logical blocks:

```
$ cat Jenkinsfile
pipeline {
  agent any
  tools {
    maven 'Maven 3.3.9'
    jdk 'jdk8'
  }
  stages {
    agent { docker 'maven:3-alpine' }
        stage ('Build') {
            steps {
                echo 'This is a Build stage.'
                sh 'mvn -B clean package'
                archiveArtifacts artifacts: '**/target/*.jar',
                  fingerprint: true
            }
        }
        stage ('Random') {
            steps {
                def browsers = ['chrome', 'firefox']
                for (int i = 0; i < browsers.size(); ++i) {
                    echo "Testing the ${browsers[i]} browser"
                }
            }
        }

        stage('Test') {
        when {
          expression {
            currentBuild.result == null || currentBuild.result
              ==
            'SUCCESS'
          }
        }
        steps {
            sh 'mvn test'
        }
          post {
```

```
        always {
          junit '**/target/*.xml'
        }
        failure {
            mail to: engineer@.yourcompany.com
        }
      }
   }
$ git commit -am 'updated jenkinsfile'
$ git push
```

So, in total, we have three stages: **Build**, **Random**, and **Test**. The global agent will create an ephemeral Docker container with Maven tools in it. Don't worry about Docker, we will get to it soon and treat it as an operating system with Maven tools preinstalled. The sh and archiveArtifacts are directives defined in the Jenkins pipeline reference.

Random shows how simple control statements, such as the for loop, are available.

Test stage has the when, steps, and post blocks. When a block is executed first, to determine whether to proceed with this stage or not, based on whether the expression block evaluates to True or False, steps are executed after that.

The post block supports additional conditional blocks within it—always, changed, failure, SUCCESS, and unstable.

As the name suggests, the always block runs irrespective of the steps result. The failure block runs when any of the steps exits with a non-zero code.

Refer to the pipeline syntax page for required and optional fields in the configuration file (https://jenkins.io/doc/book/pipeline/syntax/#pipeline-syntax).

Jenkins usually runs in a master-slave configuration. Master reads the configuration and orchestrates jobs. Slaves have executors in them to run jobs. One executor can run only one job at a time. The important thing to remember is that all pipelines are parsed and executed at the master node. The actual build steps, which is the CPU/memory intensive task, are run on slaves (or agents)

All the pieces fit together with each other and fine tuning is required on a team basis. The preceding examples are guidelines, and I would advise you to discuss it with your team and tweak it.

Some of the core features of a good CD pipeline would be as follows:

- Good notification system and emails on success and failure.
- Each code push to dev-*, feat-*, and bug-* and should trigger jobs. Report results in VCS (GitHub).
- Time-travel. Rollback deployments easily.
- Requires minimal manual intervention. Actions should be no more difficult than single UI clicks.

Traditional deployments and machine images

Almost every **operating system (OS)** has its own package manager to install a new software in a manageable way. Let's say you want to use git on a Ubuntu 14.04 Linux OS to download your source code repository from GitHub; you will issue the following command:

```
apt-get install git
```

The apt-get command will search for the git package in its package repository server and download the dependency graph, and packages on top of git will be built. It will issue install commands for each package in the graph using the dpkg utility, run the following command:

```
$ apt-cache rdepends git
```

Running the preceding command lists out all dependencies of git, which is over 100 packages! Clearly, it's humanly impossible to install these dependencies in the correct order by hand without losing sanity.

For almost all platforms, whether a programming language or OS, a package manager is essential. They excel at dependency resolution, caching a client, and configurable internal/external repositories.

```
APT ( frontend. Dependency resolution ) -> dpkg ( backend. low level
utility. install) -> debian based Linux OS
```

These frontend tools (`apt-get`) use a low-level utility (`dpkg`) whose only responsibility is to actually talk to the OS to install, remove, and upgrade the packages. These low-level managers have no knowledge of the dependency graph. They plainly fail if a dependency is missing.

Alternatively, you can compile your code on the server directly using `dpkg`, instead of downloading it from the `package` manager. Then, run the compiled binary with all the correct dependencies.

If you want to share your source code as a package, it needs to be packaged correctly for an OS type/version and uploaded to an `APT` repository, before you can install them globally:

```
Source packages ----(build parameters for specific OS)--------> binary
packages
```

Dependency versus package manager

So, package managers are great for setting up a system-wide software. A similar approach utilized for project-level dependency resolution is called **dependency management**. Popular tools are Maven, PyPI, and npm.

Scala **SBT,** which we have used extensively throughout the book, is a build tool that uses `ivy` for dependency resolution. In SBT, the developer can define the dependency list via an SBT build file (the `build` file is ultimately a Scala program). Similar to APT, SBT generates and installs the dependency graph using public/private Maven repositories. Nexus and Artifactory are popular open sourced maven-based artifact repositories.

The advantages are very similar to code versioning. On top of the ease of dependency resolution, it helps in rollbacks and time travel as the artifacts are versions and tied to commit hashes in the repository. This makes time-traveling to any atomic point in the past by redeploying the corresponding artifacts.

Another form of deployment which is popular is using **virtual machine** (VM) images. Virtual machine that is stored as a the VM image is built using a configuration file, for example, `VagrantFile`, to define the base operating system, memory limit, and CPU cores. It allows us to run shell commands to fine tune the VM precisely.

For example, let's use `VagrantFile` to create a Ubuntu VM with one GB memory, with `openssl` and `git` packages:

```
Vagrant.configure(2) do |config|
# You can search for boxes at https://atlas.hashicorp.com/search.
```

```
config.vm.box = "ubuntu/trusty64"
# Provider-specific configuration
config.vm.provider "virtualbox" do |vb|
vb.memory = "1024"
vb.name = "dev_machine"
end
# Sort of the init script
config.vm.provision "shell", inline: <<-SHELL
sudo apt-get update
sudo apt-get install -y build-essential git
sudo apt-get install -y openssl
SHELL
end
```

VagrantFile can invoke init scripts to download or build our application binary onto the VM image. Now, VagrantFile itself can be versioned. Taking one step forward, we can create a VM instance from the VM image , snapshot it, and save it to the disk. Now this snapshotted image has already run the init scripts, thus have the binaries all setup. The images themselves can and should be versioned via tags or suffixes or prefixes in the names.

We have concluded our exploration of the feedback loop and the essential principles to keep in mind while designing it. Ideally, I would recommend borrowing ideas from the preceding descriptions while you go about building your own feedback loop.

The rest of the book will deal with containers and how they improved our effective development process.

Containers

Before we get started with virtualization and containers, let's briefly go over some basics of operating systems. An operating system is a piece of software that sets up a platform for user apps to run seamlessly and these apps share low-level system resources, such as memory and CPU cycles via the OS.

The application calls to access resources are translated to system calls. The system calls access the kernel (embedded within the OS), which talks to connected hardware via drivers. A popular family of operating systems, such as macOS, Windows, and Linux are packaged with a robust kernel and supporting drivers for all the major hardware products. The preceding description of the operating system is highly shortened to keep things simple.

Introducing hardware virtualization

Virtualization is a fairly old concept of creating a version of a thing that behaves exactly like the actual thing, such as a storage device, network device, or a computer. To the user of this virtual thing (virtual machine), it looks and feels like the actual thing (real computer). The actual implementation and internal execution will be different. The most common reason for doing virtualization is cost and optimized resource utilization.

We will focus on **Hardware virtualization** (**HV**) in this section since it sets the base for our introduction to containers. HV has played a pivotal role in cloud revolution, which we have been witnessing this decade. HV is running a **virtual machine** (**VM**) with an OS without actually running it directly on dedicated hardware. This enables us to run multiple virtual machines sharing the same metal hardware using some middleware code. This middleware code is called the **hypervisor**. The actual physical machine on which virtualization takes place is called the **host machine/host OS**. The different operating systems running on top of the host machine are the virtual machines and are sometimes called **guest machines/guest OS**.

So, essentially, any application can be run in isolation inside its own VM, which is great. More importantly, this can be done on-demand via code. This has tremendous value as it models a behavior to treat compute resources (metal hardware) as a utility that can be shared and used on demand, improving utilization and overall efficiency, and reducing cost drastically. This is how Amazon, Google, and Microsoft, the three biggest players in the cloud, are trying to make money. Build world class datacenters with metal hardwares. Provide GUI tools, APIs, and CLI tools for customers to commission virtual environments on top of the metal hardware for their workload and pay for the usage.

OS-level virtualization

There has been another form of virtualization at the operating-system level that has been gaining traction. A few Linux kernel features have made it possible to run many applications within the same host in isolation without the need to create one VM per application.

These applications share the OS kernel. Instead of the host OS needing hypervisor code, it runs a container runtime. These isolated applications running on the container runtime are generally referred to as containers.

A container runtime allows developers to make use of the isolation process, CPU resource allocation by providing APIs and abstracting low-level technical details. The following diagram shows how Docker container runtime runs the application directly without needing Guest VMs. While using Docker, we get all isolation benefits but no overhead of running VMs:

What do we expect from containers?

OS-level virtualized containers are faster than VMs because they get native access to shared host kernels, also VMs run a full operating system making them bulky and resource intensive. Thus, OS-level virtualization runs smoothly on commodity hardware compared to HW virtualization. Containers are not a complete replacement for VMs, but it can be used in conjunction to maximize utilization.

We need a lightweight environment for our application to run in isolation. We also want portability of this lightweight environment, so it can be run anywhere easily. Fine-grained resource allocation per container. We will see later on in the chapter how containers offer all of the preceding concepts.

Container runtime - Docker

Docker claims to be the *world's leading container platform*. They managed to be the poster boy for the containerization movement. So, what exactly is Docker?

Docker is a collection of software that lets you develop, test, and ship applications efficiently. They are a really good fit for microservice-based architecture. At the core, the Docker engine lets us create and manage container life cycles easily via an API. The key parts of the Docker engine are the daemon, the API server, and the client.

The daemon is a self-sufficient container runtime, the heart of Docker. It is a wrapper on top of Linux containers (LXC, now `libcontainer`) and provides other useful features on top.

The REST API server exposes functionality in a nicely versioned API for primarily the client and third-party developers. The client is a command-line tool that is the main access point to run Docker commands against:

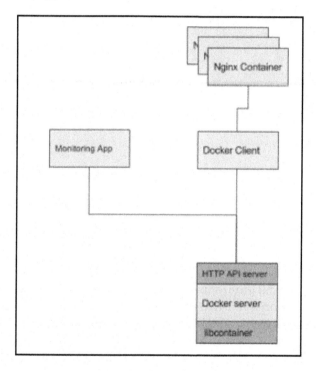

What made Docker a possibility?

Containers have been around for a while. In 2000, Virtuozzo pioneered an OS-level virtualization using containers. FreeBSD has BSD jails, Solaris came up with zones, now Linux has LXC containers, all working under the same principle explained in the preceding section. In this book, we will focus on Linux containers and how they work, especially the Docker technology Stack.

Docker's success, however, is partly shared with **Linux containers** (**LXC**) and certain key kernel features, which were added in recent years. A few key milestones in Linux and the open source world happened in the past two decades, thus making it possible to make these lightweight containers. The following image depicts these milestones:

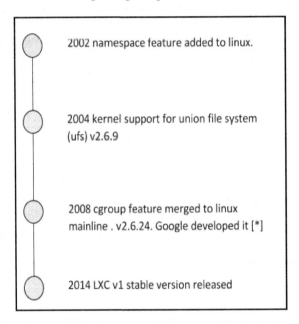

At the start of this section, we talked about the features we expect from containers. Let's see how a Linux container offers all those features from its runtime environment:

- **Isolation (process trees, mount files, filesystem)**: Containers need a completely isolated sandboxed environment. Applications inside containers would feel as if they're running on a full-fledged OS. This is made possible with kernel namespaces. For every container, five new namespaces are created (`pid`, `net`, `ipc`, `mnt`, `uts`) that are not accessible by other processes. This provides security to the host; if the process is compromised, the access is restricted.
- **Resource allocation**: Clear limits on resources allocated for each container are important to avoid containers crashing the Host VM due to resource exhaustion. A Control group in the Linux kernel is used for fine-grained resource management, allocating specified memory limits, and CPU limits, via a `.conf` file. **Control groups** (**Cgroups**) runs as a daemon service in Linux.

- **Lightweight images**: Containers are instances of container images. All the binaries and libraries needed for the container are baked into the container image. Running multiple instances from the same container image is a very real use case. Making copies in every single container will make it disk space intensive. The Union file system was added to the Linux kernel and is used by Docker. It works by creating the file system in layers and saves space by sharing layers between containers. This feature is explained in more detail in the next section.

This book's primary focus is not to serve as a devOps or automation guide. There are better books for in-depth analysis and a comparative review of all container runtimes. Our primary focus is on deploying microservices, and Docker does a great job. One of the amazing things about Docker is its strong open source community. Docker established the open container initiative in 2015 to set open, industry runtime specifications and image specifications for interoperability.

 Everything talks to Docker via an API server, which is written in golang (`https://docs.docker.com/engine/api/`).

Container images

At this point, you should be familiar with how containers work at a high level, and their benefits.

According to Docker, a container image is a lightweight, stand-alone, executable package that includes everything needed to run a piece of software, including the code, a runtime, libraries, environment variables, and config files.

Container images, when issued a run command, create a container instance or simply a container.

Similar to `VagrantFile`, a Docker container image is created using `Dockerfile`. `Dockerfile` has its own **domain specific language** (**DSL**) to define and create Docker container images. They are akin to a shell script, containing a list of commands to be run in order, and the output is a container image. The Docker website has a list of valid directives that can be used in `Dockerfile`. You can head over to `dockerhub.com` or GitHub to look at `Dockerfile` for popular container images, for example `https://hub.docker.com/_/redis/`.

Docker has a widespread support for all popular operating systems. Now head over to the Docker website and install Docker (https://docs.docker.com/engine/installation/) for your operating system. Since 2016, the Docker setup has become very easy, so the setup should be fairly intuitive.

 Please follow the instructions on https://docs.docker.com/engine/ installation/.

To test your installation, start the Docker service and open your terminal and run the following command line:

```
$ docker info
```

Create a text file without extension and name it Dockerfile:

```
$ cat Dockerfile
FROM busybox
CMD /bin/sh -c "while true; do date; sleep 5; done"
```

FROM is a mandatory directive and it refers to base a Docker container image that is to be used. This tells Docker to use it as the starting point and to apply changes on top of this container image. For example, a base image can be an ubuntu image with Java 8 installed.

In our example, we are using busybox as a base image (https://hub.docker.com/_/ busybox/).

Now, it's time to build your first Docker container image. Run the following command line:

```
$ docker build -t awesome-date-generator .
```

Since this is the first time we are running the Docker build, don't have the busybox image locally in your machine; Docker downloads it from the dockerhub public repository. You can pull images from other compatible Docker registries (public/private) as well, it defaults to dockerhub.

Let's break down the preceding command. We are asking the Docker daemon to build an image and name it awesome-date-generator by looking for Dockerfile in the current directory '.'. Docker generates a container layer for the line mentioned in the Dockerfile and stacks it on top of the base image one by one. After all commands are done, the final result is a new container image called awesome-date-generator.

You could alternately run the following:

```
$ docker build -t awesome-date-generator -f /path/to/docker_file .
```

To view your Docker image, run the following:

```
$ docker images
```

To create a container instance using this image, you need to just invoke run. The CMD defined in the Dockerfile will be used to start the process with pid 1. The container's lifespan is tied to this process. If, for any reason, the process exits, the container will die with it.

```
$ docker run awesome-date-generator
```

When a new container instance is created with the run command, internally, the Docker container runtime creates a thin Read/Write container layer and applies it on top of the awesome-date-generator container image. Any new writes performed in the lifespan of the container are added to this Read/Write container layer. This makes two important things possible:

- Reusability of the base container image
- Immutable base container image

Let's explain that with the following example:

```
$ docker run --name=generator-1 awesome-date-generator
$ docker run --name=generator-2 awesome-date-generator
```

The same container image, awesome-date-generator, can be used to run multiple containers. Both generator-1 and generator-2 are using the same container image; they are *NOT* duplicated for each container instance. Each container will have its own thin R/W layer for container on top of the awesome-date-generator image.

In the preceding image, you can see how the containers share the same container layers underneath; this saves a lot of duplication. Also, each container layer is immutable and has crypto hash, so it is easy to verify its integrity.

 A container image is a stack of container layers. Every command in Dockerfile translates to exactly one layer.

Volumes is an interesting feature that help the `mount` directories into a container at runtime. This allows dynamically loading configurations, libraries, and so on. The syntax is pretty simple as well:

```
$ docker run -e "NAME=selvam" -v config/:/opt/config awesome-date-generator
```

Docker lets you create and attach multiple network interfaces to a container. This allows complex, many-to-many combinations of networks and containers. To create a new network:

```
$ docker network --create
```

To use the host machine's network interface, execute the following command:

```
$ docker run --network=host awesome-date-generator
```

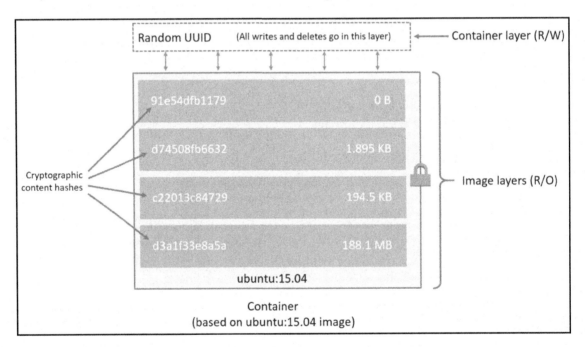

After the image has been generated, it can be useful to persist them. This helps cut down on build and setup time. Docker Registry is an open source project that provides a stateless server to efficiently store and distribute docker images. Other open source projects such as Clair for **Common Vulnerabilities and Exposures (CVE)** scanning can be used for better security. Thirty percent of the public images hosted on `dockerhub` registry have CVE security vulnerabilities.

Deployments with containers

In this section, we will be creating two web services: `time service` and `hello service` written in Flask, a Python framework. Instead of using Scala, we will intentionally look at another language to validate the simplicity of Docker container deployments.

It is highly recommended that you install Docker and run the example commands from the previous section before proceeding.

The following are the prerequisites:

- Docker installed
- Text editor

Create a new project folder as follows:

```
$ mkdir path/to/hello-world-service
$ touch server.py
```

Now, let's write our own `hello world` HTTP server. The following is the `server.py` file:

```python
from flask import Flask
import socket
app = Flask(__name__)

@app.route('/')
def hello_world():
  hostname=socket.gethostname()
  return 'Hello, World! Yours truly, '+ hostname
```

It uses a lightweight Python server called Flask to set up one HTTP route, /, which returns `Hello World!`.

Now let's dockerize `hello-world-service`:

```
$ cat Dockerfile
From jfloff/alpine-python
COPY server.py server.py
ENV FLASK_APP server.py
EXPOSE 5000
RUN pip install flask
CMD flask run --host=0.0.0.0
```

Run the Docker container to verify it as follows:

```
$ cd path/to/hello-project
$ docker build -t hello-world-service .
$ docker run -p 5000:5000 hello-world-service
```

The -p flag allows us to map <host port>:<container post>.
Open http://localhost:5000 on your browser; you should see the Hello World! message. This confirms that your Docker container is running your Flask server. Moving onto the next service, time-service. Please refer to the following code:

```
$ mkdir path/to/time-service
$ touch server.py
```

The following piece of code would be the Dockerfile file:

```
$ cat Dockerfile
From jfloff/alpine-python:2.7
COPY server.py server.py
ENV FLASK_APP server.py
EXPOSE 4000
RUN pip install flask
CMD flask run --host=0.0.0.0 --port=4000
```

Run the Docker container to verify it as follows:

```
$ cd path/to/time-service
$ docker build -t time-service .
$ docker run -p 4000:4000 time-service
```

Please visit this link—http://localhost:4000 on your browser.

Now we have both services, dockerized and functional. Before we proceed to deployment, we will make the REST call from hello-world-service to time-service. So, the following output:

```
"Hello, World! Yours truly, {hostname}"
```

Now looks like this:

```
"Hello, World! Yours truly, {hostname} , Time: {curr_time}"
```

The code changes for this `hello-world-service` are available in the GitHub repository:

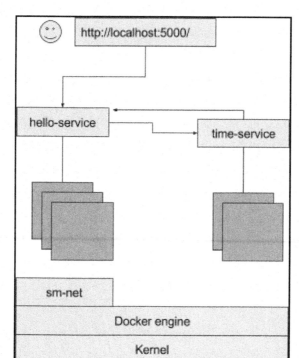

Our deployment topology is explained in the preceding diagram:

- hello-world service
- **time-service**
- **sm_net** network
- 3 replicas hello-server container
- 2 replicas time-server container

We will define this topology as a `docker-compose` file. The `docker-compose` file allows us to define Docker resources and their relations. Along with services, other configurations such as volumes, networks, and `env` variables are also defined in this file:

```
$ cat docker-compose.yml
version: "3"
services:
hello:
image: hello-world-service:latest
deploy:
```

```
replicas: 3
resources:
limits:
cpus: "0.1"
memory: 50M
restart_policy:
condition: on-failure
ports:
- "5000:5000"
networks:
- sm_net
time:
image: time-service:latest
deploy:
replicas: 2
resources:
limits:
cpus: "0.1"
memory: 50M
restart_policy:
condition: on-failure
ports:
- "4000:4000"
networks:
- sm_net
networks:
sm_net:
```

A service will load balance traffic to multiple containers based on parameters. It is one of the most needed features to avoid single points of failure and share load across containers for better performance and fewer bottlenecks. We did briefly discuss load balancing in earlier chapters using Lagom's in-built functionality. Docker's sub-component called **service** offers load balancing and scaling features.

All services and containers are part of the same new sm_net network. Since we didn't configure sm_net, the default network type is assigned; Docker puts all the containers and services in the same CIDR range. It ensures that all containers in the same network have access to all ports of other containers. It's important to pay attention when adding new services to an existing network, as it could introduce us to security vulnerabilities.

To start the service, run the following command:

```
$ docker swarm init
```

To deploy services, you will have to set Docker in swarm mode. Swarm mode enables service discovery and orchestration features. We can add additional slave Docker nodes and scale from your laptop to many machines. Moving on, run the following command:

```
$ docker stack deploy -c docker-compose.yml scalamicroservices
```

The `hello-service` uses `time-service` to show `Hello, World! Yours truly,` `{hostname}` , `Time: {curr_time}` at `http://localhost:5000/`.

Visit the GitHub repository for detailed code explanation.

To effectively run and manage containers at scale (> 50 containers), orchestration tools are necessary. Orchestration helps in scheduling, placement, and uptime of containers in a farm of similar VMs. We will be dealing with orchestration exclusively in the next chapter. This example code is not really scalable, but sets the stage for the next chapter.

If you notice, the runtime is now defined using a single `.yaml` file. This is super helpful when you want to automate this process using a **configuration management system (CMS)**, such as Chef, Puppet, or Ansible. Define the template, and add to source control. CMS will get the configuration from a config-store and populate the `.yaml` skeleton file.

Container concerns

We have seen the bright side of containers and the benefits they bring to the table over hardware virtualization. It's only appropriate to see the current issues the world of containers face.

A word of caution on container security: containers are not super secure out of the box. A good amount of work needs to go in before you are truly isolated and have a low attack surface. Docker containers run root user as default, and create and set a user in your `Dockerfile`. Please refer to the following code:

```
$ cat Dockerfile
FROM busybox
....
USER newuser
```

Make sure the containers are run in secure networks, such as virtual private networks, and have read-only access to important host file system directories, such as `/sys` .

The container ecosystem is still fragmented between few ecosystems (Docker, rkt, and so on). Major progress has been made with the **open container initiative (OCI)** where industry leaders have started to create open specifications.

Early movers, notably ADP, Goldman Sachs, and the US Department of Defense, are running critical production apps on Docker. Yet, there is reluctance due to either the Docker codebase not being stable enough or the lack of tooling around it. Major progress is being made in tooling around Docker deployments, especially orchestration and native cloud support. This will be a major step toward being production-ready for more clients.

Linux containers are still far from being a stable mature ecosystem, but they are moving in the right direction.

Summary

We covered a lot of different topics in this chapter. We looked at the feedback loop and its importance. The major takeaway is that it's very valuable to spend time to create your own feedback loop; measure everything, distill it into actionable takeaways, keep it as simple as possible.

Container images are a lightweight binary that contain everything needed to run as a container. Containers are just running instances of the images. Docker is a suite of software to manage the life cycle container instances. They provide services and Stack features to load balance services. Also, it is a great tool to test, develop, and deploy applications quickly and reliably.

Rapid growth in containers around the world led to the development of an open specification of easy interoperability of different vendor images on different runtimes—the open container initiative. Enterprise companies are investing in the technology and there is an industry-wide push towards containerization. The future doesn't look clear, but containers surely have a place in there.

10
Production Containers

In the last chapter, we looked into the setup of an effective development process, server virtualization, and Linux containers. In continuation, we will be learning how to deploy and manage containers on production workload. As production systems need monitoring, access control, load balancing, scheduling, we need sophisticated distributed software to run them, enter kubernetes, a container orchestrator. This chapter talks about the critical components needed by kubernetes to run clusters of containers. Server automation tools are another important section explaining how we can prepare the virtual servers to run kubernetes. We look at one of such tools, Ansible, with a detailed example. We deep dive into kubernetes internals and run example apps. Lastly, we focus on monitoring and security features to keep in mind when using kubernetes.

The following are our objectives in this chapter:

- Learn common traits of a distributed system
- Learn basics of server automation, run Ansible example
- Learn how kubernetes distributes by understanding its internals
- Install and run a kubernetes deployment

Learn basic ways to monitor and secure a kubernetes cluster

Distributed systems and their essentials

There are distributed systems all around us. When there is a coordinated effort by lot of stakeholders to achieve a common goal, we can call it a distributed system. In our daily lives we encounter technology at every turn. The phone call we make, the email we send, the Instagram picture we upload, the Google search we perform. All of them are made possible with a distributed system running behind it.

Distributed system - definition

A **distributed system** is one in which components located at networked computers communicate and coordinate their actions only by passing messages.

There are a few key traits we can use to identify a distributed system; they are just pointers, not a complete list by themselves:

- **Geo separation**: When you interact with an application service that is geographically separated and communicates using networks, it is a very good indicator of a distributed system. Telecom networks and banking services are good examples.
- **No shared memory**: Systems that don't share a common memory address space to talk to each other. So, two processes running on a operation system are isolated but not distributed.
- **Fault tolerance**: In face of failures, physical or network, the system will most likely be up.

It's important not to forget that systems should work towards a common objective for it be a distributed system. It could be serving a simple web request for Google website, a Facebook status update, or relaying a message to the ISS.

Reasons to distribute

You might wonder, why we need a distributed system to serve a `www.google.com` webpage, seems like a simple static website. Actually, a lot of work goes on the server side in building a customized web page before it loads on your web browser. Google checks for your location, and redirects you to a regional domain , for example `www.google.ca` . It then checks if there are any active Google doodles for your region. It logs you in using an authorization server based on your browser cookies. These are few from hundreds of such actions in that simple webpage.

All these actions cannot be performed by a single server, neither in a scalable nor a performant way.

Also, some applications are distributed geographically. For example **Domain name service (DNS)**, your browser requests DNS to translate `www.google.com` to an IP. The response IP (`172.217.1.164`) is an address of some machine in California, which then is used by your router to send `GET` requests. Banking is another example where transactions are generally not localized to one geographic location, customers for a bank are all over a country. Machines are distributed in order to:

- Share infrastructure resources
- Remove performance bottleneck
- Create resilient system
- Lower cost
- **Scale linearly**: cheap, granular control over scalability. It is easier to scale throughput by adding more servers. Instead of using more expensive and powerful microprocessors on the same machines.

Don't worry if you are not able to grasp the internal working, distributed systems is a fairly complex topic. We won't be going into detail as it's a beginner's book on microservices. I highly recommend reading a book on an introduction to distributed systems.

Let's look at the software components we should expect from a distributed system to achieve the problems it claims to solve. Like how a distributed system is able to be resilient to power outages, natural calamities?

Components of a distributed system

For a distributed system to work properly, it needs certain software constructs in place. If the distributed system is a car, the application is the people it carries, then the software constructs are steering wheel, engine, axle. We will briefly look at some of these software constructs. Please refer to the following points:

- **Service discovery**: In a distributed system, a group of networked services (or apps) work together. For service A to use service B, it needs an internal service discovery tool to get an address, in most cases, an IP address.
- **Monitoring**: Unlike a monolith, system monitoring is essential as points of failure are higher, and they cascade very quickly.
- **Message queue:** Distributed systems use message passing extensively to be asynchronous to scale well.

- **Load balancing**: Application layer (L4 and L7) load balancing is essential for high availability. Multiple copies of service machines are run behind a load balancer. For external service B, it only needs one logical address to interact with, that is, the load balancer of service A.
- **Auto scaling:** Scale machines running different services based on certain parameters. To be highly available and reduce cost.

Domain name service

DNS is a classic distributed database in use since 1985, the early days of internet. It is one of the backbone software systems that enable the smooth functioning of a free internet.

Domain name service is a hierarchical decentralized naming system for computers, services, and other resources connected to the network (private or public).

DNS allows translation of human memorable names to IP addresses for routing requests and traffic. There are in total 13 geographically distributed root servers worldwide which own **Top level domains (tlds)**.

Instances of the DNS software is run primarily at those 13 locations to support the internet, but the software can be run in an internal network to provide resolution of internal names to internal IPs as well.

When a machine requests to resolve a DNS name (such as `www.google.com`), the request goes to local name server. Usually to increase performance, the local ISP caches this DNS resolution. If mapping is not present, the request is forwarded to local name server, then the request forwarded to root server, then finally to authoritative name server.

Each root server maintains a fairly small database of IPs. Lot of caching mechanisms in place are to speed up DNS lookups. Please refer to the following diagram:

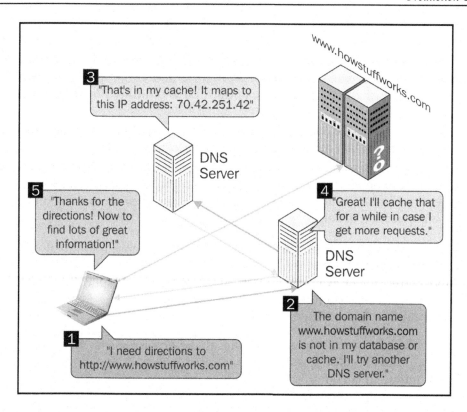

DNS is hierarchical database. All DNS entries are sub-divided into TLDS and then zones. These zones are hosted separately by physical servers called **name servers**. The preceding diagram explains how requests for specific TLDs are routed through to the network of **Geo distributed**, **non-shared memory**, **fault tolerant** machines and fulfill the user request.

Server automation

Humans are known to make trivial errors, we discussed the *feedback loop* in `Chapter 9,` *Development Process*, to solve this problem. If you noticed, most of the steps in the feedback loop were automated such as testing, continuous integration, and deployments. Automation helps us achieve predictable outcomes, prevent trivial human errors, and should be generally used everywhere in the company, not just in your software project.

I am going to define some terms we will be using extensively in this chapter:

- **Environment**: An environment usually has a collection of machines, comprising application servers, databases, network disks and so on, each environment, in turn, is sub-grouped based on business groups or utility (logging, monitoring, storage).
- **Cluster:** A cluster is loosely defined as a collection of servers which are dependent on each other in some way to perform their action.
- **Servers** or **virtual machines**: They are all synonyms in the context of this book. They are generally virtual compute machines running on metal servers in a data center. These virtual machines have an operating system running on it, where the application developer can SSH into to do run software.

Server automation has a high **return on investment (ROI)** because it indirectly impacts the revenue in many ways. In a **Software as service (SaaS)** company, automation can impact revenue almost directly. For example, more time to deploy important code fixes to production equals more loss in revenue, more time to scale machines to handle increasing traffic equals more loss in potential revenue.

Every software development setup generally has tiered-environments such as development, staging, testing, production for sandboxing to ensure high-confidence, high-quality releases. The process of setting up an environment, for the software to run, should also be automated to ensure there is **no unprecedented drift** between them. We will focus on how this can be achieved in this section.

This hinted for a need for a more comprehensive IT automation framework for sysadmins. A framework that provides:

- **Idempotency**: We tell Ansible the desired state to achieve for a server, not the process. so it won't run unwanted change commands if the desired state is already achieved.
- **Extensibility**: Modular code. Team members can contribute and grow the codebase.
- **Portability**: Works across all popular operating systems and cloud providers.

There are a few more task-specific requirements from this automation framework:

- Install and run language-specific applications/native binary applications on these servers
- Manage runtime of these deployed applications using task execution tools such as `pssh`, `ps2`, `systemctl`
- Restart application processes on failure
- Scale VMs or application based on load and traffic
- Application log aggregation
- User defined scripts

Ansible was born out of the need for merging all the preceding feature need, into a single tool with a simple declarative syntax. It still falls short on a few expectations, such as task execution and scheduling, but it is one of the most well supported automation tools out there. We will look at it in detail in the coming sections.

Use of shell scripts is still a reasonable solution, and it's still used in production by a lot of companies. Shell scripts are still essential for automation of specialized tasks. But an automation framework helps build on top of a strong foundation and a community toolkit; it's prudent to take advantage of it.

What does an automation framework look like?

We expect the framework to allow **extensibility** via plugins, **idempotency** to reduce errors, **declarative** syntax to allow readability, and a lot more.

Good use cases for automation framework are tasks that keep recurring, such as user management, secret key rotation, install OS packages, managing application configurations and secrets, health checks, replicating infrastructure for a new environment and more.

Automation framework builders have different design approaches. Some have chosen to be agentless (no agents on machines managed by the framework), some run in a master-slave configuration. Each design has made trade offs so it's important to read the philosophy of the builders before choosing one for your team. We will stick to Ansible's design to go in some level of depth, instead of contrasting all tools. I highly recommend doing POCs of all tools to see which tool suits your needs.

Automation code usually looks like any other application code. These tools have made system administration, or devOps if you may, more accessible to everyone. It is very reasonable now to expect a general software engineer to manage and scale production systems efficiently.

Infrastructure as code - Ansible

Ansible is a powerful IT automation tool which focuses on deployments, configuration management, and orchestration. It has been rising in popularity and has great community support. It is an important point to check before picking up an open source tool—the community support. Ansible was started in 2013, and was quickly acquired by Red Hat in 2015. Red Hat offers enterprise support in the form of Ansible tower.

In an oversimplified two-line description, Ansible takes in a list of virtual machine as inventory file and using public-private key authentication in the form of `ssh` keys, logs in, installs, configures based on the user supplied configuration YAML files.

Ansible only needs `ssh` service running on each managed virtual machine mentioned in the inventory file. Ansible, unlike other popular IT automation tools (chef, puppet, and so on), claims to be agentless but it rides on `sshd` and Python being present on the VMs. This avoids any additional software installation on the machines and is one of the ways Ansible stands out.

To interact with Ansible, you can use `ad-hoc cli` commands. A better, more scalable way is to define commands as configuration YAML files. These YAML files can be versioned for collaboration and persistence.

Ansible primitives

You can run Ansible from a local workstation or a dedicated machine on your cloud. Please follow instructions at `http://docs.ansible.com/ansible/intro_installation.html`. Only requirement here is that all the machines mentioned to be managed by Ansible should be reachable from your Ansible workstation.

Ansible is just like any other framework. It offers lot functionalities such as modules, primitives and more. To understand and use Ansible, we need to learn the core primitives of Ansible, that is, the building blocks; this is not an exhaustive list. Please refer to the following points:

- **Inventory File**: A simple text file listing the servers we want Ansible to manage. The default inventory file is `/etc/ansible/hosts`, where Ansible will look for. Refer to the following command:

```
$ cat /path/to/your/inventory_file
[machine_group_1]
10.0.0.1
10.0.0.2
10.0.0.3
```

- **Modules**: Modules are wrappers around certain functionalities. For example, to install an `apt` package, you can directly invoke the `apt` module which is shipped with Ansible. Running modules are idempotent, which is great. Please refer to the following command:

```
- name : installing vim apt package
apt : package=vim state=present
- name : installing nginx
apt : package=nginx state=present
```

- **Tasks**: This is a logical grouping of modules invocations. It is an action that needs to be performed on the virtual machine, such as installed Docker and running a container. Please, refer to the following command:

```
$ cat /path/to/some/task.yaml
tasks:
- name: installing docker
apt: package=docker-ce state=present
- name: running busybox container
command: docker run busybox
```

- **Roles**: Roles are a set of tasks to be performed. Before you implement your own role, please checkout Ansible galaxy for existing community developed roles.
- **Playbooks**: Is a mapping between roles to hosts inventory. Playbook you want to create for infrastructure is just composed of the preceding mentioned entities.

Ansible documentation captures it well with a couple of lines:

> *Each playbook is composed of one or more 'plays' in a list. The goal of a play is to map a group of hosts to some well defined roles, represented by things* **ansible** *calls* **tasks**. *At a basic level, a* **task** *is nothing more than a call to an* **ansible** *module*

Ansible - creating a Pageview counter

Setting up and using Ansible for a few servers or type of application should be fairly simple. We are going to learn about Ansible by using an example. It's important to go through this example as we will be using it throughout this chapter.

The problem statement at hand is--install Docker on four virtual machine servers, install **Redis** one machine, a **PageViewCounter** application on 2 servers, **Nginx** on one host to load balance traffic.

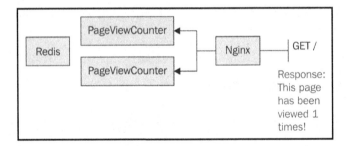

The implementation of **PageViewCounter** is not so important for our example, we are going to just use a Docker image for all the components, **Redis**, **Nginx**, **PageViewCounter**.

We are going to use Ansible to create the preceding example infrastructure. Following are the steps.

 Ideally the example virtual machines can be created locally using virtual box or on a public cloud such as AWS or Azure. I recommend using cloud to get a real feeling of the setup, but it might incur cost.

1. First step is to install Ansible on your workstation, which could be your laptop or a cloud virtual machine. Installation instructions are here http://docs.ansible.com/ansible/latest/intro_installation.html.

```
$ pip install ansible
$ mkdir ~/selvam/example-ansible/
```

2. As per the requirement, we need to create four new servers. You can create virtual machines locally or a popular cloud provider such as AWS. Lets use Ubuntu 16.04 as our OS for all servers. Add the list of IPs of these newly created machines to hosts file (inventory file).

```
$ cat ~/selvam/example-ansible/hosts
[dockerhosts]
10.0.0.1
10.0.0.2
10.0.0.3
10.0.0.4
[webservers]
10.0.0.1
10.0.0.2
[databases]
10.0.0.3
[loadbalancer]
10.0.0.4
```

We have defined four groups of hosts. A server can be part of more than one group, this logical grouping helps us run different tasks to run on which group.

3. Please ensure that all the machines created in step 2 can be connected from your local terminal. Now let's test if all servers are reachable. Run the following command on your local terminal:

```
$ ansible all -m ping -u ubuntu
```

-m flag specifies the module to use. In this case it is ping.

4. Let's create a sample file in the all the machines using a module **file** as follows:

```
$ ansible webservers -m file -a "dest=/home/system/test mode=755
owner=ubuntu group=ubuntu state=directory" -i inventory -u ubuntu
```

The preceding command runs the ansible module **file** to create /home/system/test file on all hosts of webservers group. -u specifies the user to connect the hosts with.

At this point you have already set up and started using `ansible` to manage systems successfully.

5. Now it is time to define all the task definitions. One for installing Docker:

```
$ cat ~/selvam/example-ansible/tasks/docker-task.yaml
- apt_key: url="https://download.docker.com/linux/ubuntu/gpg"
state=present
- name: add deb repo
command: add-apt-repository "deb [arch=amd64]
https://download.docker.com/linux/ubuntu $(lsb_release -cs)
stable"
- name: update apt
apt: update_cache=yes
- name: install docker
apt: name=docker-ce state=present
```

The other task definitions are present on GitHub. Please refer to repository for the complete example.

6. Now let's put this all together as an Ansible play. Running Ansible playbook is simple. Invoke `ansible-playbook` with the `play.yaml` file along with inventory file:

```
$ cat ~/selvam/example-ansible/play.yaml
- hosts: dockerhosts
vars:
key: value
become: yes
become_method: sudo
tasks:
include docker-task.yaml
- hosts: webservers
vars:
http_port: 80
remote_user: system
tasks:
include app-task.yaml
- hosts: loadbalancer
vars:
http_port: 443
remote_user: system
tasks: lb-task.yaml
include lb-task.yaml
- hosts: databases
vars:
http_port: 6379
```

```
    remote_user: system
    tasks: db-task.yaml
    include db-task.yaml
    $ ansible-playbook play.yml -i hosts ( you might have to set
    ANSIBLE_HOST_KEY_CHECKING=false)
```

7. We could have achieved some of these tasks using `ansible galaxy`, a website for users to share roles. Searching for Docker role gives us a popular `mongrelion.docker` role. Before using it in our playbook, we need to install it first.

   ```
   $ ansible-galaxy install mongrelion.docker
   ```

8. In our `play.yaml` file we need to update `dockerhosts` to use this role. Then run the playbook according to step 6:

   ```
   - hosts: dockerhosts
   roles:
   - mongrelion.docker
   ```

   This was a contrived example but sufficient enough to give you a task to show how you can go about using Ansible.

Ansible cloud modules

With the move to manage data centers and public cloud services, we encounter another problem when creating infrastructure with shell scripts or basic Ansible modules. These public clouds, popularly AWS, GCE, Azure, have exposed various interfaces such as REST API, CLI tool, language sdks, to interact with their software to deploy infrastructure, and they are richer in terms of detail and control of the cloud resources.

We can of course write code to consume this REST API. To get the same experience with stock Ansible and shell scripts will be tedious. This goes back to what we wanted from this automation framework, **idempotency**, **extensibility**, **declarative**.

Ansible cloud modules are wrappers around these sdks to call methods specific to cloud provider, for example, Ansible in the newer versions (> `1.9`) does provide AWS bindings via modules. It uses `boto3 aws python` package internally. This is great because you can leverage all the Ansible primitives while not missing out on cloud specific functionalities. Since the community support is great, these modules are well tested. You can focus only on building your infrastructure well.

An introduction to cluster orchestration

So, we have looked at automating infrastructure of a Docker-ready cluster using Ansible. We already discussed the benefits of using Docker as a first-class citizen as our execution plane, instead of using operating systems. To recap, I will list some of the most important benefits of using Docker, a container runtime:

- Lightweight isolated execution environment
- Fine-grained resource allocation, allows more isolated apps to run on the same infrastructure

To construct complicated softwares such as a riding share commerce app, we need a lot of these microservices to work together resiliently. Containers are great at running microservices. Orchestration mainly involves scheduling, resource allocation of containers. It becomes non-trivial when the number grows beyond few containers. Also, orchestrator becomes especially important for ephemeral computational jobs.

Among other things, orchestrator gives us :

- Easy scaling of apps
- Life cycle management of apps/containers
- Load balancing of inbound traffic to many containers
- Internal DNS server
- Scheduling jobs based on time or events
- Efficient resource allocation

Fault-tolerance. If a cluster node goes down in the cluster, orchestrator should find a new home for the now killed containers.

It is very common for an engineering team to end up running multiple distributed cluster to solve specific problems. For example, push notifications workers, data warehousing pipeline, analytics pipeline, logging. A common orchestration framework to run all such jobs will help teams manage, monitor less infrastructure. The framework generally tries to expose high level API exposing the above mentioned functionalities for use. Also, usually they are multi-tenant allowing different kind of workload sharing the same orchestrator.

Kubernetes

Early on in this chapter, we briefly discussed what a distributed system is. Microservices essentially form distributed systems, at least they shine in solving distributed computational problems. Each microservice is supposed to solve one problem. They work in consortium with services to fulfill the task at hand.

Kubernetes (k8s) is a container orchestrator which is platform agnostic and cloud agnostic. Google, inventor of k8s, donated this project to the Linux foundation in 2015 to help the Ops community better scale services, also to position itself better in the container era. Google has been running production workload on containers for over a decade, everything from bigtable, map-reduce runs as a container. Borg, the predecessor of k8s, is a proprietary orchestrator by Google, which they published in 2015. Google is moving onto omega, more automated Borg, led by John Wilks. Interesting articles on K8s and Google's vision for it can be found here:

- https://www.wired.com/2014/06/eric-brewer-google-docker/
- https://www.wired.com/2013/03/google-borg-twitter-mesos/
- https://www.wired.com/2014/06/google-kubernetes/

Almost any software application can be deployed using automation tool like Ansible. A playbook can create Docker image of the source code, save it to a Docker registry, then create a VM, install Docker, log into it, pull the Docker image, start the container, register itself behind a load balancer. All this can be done via a well written Ansible playbook. You might wonder, why there is a need for a complicated orchestrator? Why can't traditional automation tool based deployments work?

Traditional deployments do work, orchestrators just promise more features. The answer lies in the cost to performance ratio optimization, better fault tolerance and easy scaling. Ansible excels at config management, environment setup, automation. Kubernetes along with Docker (or some other container runtime), offers well beyond just automated deployments and config management. To name a few, k8s does auto-healing of services, application load balancing (L7), health probes for containers, cluster resource management, dynamic persistence storage provisioning. All this on top of what Ansible offers.

K8s internals

Now that the value proposition of k8s is clear, we can delve into how it is able to achieve all these features out of the box.

Kubernetes runs in a single master + multiple agent nodes cluster configuration. Master node houses all critical services (also called **control plane**) for the cluster's functioning. There is a fairly advanced deployment guide for a multi-master setup available at `https://github.com/kubernetes/kubernetes/blob/release-1.1/docs/admin/high-availability.md`.

K8s control plane is **a collection** of softwares that run as containers themselves on a cluster of machines, mainly the master. It is the K8s control plane's job to reach the desired state by creating new containers, resources, scheduling jobs and more. The state of the cluster is altered using user supplied configuration files, which triggers the control plane to reach the new desired state.

Control plane components *present on master node*:

- **Kube-apiserver**: REST API for cluster's shared state. All other components rely on `api-server` to perform CRUD operations to the state.
- **Etcd**: Distributed key value store. Persists the shared state. Used by `api-server`.
- **Kube-controller-manager**: Daemon control loop which watches the `api-server` for state changes. Responsible to move the current state to desired state of the cluster.
- **Kube-scheduler**: Heavy lifter inside k8s. Schedules containers based on policies, cluster topology, available resources.

Control plane components *present on agent node*:

- **Kube-proxy**: This container acts as a network proxy. It forwards packets arriving on TCP, UDP on node ports to containers port.
- **Kubelet**: It talks to master to get instruction on which pods to run on the node agent and runs them.

Everything inside a kubernetes cluster is defined by an API object, which can be accessed via the `api-server` running on master node. User creates application and other workloads in the form of API objects using `api-server` or `kubectl` (which takes to `api-server` internally). The API objects or the desired state is persisted in distributed key-value store.

The API object definition specifies configuration such as the number of replicas, which container images to use, type of network, ports to expose. This is the desired state of the cluster, as defined by the user. API object definition follows a spec published by k8s for each version.

The following diagram is a depiction of how these components work together:

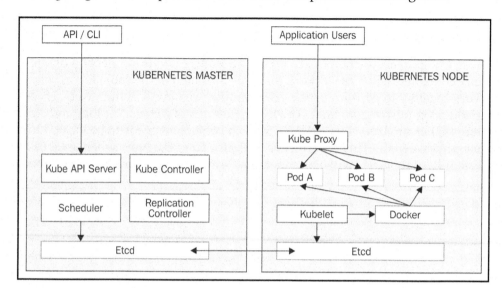

As you would have guessed, containers are the smallest functional and structural unit inside k8s cluster. There are more abstractions created on top of containers to better manage, scale and auto-heal applications efficiently. In the subsequent sections, we will explore the different kinds of abstractions present in k8s.

API objects

Any CRUD operation on this object to change its state triggers the control plane to act on the cluster to move closer to the desired state.

New bleeding edge features in kubernetes are added frequently. Also the fact that kubernetes has so many feature sets, their API is structured into API groups such as Core, extensions, batch and so on.

There are a lot of API objects supported by k8s as of v1.7 . Please explore the kubernetes API to see the exhaustive list of objects `https://kubernetes.io/docs/api-reference/v1.7/` . We will be looking at the following objects as they are more commonly prevalent in most use cases.

- Pods
- ConfigMaps
- Secrets

- Deployment
- Services
- Namespace

The most basic logical abstraction in k8s is called a **pod**. A pod is a collection of one or many Linux containers (such as Docker), that are co-located in the same k8s agent node and need to work together to perform a task. For example, we have a Python web-server container and a log-pusher container. The log-pusher reads web-server logs and stores them in a filestore (S3) in Amazon cloud (AWS). So both containers needs to be located together in the same physical node. This is perfect use-case for K8s Pod. Now when scale up, pods get replicated. Each replica is with container one Python web server and one log-pusher:

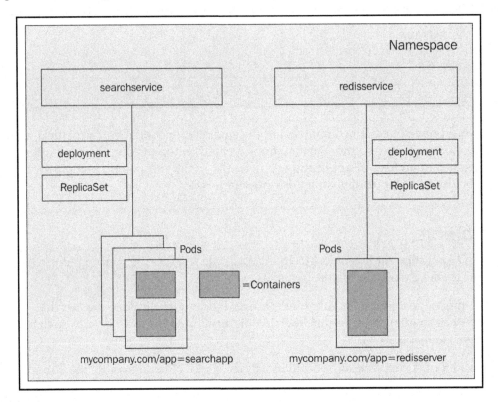

K8s ConfigMaps are just hashmaps that can be used to carry application runtime parameters. They are just plain hashmaps, so any string can be stored in it. The primary way to consume them is as volume mounts onto containers inside pods.

K8s Secrets are the same as ConfigMaps except that they are used for storing sensitive information. This gives us more flexibility in handling passwords and access keys.

K8s Deployments are definitions on on how to run Pod along with associated volumes, ConfigMaps, Secrets.

K8s Services are proxy to load balance traffic between pods. Services are accessible across the cluster via the DNS entry `servicename.namespace:serviceport`. Services API object requires a selector field where labels are to be defined. All pods across deployments that have the same label, receive routed traffic from the service on the service port.

The biggest logical grouping or abstraction in k8s is namespace. Namespaces are a simple way to sandbox K8s resources (also known as API objects) to not collide with other logical namespaces. A namespace can span across few or all physical k8s agent nodes. They are just logical groupings, just like closures in software programming. Remember, some services and API objects work across namespaces, so always read the documentation properly.

Config management

Config management is a very important feature needed in a distributed system. This helps network attached systems to share control plane information. Also user applications can make use of config management. As you would have hoped, config management is an API object called ConfgMaps.

ConfigMaps are just key value pairs scopes to namespaces. They allow us to keep our application code portable by loading configuration at runtime. These key value pairs can be mounted onto a pod's containers as volumes. Please refer to the following code:

```
kubectl create configmap test-config --from-file=/etc/test-app/
kubectl create configmap test-config -from-literal=special.how=very
--from-literal=special.type=charm
```

Secrets are a `configmap` of sensitive information. Only difference is that the data is stored as Base64 instead of plaintext for protection. The best way to further protect them is to restrict access via RBAC rules which we will talk about later in this chapter.

Incase of Secrets and ConfigMaps, pods using them needs to be restarted for the application within it to use the new changes.

All other API objects values can be changed, updated or deleted from kubernetes dashboard UI (with correct permissions) or using `kubectl`.

K8s setup guide

Kubernetes cluster deployment involves configuring virtual machines with the right software binaries installed. All of the VMs will need Docker installed on them, which implies any operating system that supports Docker can be used.

Master and agent node distinction is strictly not necessary, though commonly done. Critical services (running as pods) such as `api-server`, `etcd`, `kube-controller` are scheduled to run on one node, as they can cause seriously obstruct the functioning of the pods. This node is usually referred to as master. Also, each node can have different machine configuration. This has no impact on functioning of kubernetes, as pods placement is done based on node resources.

Deployment of k8s in high availability configuration is beyond the scope of this book, but is well explained in the official documentation of kubernetes. Using auto-scaling features of public cloud and infrastructure as code, it should be fairly easy to scale kubernetes cluster beyond few nodes.

That being said, the easiest and robust way of deploying K8s cluster in a cloud agnostic way is by using **kubeadm**. Creating a K8s master on a VM is as simple as running `kubeadm init`.

Subsequent nodes to this cluster can be added by running kubeadm join `token <token> <master-ip>:<master-port>`.

Follow official instructions are here `https://kubernetes.io/docs/setup/independent/create-cluster-kubeadm/`.

K8s example app

We are planning to deploy the sample application we did with Ansible in **server automation** section earlier. This will help us compare and understand the superiority of k8s as a runtime. It is interesting to note that Ansible can be used to manage and deploy containers on kubernetes using Ansible modules.

We are going to use `kubectl` to post our API objects to the cluster. We need to make sure you have access to the cluster. At the end of K8s setup, you should get a `kubeconfig` file. Please refer to the following command:

```
$ export KUBECONFIG=/path/to/kubeconfig_file
$ kubectl get nodes
$ kubectl cluster-info
```

Kubernetes dashboard is fairly new feature. We can view the current state of most of the API objects in k8s cluster such as Pod, Deployment, Service, Node, ConfigMap, Secret and so on. The list is growing as more features are getting added.

Run `kubectl proxy` to establish a reverse tunnel between master node, where the dashboard pod is running, and your workstation. Now you can visit, `http://127.0.0.1:8000/ui` to see the dashboard. Please refer to the following command:

```
$ kubectl proxy
```

Before we start, we need a K8s namespace to create all our resources, as follows:

```
$ kubectl create namespace ns-pagviewcounter
```

You can directly use `kubectl get {API_OBJECT}` to get more details.

Let's get started by deploying a single replica Redis server and a k8s service as well. We are using the stock Redis Docker image for this, as follows:

```
$ cat redis.deployment.yaml
apiVersion: extensions/v1beta1
kind: Deployment
metadata:
labels:
my.company.com/app: redis
name: redis-deployment
spec: ←------------ ReplicaSet Spec
replicas: 2
template:
metadata:
labels:
my.company.com/app: redis
name: redis-pod
spec: ←------- POD Spec
containers:
- name: redis-container
image: redis:latest
imagePullPolicy: Always
ports:
- containerPort: 6379
- - -
  kind: Service
apiVersion: v1
metadata:
name: redisservice
spec:
selector:
```

```
my.comany.com/app: redis
ports:
- name: tcp-port
protocol: TCP
port: 6379
targetPort: 6379


$ kubectl apply -f redis.complete.yaml -n ns-pagviewcounter
```

We defined both service and deployment in the same file `redis.complete.yaml`. Our application pod running in the same k8s cluster can access `redisservice:6379`. Let's deploy the `pageviewcounter` application with two replicas. We are going to load balance behind a k8s service in the next step:

```
$ cat pageviewcounter.deployment.yaml
apiVersion: extensions/v1beta1
kind: Deployment
metadata:
labels:
my.company.com/app: pageviewcounter
name: pageviewcounter-deployment
spec:
replicas: 2
template:
metadata:
labels:
my.company.com/app: pageviewcounter
name: pageviewcounter-pod
spec:
containers:
- name: pageviewcounter-container
image: chartotu19/pageviewcounter:v1
imagePullPolicy: Always
ports:
- containerPort: 80


 $ kubectl apply -f pageviewcounter.deployment.yaml -n ns-pagviewcounter
We are going to make a corresponding k8s service , which will route traffic
to .
$ cat pageviewcounter.service.yaml
kind: Service
apiVersion: v1
metadata:
name: pageviewcounterservice
spec:
selector:
my.comany.com/app: pageviewcounter
ports:
```

```
- name: http-port
protocol: TCP
port: 80
targetPort: 80
type: LoadBalancer ← optional
$ kubectl apply -f pageviewcounter.service.yaml -n ns-pagviewcounter
```

To test the application, we could map the service to a cloud L4 load balancer to get a public IP to access the server. If you don't want to do that, log into any of the k8s nodes in the cluster, and run:

```
$ curl http://pageviewcounterservice:80
```

This example demonstrates the ease which we can deploy a load balanced application using simple YAML configurations.

The YAML file structure is defined in the kubernetes API specification. Pay attention to the API groups as it is a fairly new project, features get upgraded from Alpha level to Beta level to Stable level `https://kubernetes.io/docs/concepts/overview/kubernetes-api/`. Some new properties or types might be added to the existing API objects.

Always rely on the API specification as blogs and tutorials get outdated pretty fast with kubernetes.

K8s monitoring

Since pods are collections of containers which are run by the container runtime, in our case docker, logs for every pod is collected based on the default logging driver used by Docker. The default is **json-file,** which writes logs for each container to a JSON file on the agent node where the pod is running.

There are a lot of pluggable log drivers available. As of Docker v17, there are nine supported drivers `https://docs.docker.com/engine/admin/logging/overview/#supported-logging-drivers`. To switch drivers, the Docker daemon running on k8s agent nodes can be started with one of these drivers:

```
$ /usr/bin/docker daemon -H fd:// --storage-driver=overlay --logging-driver=fluentd
```

Docker also lets us specify logging driver per container.

The `fluentd`, one of the nine drivers, claims to be an *is an open source data collector for unified logging layer*. `fluentd` driver runs on the application server to stream logs to lots of possible sinks such as a `fluentd` server, Elasticsearch, kafka, S3, Azure Blob Store and so on using plugins.

To use `fluentd` logging driver to stream logs to a `fleuntd` server, we need to specify two things. `fluentd` server host and port (default is `24224`).

```
docker run --log-driver=fluentd --log-opt fluentd-
address=fluentdserver:fluentdport
```

Consistent and reliable log aggregation of pods across the cluster is very important to perform any sort of monitoring and eventually alerting. For example, An application such as the `pageviewcounter` configured to run multiple replicas, can run on many distributed k8s nodes/agents. This leads to system partitioned log files.

Please refer to the previous section to see the `pageviewcounter.deployment.yaml` file. To view logs for this deployment in K8s.

```
$ kubectl get pods -n ns-pagviewcounter
// log for just one pod.
$ kubectl logs -f deployment-pod-name -n ns-pagviewcounter
```

We are running `pageviewcounter` as a kubernetes service (a.k.a microservice), which routes traffic to two replicated pods. It is non-trivial usecase to search across all log files at the same time.

There are many strategies to solve this problems explained in the official kubernetes documentation `https://kubernetes.io/docs/concepts/cluster-administration/logging/#cluster-level-logging-architectures`.

We will look at a very simple solution for now. Instead of using `json-file`, we will switch to `fluentd` driver. A `fluentd` server needs to be running to direct all logs to it. All our kubernetes cluster nodes should be running docker daemon with `fluentd` driver.

We will switch our Docker daemon's default log driver by starting the `dockerd` daemon by setting it in `/etc/docker/daemon.json`.

```
{
  "log-driver": "fluentd",
  "log-opts": {
    "fluentd-address": "fluentdserver:24224"
  }
}
```

All logs from all Docker engines in the kubernetes cluster should be started with docker logging driver as `fluentd`. This will forward all our logs to `fluentdservert:24224` server. Now that logs are streaming from all containers to `fluentd` server, it is easy to push these logs onward to kafka, Elasticsearch, backup server(S3, Blobstore and so on). This can be done with a declarative `fluentd.conf` file on the server. The syntax and plugin usage is explained on `fluentd` website. The following is a `fluentd.conf` for our example:

```
<source>
@type forward
port 24224
bind 0.0.0.0
</source>

<match *>
@type copy
<store>
@type elasticsearch
log_level info
include_tag_key true
host {{ELASTICSEARCH_HOST_HERE}}
port 9200
</store>
</match>
```

Once all log data is streamed inside Elasticsearch, alerting is a breeze. Application specific queries can be defined and polled at regular intervals to Elasticsearch to detect anomalies, `https://github.com/Yelp/elastalert`. Explaining how to use ELK (elasticsearch + logstash + kibana) stack is beyond the scope of this book.

K8s security

It's important to secure your kubernetes installation using cryptographic encryption. Especially by letting the application developer pick and choose the technology stack to define container images, cluster ends up with a diverse set of containers running. The chances of vulnerabilities showing up is high.

There are many security features in kubernetes and in public cloud to secure your business data. There are two broad levels of protection that can be configured.

Based on your team's knowledge and expertise, you should decide which level to invest more in. It is important to note that the simplest security features, sometimes have the maximum impact. It is important to understand the security implications of each level, before working on it.

Network level

Firstly, the host VMs on which kubernetes is running should be secured. The attack surface can be greatly reduced here by moving all machines into a virtual private network. A virtual private network is a construct where machines are placed in an isolated private network, with limited restricted inbound traffic. Routes and security rules can be defined for ingress and egress traffic on specific ports. Most popular public clouds offer VPNs at fraction of cost than self hosting.

This is a probably the easiest security measure that you can take with a very high return on investment. Doing this right should be high on the priority list. The premise is that it is very hard to hack into a machine, if there exists to internet route to reach it. The machines will have a publicly reachable IP, only if they are really need to be.

Move all VMs, Databases into a virtual private network preferably on public cloud.

All machines within a VPN will be assigned static IP from the private address space. Remember, it is a usual practice to allow all protocols (HTTP, FTP, SSH , RDP and so on) and all ports (0-65355) between VMs are allowed inside a virtual private network through a master route table or route entry. This greatly simplifies the network topology, as every machine is discoverable and accessible right out of the box without any configuration. Since the exposure of VM ports to the outside world is highly restrictive, this should be fine.

VPN is a safe environment for your resources, so it's important to not install any random software on it without verifying.

The following figure shows an example configuration of servers within a virtual private network. We are using an example of AWS here, though this trivial setup can be done on any cloud or self hosted servers.

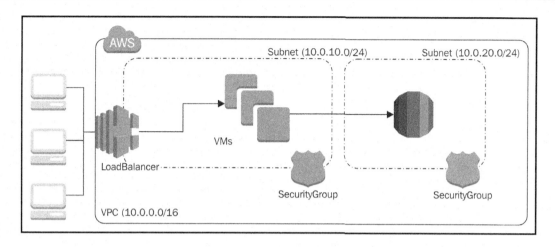

Service level

We are referring to k8s service here. Kubernetes is a group of software which runs on a cluster of VMs. Each VM will need to have Docker installed, `openssl` binary, `ssh` and few more. All internal communication between nodes, node and `api-server`, is encrypted using x509 certificates generated by default. You will find the certificates in `/etc/kubernetes/certs/`.

Certificates

Kubernetes uses a **certificate authority** (**CA**) to sign certificates for internal communication. A public-private certificate pair is generated at cluster initiation for `apiserver` (`apiserver.crt`, `apiserver.key`) and node (`client.crt`, `client.key`). Based on which tool you are using (`kubeadm`, `acs-engine`, `GKE`), the certificate pairs will be generated automatically or will have to be provided by the user at install time.

This certificate authority is exposed via API group `certificates.k8s.io/v1beta1` for users to send **certificate signing requests** (**CSR**) to generate new signed certificates for user defined k8s services.

Authentication

There are pods and users who need access to the API server. As discussed, API server, persists the state of the cluster and exposes a frontend for all K8s elements (such as pods) to interact. For example, If we wanted to create a new service, we will have to make a HTTP POST call to the /service API endpoint of the K8s cluster apiserver. (Kubectl internally makes REST calls).

So authentication is necessary to perform CRUD operations on the cluster. User authentication is restricted initially to one admin account which is auto generated and is done via x509 cert. The admin can decide to create more user accounts and restrict access to specific resource types or namespaces via the RBAC rules which we will discuss now.

Authorization using RBAC

Role based access control (**RBAC**) is a common authorization feature in most shared software. It allows administrators to define roles , assign permissions to it, assign users to these roles. Authentication, which is verifying if the user is really who he/she claims is done by different software which in our case is using kubectl and certs (kubeconfig) .

Services translate to microservices and are central to our design. Access to API resources to services is restricted via service account.

RBAC features were added to kubernetes in 1.6 version.

Access to kubernetes control to grouped into services and users. Service accounts are used by non-humans (pods, containers) to access kubernetes. User accounts are used to access kubernetes clusters from outside. Kubernetes gives scoped access to users.

The complete source code for the example with RBAC rules is on GitHub. Please check it out for more documentation and the help guide.

Caveats

Looking back at what we have learnt in this chapter, it might seem like kubernetes has it all. That is not true. There have been documented concerns with production use of Docker. Having said that Docker is being used in production by a lot of companies and notably the federal government of the United States. Kubernetes is also in a similar state, being run in production by notable companies such as SoundCloud, NY times. Being developed by the community, Google engineers still contribute a lot to its source still. This has given lot more confidence to adopters. Some common concerns with docker and kubernetes is around :

- **Actively developed:** Docker engine is fairly stable with its feature set. Kubernetes has lot of important features still in alpha or beta. Alpha features can be changed completely in future releases, deterring engineers from using to for production workloads.
- **Ephemeral:** Containers are by design ephemeral. This is starkly different from traditional VM workloads. Even though kubernetes is capable of running stateful applications and database with persistence, there is hesitation from engineers to run persistent services on k8s.
- **Cocktail of new technologies:** Docker rides on some major advancement in Linux kernel. Kubernetes evolved from Google's famed Borg system. For new teams to adopt these new tools, there is a learning curve.

Summary

This chapter has given an overview of running containers in a scalable way. We looked at current state-of-the-art in server automation, and how Ansible can be used to create repeatable infrastructure in an automated fashion.

While designing a microservice based architecture, understanding the key features of a good distributed system is important. Running microservices at scale requires a lot of support services and there are good tools such as kubernetes to use. With the advent of kubernetes, and notable predecessors, it has become easier to run and scale microservices as they are first-class citizens.

For here it is important to read up on kubernetes documentation, to understand all the resource objects provided by k8s. Read up on more complex deployments done by community members.

The key takeaway regarding kubernetes is that it is a formidable orchestrator for containers. It is not a fit for all solutions (at least not yet), and but it is definitely a great fit for some. In the next chapter, we will work on deploying a full fledged application on kubernetes!

11

Example Application in K8s

In the last two chapters, you learned the problems and possible solutions for how to write and run applications in production. Chapter 9, *Development Process*, focused on processes to do software engineering better, especially in microservices-based architecture. Chapter 10, *Production Containers* focused on container technology and on how to use it effectively for more development speed and better ratio of cost to usage of infrastructure.

In this final chapter, we will look at how to use what you learned about Kubernetes in Chapter 10, *Production Containers*, to containerize the Chapter 4, *Dive Deeper*, example, **Talent search engine**. The Chapter 4, *Dive Deeper* example had many microservices (such as auth, Stack Overflow, GitHub, web) working together to find the best developers in a queried city.

We will look at making docker images for each service, push the images to cloud docker registry, write kubernetes configuration for each to use those images, and deploy! Once the application is functional in kubernetes, that is, once we are able to see and perform searches, we will do rolling deployments of new code to one of the services to illustrate how easy it is to update in kubernetes. Each section is accompanied by a GitHub code to support it. It is very important to walk through the code while reading this chapter.

As per the effective development process, the code owners (it might not always be you) can push fixes, which in turn lead to new docker image versions. These images then can be directly picked up by the devOps team to deploy into kubernetes as an update. We will see how to do that in the *Blue-green deployment* section.

In this chapter, we will cover the following topics:

- How to create and set up a kubernetes cluster
- How to dockerize a piece of code
- How to write kubernetes configurations
- How to run a kubernetes deployment
- How to roll deploy code changes to kubernetes cluster

Talent search engine example

The reason we will revisit the talent search engine example is because the software logic has already been discussed and implemented. We can focus purely on deploying them. In this chapter, with minimal effort, we will containerize each of the services.

The deployment of it in the kubernetes cluster is going to require basic information about each individual services such as port, statelessness, traffic, and external DNS entry.

This is a sample example of a play framework application discussed in depth in `Chapter 4`, *Dive Deeper*. It comprises many individual microservices working together to help search for developers based on two parameters: location and speciality (Scala and Java). Check out the Github repo for an in-depth walk through of the code logic, as this chapter won't be dealing with that. Also, *among the many microservices, we will deploy only three of the most important services to demonstrate a working example in kubernetes. The three services are as follows:*

- **Auth-app**: This app is a REST API server that authenticates and authorizes requests for account
- **So-app**: This is the REST API server that returns stack overflow users based on query parameters
- **Web-app**: This is the Javascript Single page app written in React and backend in Scala

The application is a web application that allows authenticated users to search for Stack Overflow users based on **location** and **tag.** The following screenshot is the landing page for the web app:

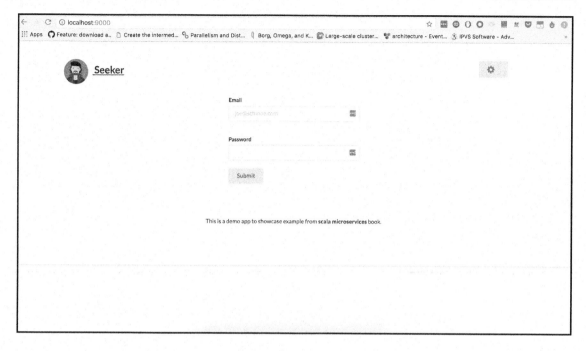

All three services are REST-based servers written in Scala. The web-app depends on the auth-app for user authentication and on the so-app for performing search.

Dockerize

Looking at the three individual applications, you will notice that all of them are Scala projects; however, this is not a necessity. This is just a convenience thing for a team to use a well-tested tool or language. Docker makes it easy to deploy any kind of application written in any language. In this section, we will focus primarily on dockerizing and deploying our seeker application.

If you remember, to create docker images, all you need is a recipe called Dockerfile. Before we get to writing a custom Dockerfile for our applications, we need to ensure your workspace has all the right tools. Follow these steps:

- Install docker by following the instructions on `https://docs.docker.com/engine/installation/`.

- Install git by following the instructions on `https://www.atlassian.com/git/tutorials/install git`, and download the source code from `https://github.com/scala-microservices-book/book-examples`
- Install sbt from `http://www.scala-sbt.org/1.0/docs/Setup.html`. Make sure you have sbt to build your project.

Ideally, the **continuous integration (CI)** pipeline is responsible for building the project. Once the test cases pass, CI builds artifacts and generates a docker image. The `dockerfile` simply copies the `.jar` file into a path and sets the docker CMD.

We will skip the CI step and directly build the project locally on our workspace:

```
$ cd book-examples/chapter-4/
```

You will enter the `sbt` prompt:

```
$ sbt> project web-app
$ sbt> dist
```

Now, the project has been packaged for distribution. You can find the JAR file at so-app/target/universal/so-app-0.1-SNAPSHOT.zip.

Creating a Docker image

Let's pick a tiny (in size) docker image that has Java in it. It is highly recommended that you use tiny docker images as your base because you will soon find that your kubernetes agents nodes are running out of disk space, as K8s master keeps providing new containers from different deployments on agent nodes and each of them may involve pulling fresh docker images.

We will use Alpine-based java docker image *anapsix/alpine-java* for this endeavor. So, let's look at the `Dockerfile` for the `web-app` container. Consider the following code:

```
$ cd path/to/chapter-4/web-app/
$ cat Dockerfile
```

```
FROM anapsix/alpine-java
MAINTAINER Selvam Palanimalai selvam.palanimalai@gmail.com
COPY target/universal/web-app-0.1-SNAPSHOT.zip /opt/scala/web-app.zip
RUN unzip /opt/scala/web-app.zip -d /opt/scala/
CMD /opt/scala/web-app-0.1-SNAPSHOT/bin/web-app -
Dplay.http.secret.key=$HTTP_SECRET -Dplay.crypto.secret=$APP_SECRET
```

The preceding `dockerfile` pulls the base docker image alpine-java. It copies over the `auth-app-0.1-SNAPSHOT.zip` file into the `/opt/scala` folder of the docker image. Then, it unzips the `SNAPSHOT.zip`. It sets the main docker command that will be started on docker.

If you pull the source for `Chapter 4`, *Dive Deeper* from GitHub, you will notice a `Dockerfile` in every service folder.

Testing the Docker image

We already know that a Dockerfile is a sort of recipe to generate docker images. So, let's build our docker image for the web-app using the Dockerfile we just created:

```
$ cd path/to/chapter-4/web-app/
$ docker build -t web-app
```

This process will take time the first time it is run; subsequent runs will be faster because of the docker image layers getting cached. If you see successfully built <image_hash>, it means your docker build went successfully. Time to create a container instance:

```
$ docker run -d -e APP_SECRET="sadsasdasdaws" -e HTTP_SECRET="@#$@#$#@WEWQ"
-p 9000:9000 web-app
```

Notice that we passed two environment variables, `HTTP_SECRET` and `APP_SECRET`, with our docker run. If you look at Dockerfile, the CMD keyword is followed by the main docker process (PID 1) of container. That process required these two environment variables.

The container's web-app is mapped to port 9000 of your workstation. Since it is a website, we can view it at `http://localhost:9000`. You should see the the talent search engine's homepage.

Pushing the Docker image

Docker Registry is a place to store and retrieve Docker images. This is to facilitate high availability of images for easy deployments. Usually, it is advised to use Docker registry in a public cloud, but it's open source and can be self-hosted too.

To push a Docker image to the official public registry from Docker Inc., you will need to create an account on dockerhub.com. It's free. Usually, there is one Docker image per code repository. So, web-app will have one, and auth-app will have its own. Another important practice is to maintain Docker image tags just like GIT (or other VCS) versions. Ideally, each Docker image tag should ideally correspond to a GIT tag or GIT commit.

To quickly push an image directly from your workstation, run the following command:

```
$ docker login
```

You will be prompted to enter your `dockerhub.com` `username` and `password` combo:

```
$ docker tag web-app {username}/web-app:v1
```

We are tagging our `web-app` as `v1`. Feel free to pick some other name here:

```
$ docker push {username}/web-app:v1
```

Dockerhub only provides one private repository for free account. So, don't end of pushing proprietary docker images as they will be publicly available.

What we did earlier manually, generating images, should be taken care of by a CI pipeline. It should be building images and pushing images to registry automatically on every code commit on specific branches (generally develop, release, and master).

Just as an example, we will look at CI setup using `circleci.com` (proprietary SaaS company). We could have very well used Jenkins here, but CircleCI is much easier to configure.

You will have to create a `circleCI.yml` file for the project at the root level and commit it. CircleCI watches for this file and triggers the pipeline based on it on every commit.

The structure of the `circleci.yml` file is shown here:

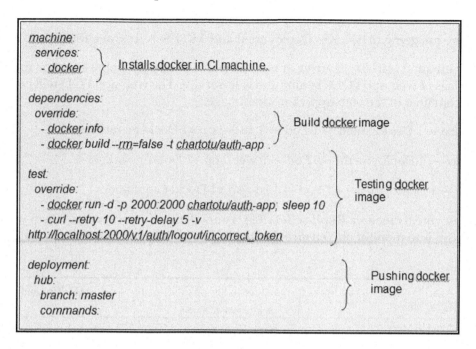

Deployment topology

In this section, we will look at the deployment strategy of our Talent Search engine app. This step is required before we proceed to write kubernetes configuration files. Since the configuration will be based on the topology.

Our focus is on running the application in with high availability and fault tolerance. What it means is that the application should always try to respond to adverse conditions such as machine failure, excessive traffic, spikes in traffic, network failure on machine, and so on.

This is also a good time to analyze the requirements and define Service Level Agreement (SLA) for each service to better allocate resources. It's impossible to predict all of it right away, but we need to start somewhere. Also, kubernetes has built-in auto scaling (`https://kubernetes.io/docs/tasks/run-application/horizontal-pod-autoscale/`) to handle unprecedented traffic. It has auto-healing abilities to detect misbehaving pods and to recreate them.

As discussed in the talent search engine example, we will deploy only three of the services from Chapter 4, *Dive Deeper* web service, auth service, and so service.

Hence there are going to be 3 K8s Deployment and 3 K8s Services, one for each.

All public inbound traffic will arrive at web-service. To support that, we will be running three replicas of web-app PODs behind the web-service. The web-app POD will contain only one container of the web-app:v1 docker image:

auth-service → 1 Deployment → 1 Pod → 1 auth-app.v1 Docker container

web-service → 1 Deployment → 3 Pod → 3 web-app.v1 Docker container

so-service → 1 Deployment → 1 Pod → 1 so-app.v1 Docker container

Every deployment creates a **Replica Set (RS)**. You will mostly never create them yourself. The job of RS is to monitor and ensure that the requested number of pods is actually running.

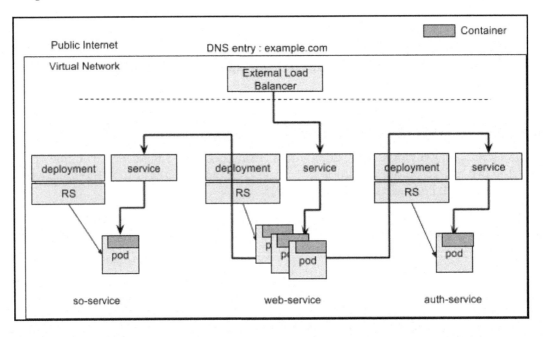

We will need a public DNS entry for the web-service. We will use a cloud-managed load balancer for the web-app service. You can very well use an Nginx-based load balancer as well. This can be achieved by adding one additional line to the service.yml file. We will take a look at it later in this section.

It is also important to take into account the k8s node agents. If there is only one agent running in the cluster other than master, we really don't have high availability (HA), as there is a single point of failure. Make sure your production deployment has many k8s agent nodes running.

K8s configurations

Now that we have docker images for each individual application and we have deployment topology figured out, it is time to write actual kubernetes configurations.

The exercise in the previous section helped us plan the number of containers per service to handle our traffic.

Before we start writing our configurations, it is always good to come up with naming conventions. We will realize that soon, as there will be too many things to name. Certain conventions that we will adopt in this example are as follows:

- Any resource created in k8s will have a name prefixed with shorthand for scalamicroservices (sm-). This is essential to distinguish between your resources and system-generated resources and also resources from other users of the cluster.
- Decide on a tool to apply changes to kubernetes, and stick to it for consistency--Kubectl or REST API, not both. We will use kubectl.
- Every resource will have its own configuration. You can stack resources in the same YAML file, but for clarity, we will break them down. For example, we can put Service, Deployment definition for auth-service in the same `auth-service.yml` file, but we will make `auth.service.yml` and `auth.deployment.yaml`.

The source for each of the three microservices are available in GitHub under `scala-microservices-book/book-examples/chapter11/1-deploy-all`.

Let's start by defining k8s deployment. A deployment resource is a very fundamental resource. It allows us to mainly specify the following:

- Pod template--volume mounts, containers, and so on
- Number of replicas of the pods
- Deployment strategy--recreate or rolling update

For the complete deployment specification, visit `https://kubernetes.io/docs/api-reference/v1.7/#deployment-v1beta1-apps`.

Kubernetes is an actively developed project. Lot of new features keep getting added with every version. Check out the API reference for your kubernetes cluster version at `https://kubernetes.io/docs/api-reference/v1.7/`.

Auth-service

If you look at source for auth-app in `book-examples/chapter-4/ github`, you will notice that the H2 database is running in memory. So, for this example, we are restricted to one pod for an auth-service. If the database is hosted on a separate server/pod, we can scale up the replicas of the auth-app pods.

The `deployment.yml` file looks like this:

```
apiVersion: extensions/v1beta1
kind: Deployment
metadata:
  name: auth-deployment
  labels:
    app: auth
    environment: production
spec:
  replicas: < Replica count >
  strategy:
  template:
    < POD template >        This template has almost all properties of pod
                            specification . https://kubernetes.io/docs/api-
```

Let's look at the pod template closely as all the container definitions are here:

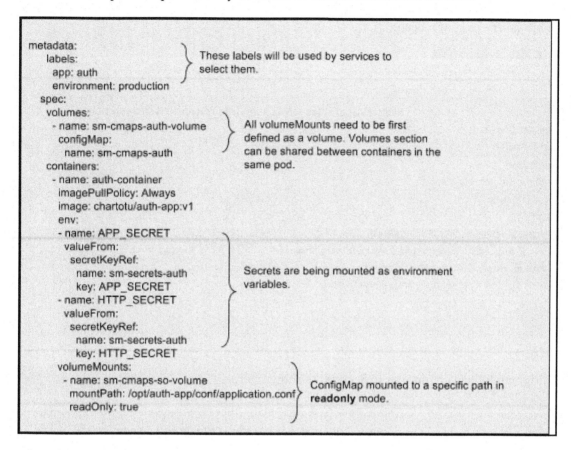

```
metadata:
   labels:
      app: auth
      environment: production
```
These labels will be used by services to select them.

```
spec:
   volumes:
      - name: sm-cmaps-auth-volume
        configMap:
           name: sm-cmaps-auth
```
All volumeMounts need to be first defined as a volume. Volumes section can be shared between containers in the same pod.

```
   containers:
      - name: auth-container
        imagePullPolicy: Always
        image: chartotu/auth-app:v1
        env:
        - name: APP_SECRET
          valueFrom:
             secretKeyRef:
                name: sm-secrets-auth
                key: APP_SECRET
        - name: HTTP_SECRET
          valueFrom:
             secretKeyRef:
                name: sm-secrets-auth
                key: HTTP_SECRET
```
Secrets are being mounted as environment variables.

```
        volumeMounts:
        - name: sm-cmaps-so-volume
          mountPath: /opt/auth-app/conf/application.conf
          readOnly: true
```
ConfigMap mounted to a specific path in **readonly** mode.

You will notice that `sm-cmaps-auth` and `sm-secrets-auth` are being used, but have not been discussed until now.

`sm-cmaps-auth` will contain the `application.conf` file. `sm-secrets-auth` will contain `HTTP_SECRET` and `APP_SECRET`. You can, of course, add more to them as the application business logic grows.

You can get really creative with Secrets and ConfigMaps by breaking it down and sharing global values across other deployment . We will keep things simple and make one secret and one configmap for every deployment for now.

K8s secret values need to be base64 encoded in the YAML file. The value will be decoded to plain string when mounted as volume or environment variable on a container. Lets look at the `sm-secrets-auth` Secret :

```
$ cat secret.yml
```

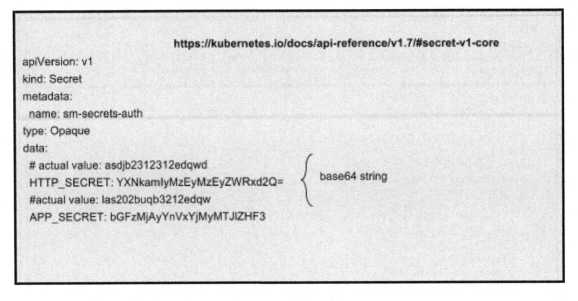

```
                    https://kubernetes.io/docs/api-reference/v1.7/#secret-v1-core
apiVersion: v1
kind: Secret
metadata:
  name: sm-secrets-auth
type: Opaque
data:
  # actual value: asdjb2312312edqwd
  HTTP_SECRET: YXNkamlyMzEyMzEyZWRxd2Q=     } base64 string
  #actual value: las202buqb3212edqw
  APP_SECRET: bGFzMjAyYnVxYjMyMTJlZHF3
```

Configmap looks very similar to Secrets, as shown here:

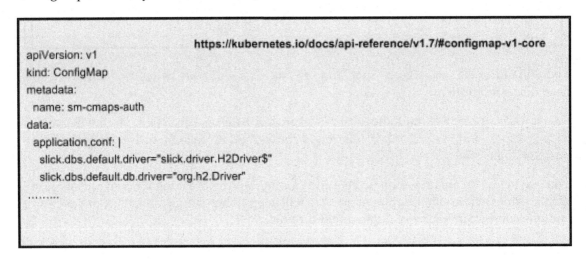

```
                    https://kubernetes.io/docs/api-reference/v1.7/#configmap-v1-core
apiVersion: v1
kind: ConfigMap
metadata:
  name: sm-cmaps-auth
data:
  application.conf: |
    slick.dbs.default.driver="slick.driver.H2Driver$"
    slick.dbs.default.db.driver="org.h2.Driver"

..........
```

The way K8s Service works is simple. It finds all pods (in the same namespace) that match the selector. Selector is just a map of labels, which is a mandatory parameter in the `service.yml` file.

Then, the traffic to this service is routed to all selected pods. In the following config, all pods with the `app:auth` and `environment:production` labels are selected:

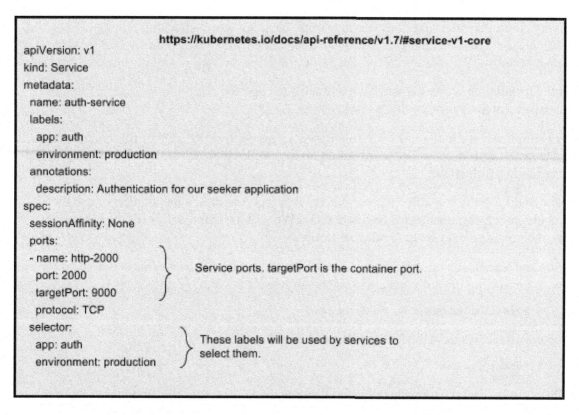

```
                    https://kubernetes.io/docs/api-reference/v1.7/#service-v1-core
apiVersion: v1
kind: Service
metadata:
  name: auth-service
  labels:
    app: auth
    environment: production
  annotations:
    description: Authentication for our seeker application
spec:
  sessionAffinity: None
  ports:
  - name: http-2000
    port: 2000             } Service ports. targetPort is the container port.
    targetPort: 9000
    protocol: TCP
  selector:
    app: auth              } These labels will be used by services to
    environment: production    select them.
```

The preceding process will be the same for so-app and web-app deployments. Take a look at the source code on GitHub.

Installation of K8s

Before we deploy our K8s configurations, we need a kubernetes cluster to connect to. Follow the instructions here to set up the kubernetes cluster using kubeadm at `https://kubernetes.io/docs/setup/independent/create-cluster-kubeadm/`. I recommend that you use a cloud account for this example even though it might cost a little bit.

Every cloud provider gives out free accounts. They are worth checking out at `https://aws.amazon.com/free/`, `https://cloud.google.com/free`, and `https://azure.microsoft.com/en-us/free/`.

If the installation was successful, we will have to copy the admin `kubeconfig` file. It is usually located at `/etc/kubernetes/admin.conf`.

For simplicity, we will not do any role-based access control (RBAC) for this cluster. We will just use the admin `kubeconfig` file to do all our deployments. This is not a recommended practice in production.

You could use the versatile `kubectl` CLI tool shipped with K8s installation or use the kubernetes cluster dashboard to create them. We will use `kubectl` as it's the easiest. So, let's set up `kubectl` on our local workstation.

First and foremost, you will you have to set the kueconfig file path. This is where `kubectl` looks for finding the auth cert and K8s cluster master DNS:

```
$ export KUBECONFIG=~/.kube/config
```

Now, let's try to access the Kubernetes dashboard:

```
$ kubectl proxy
```

This creates a proxy from a localhost address to the Kubernetes apiserver running on the K8s master node. Visit `http://127.0.0.1:8001/ui` to see the kubernetes default dashboard:

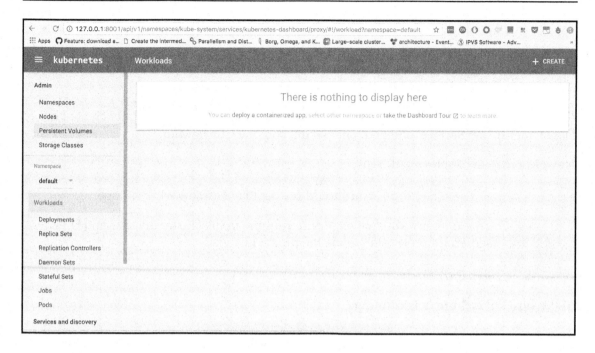

Deploy!

The difficult part is done. Deploying kubernetes configuration is a breeze. First and foremost, we need to create a K8s namespace, as shown here:

```
$ kubectl create namespace "sm-talent-search-engine"
```

Let's focus on auth-service first. ConfigMaps and Secrets needs to be deployed before the Deployment, as they are used it. We are mounting Secrets and ConfigMaps into our pod. If they don't already exist in the same namespace, the deployment will fail:

```
$ cd auth-app/
$ kubectl apply -f 10-cmaps.yml -n sm-talent-search-engine
$ kubectl apply -f 10-secrets.yml -n sm-talent-search-engine
```

The creation is almost instant. You can verify it by visiting the dashboard at `http://127.0.0.1:8001`. Switch the namespace from `default` to `sm-talent-search-engine` first. In the sidebar menu on the left-hand side, click on **ConfigMaps**.

Then, we will deploy `deployment` followed by service:

```
$ kubectl apply -f deployment.yml -n sm-talent-search-engine
$ kubectl apply -f service.yml -n sm-talent-search-engine
```

You are done! It is that simple. If you visit the dashboard, inside the `sm-talent-search-engine` namespace, you should have one Deployment, one RS (automatically created by Deployment), one **Service**, one **Pod**, one **Secret**, and one **ConfigMap**.

Now, to verify the deployment, visit `http://127.0.0.1:8001/api/v1/proxy/namespaces/sm-talent-search-engine/services/auth-service:3000`. You should see the Play Framework `404` page.

 To access any kubernetes service running in the cluster that has an HTTP server, it's pretty simple via the proxy. Just visit `http://127.0.0.1:8001/api/v1/proxy/namespaces/{servicenamespace}/services/{servicename}:{serviceport}`.

Make sure kubectl proxy is running.

The same steps can be followed for web-app and so-app as well. All source code is present in the GitHub repository.

How to use platform-specific load balancer?

To deploy the service behind a managed load balancer, a minor code change to our `service.yml` configuration file needs to be made, as shown here:

```
. . . . .
spec:
type: LoadBalancer
sessionAffinity: None
ports:
. . . . . . .
```

K8s is platform aware and using the appropriate cloud provider (AWS, Azure, GCP, and so on) plugin. It will create a managed load balancer and link it with this service.

You need to reapply `service.yml` to the K8s cluster with the code change:

```
$ kubectl apply -f service.yml -n sm-talent-search-engine
```

In the Services section in the dashboard (check the following screenshot), against **auth-service**, you will see the **External endpoints** column populated with an external IP. This is the load balancer IP. This might take few minutes though.

You can link this external IP to a DNS name, such as `auth.example.com`, if you want it to easily consumed by other outside services. The procedure for that is out of the scope of this book.

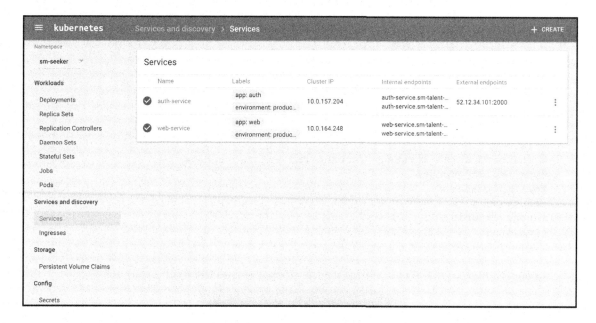

Rolling deployments

Now that our application is fully functional, it's time to test deploying new code updates to simulate active software development cycle.

Let's assume there is a change in product design of the homepage. It will lead to code change to the web-app source code. The product team feels the title of the web-app should be not be `Seeker`, but `New-Seeker`.

```
$ vim chapter-4/web-app/app/assets/javascripts/components/Layout.js
```

On line 60, I will change the `<Header>` value from `Seeker` to `New-Seeker`. So, when we open the web-service homepage, we should see the change, as shown here:.

```
$ cd chapter-4/web-app/app/assets/javascripts/
# The homepage code is written in ReactJS and uses Webpack. For more
details, checkout chapter4/web-app/Readme.md
$ npm run build
$ sbt "project web-app" dist
```

Build and push the new docker image with a distinct tag:

```
$ docker build -t {username}/web-app:v2
$ docker push {username}/web-app:v2
```

With our changes safely packaged into a docker image, all we have left to do is modify the kubernetes deployment for web-app. Add the `RollingUpdate` strategy to the `spec` section of the deployment file.

```
. . . . .
spec:
replicas: 3
minReadySeconds: 5
 strategy:
 # indicate which strategy we want for rolling update
 type: RollingUpdate
 rollingUpdate:
 maxSurge: 1
 maxUnavailable: 1
 template:
. . . . . . . .
```

The second change to make is to bump up the docker image tag from v1 to v2:

```
. . . . . . . . . .
containers:
- name: auth-container
imagePullPolicy: Always
image: chartotu/auth-app:v2
. . . . . . . . . .
```

Before you deploy the new configuration, run the following command on shell:

```
$ while true; do curl -s -o /dev/null -w "%{http_code}" ;
http://WEB_APP_URL; done
```

This will return the HTTP code for the request. The response should be a consistent 200 (HTTP code for success) during and after the deployment. This proves that there was no downtime on the service, and new code was deployed rolling over one pod at a time.

The WEB_APP_URL will be something like
`http://127.0.0.1:8001/api/v1/proxy/namespaces/sm-talent-search-engine/s
ervices/web-service:2000` and can change based on what namespace, service name,
port number you specified in your deployment.

On a new terminal window, apply the new deployment:

```
$ kubectl apply -f deployment.yml -n sm-talent-search-engine
```

You should also visit `http://WEB_APP_URL` to see the application heading change from
`Seeker` to `New-Seeker`. Keep refreshing until you see it. What we did earlier is a rolling
update!

Persistent workloads

K8s Deployment resources are great for stateless applications where we can scale replicas
very easily.

For stateful applications such as databases, K8s Deployment resources don't work well.
There are K8s stateful sets to address this use case, but personally, I recommend that you
run databases on the cloud-managed service. This is because database backups are very
critical and they are very cheap. Disaster recovery is also easy in a managed service.

Persistent disks

There is another form of persistence that we can leverage with kubernetes. Let's say you are
running Jenkins as a pod.

When we `delete`/`restart` the pod or when K8s moves the pod to a different agent node
on a scaling event, the data folder is lost and a fresh copy is created.

To avoid this problem, K8s allows us to mount volumes that are backed by a real disk at the
location where the data folder will be created inside the container (of Jenkins Pod). This is
done via **PersistentVolumeClaim (PVC)**, **StorageClass**, and **PersistentVolume (PV)**.

Storage class lets us allow dynamic provisioning of persistent disks. This means that K8s will create disks on the fly when it receives an API request for a PVC:

```
$ cat storage-class.yml
```

```
                          https://kubernetes.io/docs/api-reference/v1.7/#storageclass-v1-storage


kind: StorageClass
apiVersion: storage.k8s.io/v1
metadata:
  name: mystorageclass
provisioner: kubernetes.io/azure-disk
parameters:
  skuName: Standard_LRS
  location: eastus
  storageAccount: mystorageaccount
```

```
$ kubectl apply -f storage-class.yml
```

There are many default `provisioner` available for use. We are using `azure-disk` in the preceding example. Each `provisioner` has its own set of parameters; refer to `https://kubernetes.io/docs/concepts/storage/persistent-volumes/#aws`

- `kubernetes.io/aws-ebs`—Amazon Web Services
- `kubernetes.io/azure-disk`—Microsoft Azure
- `kubernetes.io/gce-pd`—Google Cloud Platform
- `kubernetes.io/cinder`—OpenStack
- `kubernetes.io/vsphere-volume`—VMware vSphere

Pods access storage using the PVC as a volume mount. Claims must exist in the same namespace as the pod using the claim. The K8s cluster then uses this claim to get the `PersistentVolume` backing the claim. The `PersistentVolume` is then mounted to the host and into the pod. In nutshell, pods access a `PersistentVolume` using PVC.

For an application developer, all they need to do is define a PVC, as the actual provisioning of disk is abstracted away in the `storageClass`. It is possible to set a `storageClass` as default, so the application developer doesn't even have to care about the `storageClass`. Note, a `PersistentVolume` can also be created directly using `kubectl` to be used by a PVC.

Here is an example of a PVC config file, `pvc.yml`:

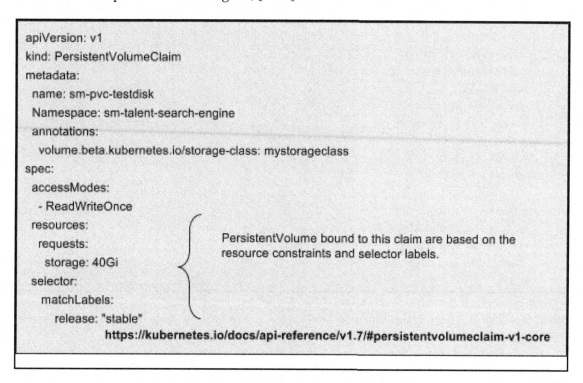

```
apiVersion: v1
kind: PersistentVolumeClaim
metadata:
  name: sm-pvc-testdisk
  Namespace: sm-talent-search-engine
  annotations:
    volume.beta.kubernetes.io/storage-class: mystorageclass
spec:
  accessModes:
  - ReadWriteOnce
  resources:
    requests:
      storage: 40Gi
  selector:
    matchLabels:
      release: "stable"
```

PersistentVolume bound to this claim are based on the resource constraints and selector labels.

https://kubernetes.io/docs/api-reference/v1.7/#persistentvolumeclaim-v1-core

We will apply it to our kubernetes cluster:

```
$ kubectl apply -f pvc.yml -n sm-talent-search-engine
```

This will trigger K8s to create a new **virtual hard disk (VHD)** from Azure cloud. To be able to create Azure VHD, it needs a Service principal, which is passed on to kubernetes on creation(`https://docs.microsoft.com/en-us/azure/azure-resource-manager/resource-group-authenticate-service-principal-cli`):

```
.....
    containers:
    - name: container
      image: chartotu/auth-app:v1
      imagePullPolicy: Always
      volumeMounts:
        - mountPath: /opt/scala
          name: sm-volume-testdisk
      ports:
        - containerPort: 22
        - containerPort: 22

    volumes:
    - name: sm-volume-testdisk
      persistentVolumeClaim:
        claimName: sm-pvc-testdisk
```

Now, this disk has been claimed, so no new `deployment/pod/container` can use the same PVC anymore unless it is hosted on the same k8s agent node.

Kubernetes has cloud-specific bindings for creating cloud resources. So, when we want to deploy a load balancer, create a virtual disk, and so on, they are created automatically.

Summary

In this chapter, we deployed our Talent search engine application in production with kubernetes, with less than 500 lines of code. It shows the ease with which K8s cluster can be operated.

We saw that microservices are first-class citizens in K8s, which makes it a great fit for lagom and play applications.

The complex orchestration, life cycle management, and resource allocation of containers is abstracted out of our way. Scaling and rolling deployments are supported out of the box, letting your workload scale without any hiccups. Kubernetes lets us focus on our business logic and prevents us from worrying too much about the operation of it.

Index

CPSIA information can be obtained
at www.ICGtesting.com
Printed in the USA
BVOW04s1145200917
495414BV00005B/42/P

9 781786 469342